COMPARING POLITICAL BEHAVIOR

Volume 28, Sage Library of Social Research

SAGE LIBRARY OF SOCIAL RESEARCH

Comparing
Political Behavior

MOSHE M. CZUDNOWSKI

Preface by HEINZ EULAU

Foreword by SIDNEY VERBA

Volume 28
SAGE LIBRARY OF
SOCIAL RESEARCH

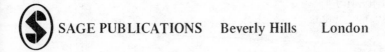 **SAGE PUBLICATIONS**   Beverly Hills   London

For information address:

SAGE PUBLICATIONS, INC.
275 South Beverly Drive
Beverly Hills, California 90212

SAGE PUBLICATIONS LTD
St George's House / 44 Hatton Garden
London EC1N 8ER

Printed in the United States of America

Library of Congress Cataloging in Publication Data

Czudnowski, Moshe M   1924-
    Comparing political behavior.

    (Sage library of social research ; v. 28)
    Bibliography, p. 167
    1. Political science—Methodology.   2. Comparative
government—Methodology.   I. Title.
JA73.C97   320'.01'8   76-5825
ISBN 0-8039-0691-9
ISBN 0-8039-0692-7 pbk.

FIRST PRINTING

CONTENTS

034857

PREFACE

That knowledge is never better than the methods by which it is created is an insight so banal that it should not need mention, were it not for the fact that it is still not generally accepted by all political scientists. Indeed, a concern with method is variously denounced as "methodism" or "methodolatry." Nevertheless, the "methodological situation" in political science today is eminently different from what it was less than twenty years ago. "Concern with methodology," I had to write in 1958, "has not been a hallmark of political science. One seeks in vain in the vast literature of politics for the kind and degree of methodological awareness easily found in the work of economists, sociologists, or psychologists." By way of contrast, there is today much lively interest in methodological problems, ranging from rather remote philosophical issues to rather immediate technical questions. Professor Czudnowski's new work is symptomatic of the ferment and, it seems to me, a more personally responsible statement of methodological problems in comparative politics or, for that matter, in political science as a whole, than most works of similar concern.

What do I mean by a "personally responsible statement?" As I read books and articles on methodological problems in political and social science, I find many of them impersonal—the author seems to have no commitment and seems to be indifferent to the consequences of methodological alternatives; or I find them second- and even third-hand—the author copies and tries to relate what others have written, but does so badly; or I find them supercilious and defensive—the author may or may not know where things are at, but he doesn't like what he sees; or I find them enthusiastically adolescent—the author thinks to have discovered something new that has been around for some time, and he doesn't know it; or I find them gauche and heavy-handed—the author has evidently had little, if any, research experience; and so on and so forth. What usually happens on these occasions is for me to pick up my Durkheim (*The Rules of Sociological Method,* 1895) or my Cohen and Nagel (*An Introduction to Logic and Scientific Method,* 1934) and convince myself that not much has happened in methodological development in the last hundred years, though a good deal has happened in the development of techniques. But techniques are not methods.

Professor Czudnowski's book belongs to the rare genre of methodological writing where one feels that the author has an intellectual stake in what he is writing; where one feels that he is coping or trying to cope with difficult questions, rather than denying them or giving superficial answers; where one feels that he is sensitive to the paradoxes and indeterminacies of the methodological life, not as it appears in the treatises of the methodologists but in the real world of empirical investigation. Above all, and regardless of whether one agrees or disagrees with a particular formulation or chain of thought, this book is a sophisticated response of a sophisticated observer of the methodological scene in political science to the challenges of a genuine science of politics.

Stanford, California

Heinz Eulau

FOREWORD

In the old days there were books *in* comparative politics, but rarely books *on* comparative politics. Books about politics outside the United States fell in the comparative politics field, but few considered what, if anything, that field was. In the past two decades, comparative poltiics has become more sophisticated; it includes the United States, it is often truly comparative. And it has become more self-conscious. The result: books *on* comparative politics.

Many of us who work in the field of comparative politics have wondered whether it is a distinctive field. Can one write books that are not about some country, or books comparing voting behavior or bureaucracies, or policy-making, but books on comparative politics per se? Is it a subject matter in itself? Is it coterminous with political science?

The works that have attempted to deal with the field generally—the ones we would use in courses entitled "Introduction to Comparative Politics"—have taken several forms. One set of works has raised broad philosophical questions as to the possibility of a systematic comparative politics. Another type of book presents a particular theory (or more usually, framework) for comparative political analysis. It sets forth categories for analysis and, at times, typologies of political systems. These general schemes have been of great help in making comparative politics a discipline; they lead us to think comparatively across nations in general and give us a language for those comparisons. Their fault is that they often lack "substance"—by which I mean that they are so general as to offer little guide to specific hypotheses for specific research topics. A third type of work has been technical. These works spell out statistical techniques for cross-national measurement. A last and most useful type deals with the overall logic of comparative analysis; with strategic choices that scholars must make in research design.

Professor Czudnowski's book represents a most interesting and useful synthesis of several of these approaches. He does not offer a general global scheme for political analysis—which may be all to the good. He does, however, range broadly over the problem of a systematic comparative politics.

He considers the philosophical stance that has been taken against systematic comparison and rejects the position that systematic comparison is impossible. Yet he also rejects (or, rather, subjects to searching criticism) macro-quantitative approaches that assume, implicitly, that systematic comparison is easy. Rather, he offers a sketch of a strategy of comparative research; a strategy that stresses cross-level comparisons and an understanding of the subjective meanings of politics to political actors. And he illustrates the strategy in relation to several substantive problems. Not everyone will accept the strategy. But students of comparative politics cannot fail to learn a good deal about their recently evolved craft from Professor Czudnowski's attempt to link substantive problems with concerns for research strategy.

May 1976   *Sidney Verba*
Harvard University

AUTHOR'S PREFACE

This book had originally been planned as an evaluative survey of the growing literature in the field of the "new comparative politics." It was still in the planning stage when a number of excellent works dealing with substantive and methodological issues relevant to this field were published at short intervals. There seemed to be no particular advantage in replicating these works, especially since I did not feel I could add important comments to those of my predecessors. In the original planning I had included a final chapter on the status and role of comparative politics in the discipline, addressing a number of methodological questions to the practitioners in the field and describing the need to develop adequate theoretical frameworks. This chapter survived, but instead of merely asking the questions, I have attempted to supply some of the answers. Thus, that postscript became the introduction to this book.

Essentially, the chapters of the book which eventually emerged from this exploration reflect the belief that the field of comparative politics is far more dependent on the development of a general paradigm for the study of political behavior than most of the various substantive subdivisions of the discipline, in which low- or middle-range theorizing has been both relevant and successful. One of the consequences of this dependence is the need to translate and integrate the knowledge which has accumulated from sub-system- and system-level research into the categories and relationships postulated in a general theoretical framework. This would involve abandoning some of the simplifying assumptions implied in systemic conceptualizations in which system attributes are held constant. The issues are, of course, further compounded by the need to seek at least an approximate equivalence of meanings across cultural, historical, and institutional diversity.

In confronting questions of such magnitude, I have frequently taken the position that the behavior observed by political scientists does not "naturally" fall into the patterns postulated or hypothesized by specific theories in the pluralistic universe of our preparadigmatic discipline. The answers we receive depend on the questions we ask. If the answers do not easily lend themselves to higher-level empirical theorizing, perhaps the questions ought to be asked in a somewhat different manner. Not questions about different issues or different aspects of politics—one would like to think that political science has attempted to deal with the politically salient and theoretically relevant issues—but questions reflecting conceptualizations congruent with higher-level theoretical integration. A corollary of this desideratum is a theoretical framework sufficiently general to allow for such integration and yet sufficiently operational to serve comparative analysis across systems.

In dealing with these questions in Chapters 3, 4, and 5, I have adopted a methodological posture attempting to stay as close as possible—though probably not close enough—to relevant empirical research. Chapter 6 is a selective theoretical survey of the recent literature on voting behavior, presented as an example of, and a commentary on, the current state of the discipline in the most researched area of political behavior. Chapters 7, 8, and 9 represent attempts to ask the metatheoretical questions "in a different manner."[1] Given the exploratory nature of this study, my answers are necessarily tentative; yet I believe they suggest that it is possible to seek common denominators of theoretical interest for areas of political study which have remained—with minor but notable exceptions—in a state of relative compartmentalization. Specialization and integration need not be conflicting emphases, and cross-disciplinary fertilization need not undermine the autonomy of our subject matter and the justification of our endeavors.

Althouth it examines issues in a number of specialized areas—including cross-national studies, ecological analysis, the methodology of comparison, voting behavior, economic theories of politics, and developmental psychology—or perhaps *because* it examines issues in such different areas, this book is merely an *introduction* to "comparative politics" and empirical theory. I have made no assumptions about the reader's familiarity with any of these subjects, and the book should be capable of serving a relatively broad variety of instructional purposes. The scholar familiar with some or all of these subjects may find this exploration as rewarding as it was for me, even if he does not agree with all my interpretations.

I wish to thank Heinz Eulau for persuading me to engage in this endeavor, for his unmitigated interest and support, and for his stimulating criticism. It is difficult to list all the scholars whose works made this study possible; but the names of Gabriel Almond, Hubert Blalock, Jr., James Buchanan, Philip Converse, Heinz Eulau, Juan Linz, Mancur Olson, Jr., Adam Przeworski, William Riker, Stein Rokkan, Erwin Scheuch, Gordon Tullock, and Sidney

Verba would certainly constitute the top of this list. My debt to my colleagues, as well as to graduate students who patiently helped me test my ideas, will have to remain anonymous.

Northern Illinois University *M. M. C.*

NOTE

1. An earlier version of Chapters 7 and 8 was presented as a paper at the 1973 World Congress of the International Political Science Association in Montreal.

Chapter 1

INTRODUCTION

In the three decades following the end of World War II in 1945, political science has witnessed a considerable expansion of one of its subfields, traditionally referred to as "comparative politics." Scholarship and material resources have been invested in the study of "foreign areas," especially the new developing areas in Asia and Africa, as well as the Communist countries; the percentage of "comparative politics" courses offered by political science departments in the United States increased considerably (in some cases by 100%; Bill and Hardgrave, 1973: 11); a new social science technology facilitated large-scale empirical studies; cross-national research became a major source for generating and testing theory; unprecedented rates and scales of political change and modernization presented both students and practitioners with an urgent need for new conceptual frameworks and plausible hypotheses. Indeed, the "new comparative politics" had become an "exploding culture."

In addition to the substantive reports and the theoretical and methodological writings which have emerged from this interest in "comparative politics," an increasing number of scholars have attempted to systematically summarize, explain, and evaluate these developments. There is, therefore, no need to replicate this exercise in stock-taking, especially if nothing of interest can be added to Eckstein's "Perspective on Comparative Politics, Past and Present" (Eckstein, 1963: 3-32) or to subsequent surveys and analyses such as those of Scarrow (1969), Golembiewski et al. (1969), Holt and Turner (1970), Merritt (1970), Merkl (1970), Mayer (1972) and Bill and Hardgrave (1973). Some of the theoretical and methodological contributions included in these works, and those of other authors who have addressed themselves primarily to theoretical and methodological issues involved in the study of "comparative politics" (and will be referred to explicitly in the chapters of this book) constitute, together with some of the substantive reports of political research, the material to which the analyses offered in this book will address themselves explicitly or implicitly. The mention of "implicit references" is intended to convey the position—reflected herein—that comparing political behavior is neither a particular method nor a specific subfield of political science and that a discussion of "comparative politics" refers implicitly to all substantive areas of the discipline.

For the present purpose, it will suffice to identify briefly the factors which have elicited the rapid expansion of the comparative "field" and the manner in which the "new comparative politics" differs from the traditional study of "foreign areas."

(1) Commenting on the "revival" of comparative politics, Lasswell (1968) wrote: "The principal point is not obscure: political scientists have been belatedly responding to the accelerated interdependence of the world arena, an interdependence which was shockingly dramatized by World War II, by the bipolarized tensions between the Communist and the non-Communist worlds, and by the anticolonialist emergence of the nation-states in Africa and Asia." And he adds: "The inference would appear to be that an effective demand for more comparative knowledge depends on the shared expectation of political elites that they will be better off if they broaden the territorial scope and depth of their political information." The concern for an expanded frame of reference in space and in time is not limited to "imperial elites" in the "phase of expansion": although "recent decades have been a period of relative decline for the empires of Britain, France and other European states . . . both official and private agencies [in these countries] have encouraged the gathering of information about the forces of dissolution." The "thirst for comparative intelligence" has also been shared by transnational economic organizations, of which the European "Common Market" is an outstanding example.

The "crisis expansion" of comparative political analysis has been determined by political factors, but its innovations in the discipline will endure, according to Lasswell, if it is accompanied by an enduring demand "to think comparatively." Most observers have indeed associated the expanded emphasis on comparative data with the "behavioral revolution," and since behaviorism has greatly contributed to the institutionalization of the scientific pattern of thought, Lasswell believes that this scientific frame of reference "will keep alive the demand for comparisons."

(2) The basic characteristics of the "new comparative politics" can be best described in contradistinction to the traditional approach. The pioneering works of Hermann Finer and Carl Friedrich notwithstanding, the traditional approach was characterized by configurative descriptions, parochialism, formal legalism, conservatism, methodological insensitivity, and nonscientific preoccupations (Bill and Hardgrave, 1973: 3-10). The "new comparative politics" went beyond descriptive case studies, expanded its interest to the non-Western world, emphasized informal political processes including elite and mass behavior, and introduced a developmental perspective, thus breaking away from the conservatism inherent in preoccupations with a precedent-sensitive law and past-oriented history. Furthermore, it espoused in varying degrees the methodology of behavioral—i.e., empirical—political science which was neither available nor relevant to the legalistic and unsystematic descriptions of the traditional approach. Finally, and most importantly, it combined an interest in substantive findings with a theoretical goal: the discovery of regularities, of patterns of behavior, across systems for the purpose of making generalizations and establishing the boundaries or conditions under which such generalizations hold true.

There seems to be general agreement on the theoretical or scientific orientation of the "new comparative politics," but there is still some reluctance to agree on the status of comparative analysis in political science. This may reflect the manner in which the professional core of political science is maintained.

Vested and sentimental interests are generated in its transmission. Since the overwhelming fraction of those who receive professional training do little subsequent research, once a given conception of comparative government is crystallized, it provides the frame of reference within which subsequent teaching and consultation is [sic] carried on [Lasswell, 1968: 5].

Thus, for some, comparative politics is still a subfield of political science, while others consider it a particular method. Golembiewski et al. (1969: 230) list six interpretations of the comparative method in political analysis:

(1) There are only three basic methods for theory-building: comparative analysis, the experimental method, and the statistical method. The underlying logic, however, is the same in all three cases: the logic of comparative analysis.

(2) There are numerous comparative methods. Different approaches and techniques can be used comparatively and have different implications for theory-building (for example: cross-cultural and longitudinal comparisons, quantitative and qualitative comparisons).

(3) There is no comparative method. Comparison is not part of science, it *is* science; it is pervasive in all areas of inquiry.

(4) Comparative methodology is essentially quantitative and, as such, represents the behavioral approach in political science. Statistics is the most highly systematized form of comparative analysis.

(5) Comparison is the substitute for controlled experimentation in the social sciences.

(6) Systematic comparative analysis is impossible. Historical and other factors give nations characteristics that are unique, and it is impossible to develop generalizations that are valid for all political systems.

Items 1, 2, 4, and 5 in the above list are variations of the statement in item 3; thus, the issue becomes one of accepting or rejecting not the comparative method but its applicability to the universe of political phenomena. Stated otherwise: those who deny the adequacy of comparative analysis for political phenomena do not believe that political "science" is—or can ever become—a science. In contradistinction, social science,

indeed all work directed toward understanding the behavior of men and women in social groups, is posited on the axiomatic assumption that behavior is nonrandom and rule-governed in the sense that "natively competent" members of social groups behave in accordance with shared understandings that simultaneously govern their own behavior and their interpretations of the behavior of other members [Grimshaw, 1973: 4].

These statements suggest two rather obvious comments:

(a) If the political universe does not display regularities which would justify the use of the comparative method, there is no justification for a "comparative" subfield in political inquiry. A nomothetic subfield in an idiographic discipline would constitute a logical contradiction. Thus the nontheoretical position excludes comparative politics both as a field and as a method. This, of course, is not incompatible with the country-by-country type of description of "foreign areas."

(b) Grimshaw's formulation of the axiomatic assumption of patterned behavior applies explicitly to intrasystemic regularities based on "shared understandings." This interpretation limits the application of the comparative method to intrasystemic behavior, whereas, according to Grimshaw's own definition, it is precisely "the particular task of comparative sociology . . . to distinguish between those regularities in social behavior that are system-specific and those that are universal" (1973: 5). Positing the existence of universal regularities implies a position which goes beyond the assumption of nonrandom behavior based on the shared understandings of "natively competent" members of a group: the latter is congruent with the belief in the uniqueness of historical societies or political systems. There is, however, a difference between assuming either the *presence* or the *absence* of universal regularities and the assumption that such regularities are *possible,* a difference to which we shall return shortly.

There is another way of examing the meaning of "comparative politics" or comparative social science in general. Those who accept the statement that there is no comparative method as opposed to other methods, that comparison is not part of science but science per se, will probably also agree that the comparative method in scientific endeavors is merely a formalization of a mental or psychological category that we encounter, in more or less developed forms, in all human experience and reasoning. For Hume (1952: 199), "All kinds of reasoning consist in nothing but a comparison." Kant did not include "comparison" among his four sets of a priori concepts, but the distinctions within these sets of categories are based on comparisons, and the "intuitions" of space and time, which according to Kant are part of our mental constitution, also presuppose the ability to compare.

What is worthwhile emphasizing is the fact that, not only formal logic, Mill's methods of experimental inquiry, or rational behavior, but also "intuitive," psychologically determined, or sociopsychologically learned behavior involve the ability to compare. We are not concerned here with epistemological theory or the cybernetics of neurophysiology, but with the more or less developed ability of human beings to perceive similarities and differences. If human beings find it difficult to orient themselves meaningfully to their environment without the use of their ability to compare, then there is nothing inherently scientific in the use of comparisons. The difference between logically or scientifically prescribed and psychologically determined or experientially learned comparisons consists in the normative character of the former as opposed to the intuitive nature of the latter. The rules of comparative analysis in the logic of the scientific method are therefore purposive means of regularizing and maximizing the benefits of the process through which human beings orient themselves to—i.e., attempt to understand, explain, and influence—their environment.

The similarity and correspondence between the processes through which the individual tests his beliefs about the environment and the purposes of comparative analysis in the social sciences are easily apparent in the following inventory of comparisons in inductive, "grounded" theorizing derived from Glaser and Strauss (1967: 22-31). Comparisons serve the purposes of:

(1) establishing the accuracy of factual evidence;

(2) establishing the generality of a fact;

(3) establishing conceptual categories and their properties;

(4) generating statements about generalized relationships between categories;

(5) delimiting the boundaries of applicability of a relationship;

(6) measuring the magnitude of a relationship within a particular group;

(7) generating substantive theory;

(8) generating formal theory through comparisons of substantive theories;

(9) verifying hypotheses obtained by logical deduction from "grand theory" or abstract models.

The first seven items in this inventory can be easily applied to nonscientific activities of everyday life.

As a formalized rule of procedure, the comparative method is an integral part of any scientific method. Viewed as a method, "comparative politics" is a tautology. Yet it is possible to identify the so-called *field* of comparative politics by the purpose for which the comparative method is used.

Any science seeks to discover and explain patterns of relationship between phenomena. The phenomena studied by the social scientist occur only in groups, societies, or political systems, and the regularities he or she seeks to discover and explain are those which can be observed in specific groups (societies or systems). This implies, however, that the explanations he can offer will be necessarily based on observations made in a specific group, society, or political system. Stated otherwise, the number of cases on which his explanation is based is one. Obviously, there is nothing scientific about an explanation based on a single case. Furthermore, he does not know which of the relationships he has observed are likely to remain relatively stable because, for example, they reflect a universal pattern of human behavior in a particular type of situation and which relationships are likely to change because, for example, they reflect a system-specific and time-bound problem which may or may not influence behavior at a future point in time.

In many cases, the political scientist is guided by the practical or political purpose of improving the ability to predict behavior in his or her own political system, and research funds are more easily available for politically "relevant" purposes than for pure scientific research. He will therefore replicate his study as frequently as he can in order to verify his hypothesis and establish which variables do and which do not display variation at different points of observation in his time-series. This strategy is certainly legitimate and reflects, in very broad terms, the development of survey research in the field of voting behavior. However, whatever their practical significance, there is little scientific value in such studies if they are not anchored in some cross-systemically verifiable hypothesis.

The political scientist who believes that cross-systemically observed relationships between variables strengthen the validity of statements based on observations made in one system only will therefore proceed to test his explanation by engaging in cross-systemic replications of his study. The so-called "field" of comparative politics will not reflect merely the interest of, say, an American political scientist in the politics of India, Finland, or Japan, but an attempt to generate or verify general hypotheses about political behavior and the conditions under which they hold true. Thus, comparative politics is neither a method nor a field, but a prerequisite for empirical theorizing—i.e., for empirical political science. It consists in using the ubiquitous comparative method in order to generate or verify hypotheses by increasing the number of independent observations.

All this is elementary and common knowledge for the empirically oriented political scientist. Yet, given the intrinsic conservatism in the patterns of transmission of the professional core of the discipline and, to some extent, the generational gap and the ideological barriers in the diffusion of innovations, empirical political science—often mistakenly identified with a narrowly defined behavioral approach—is still considered one of several possible approaches in political "science." Some would go even farther claiming that there can be no cross-systemic regularities in political behavior, although more or less stable patterns of behavior can be observed within systems. Arguing against this position, Przeworski and Teune (1970) have called for the elimination of proper names of systems (e.g., *French* political culture, the *Italian* party system, etc.) from explanatory propositions in political science. This problem will be discussed in some detail in a subsequent chapter of this book.

Accepting the *possibility* of universal generalizations does not imply a negation of the impact of system-specific variables, especially those associated with national political systems. In fact, it will be argued that no behavior can be meaningfully interpreted, let alone explained, if it is dissociated from the context in which it occurs and the environment to which it addresses itself. One of the most difficult tasks consists in translating system-specific structural configurations into a language allowing for conceptualizations and models that can be applied across systems. This is part of the problem of structural equivalence in comparative analysis.

Assuming the *possibility* of universal generalizations also poses the problem of functional equivalence in the comparison of political behavior. Combining the quest for functional equivalence with methodological individualism (i.e., seeking equivalences in the meaning of political behavior for the actors involved, rather than functional interpretations at the systemic level) raises no lesser an issue than the difficulty of defining politics in substantive rather than institutional, procedural, or normativist terms. This book represents an attempt to seek some answers to these questions.

In a discipline which has been dominated until recently by normative theories, historicism, and legal institutionalism, much work remains to be done in formulating the relevant questions in an adequate manner before empirical research can provide some indication whether the scientific posture in political science is justifiable. However, the issue whether or not a science of politics is possible can be settled only by the empiricist, because it is incumbent upon the empiricist to supply the evidence challenging the non-theoretical position that there are no universal patterns in political behavior. The axiomatic belief that there can be no science of politics is indeed a comfortable position, since it need not, and cannot, be shown to be true. The theoretical approach denies this belief the status of an axiom and treats it as a hypothesis that can be falsified and rejected.

Before we engage in formulating what seem to be relevant questions and examining available theories, methods, and findings, we shall discuss, in Chapter 2, some of the arguments put forward by those who support an idiographic model of political "science."

Chapter 2

OBJECTIONS TO AN EMPIRICAL

SCIENCE OF POLITICS

Uniqueness and the Impact of Time

The position that political behavior can be analyzed in terms of universal generalizations has come under attack from different directions. Historicist political philosophy has maintained that a science of politics is impossible, or should it be possible it would be irrelevant, or, at best, incomplete. Others have emphasized an evolutionary dimension challenging the appropriateness of universal generalizations. The impact of time has also been associated with localized traditions which prevent uniform changes through time. Furthermore, anthropologists have raised the issue of cultural diffusion—i.e., the borrowing of institutions and patterns of behavior which could be responsible for some observed uniformities across systems. In this chapter, we shall discuss briefly the merit of these positions.

The historicist philosopher contends that a science of politics is impossible because historical events, and sequences of historical events, are unique. One cannot generalize from unique events occurring in different historical and cultural contexts, nor from unique personalities who have contributed to shape these events. Although each event can be explained within its own context, no generalization is possible. However, speaking of events and a fortiori of sequences of events tends to obscure the fact that one never describes or explains the totality of observable occurrences. An event is always a cluster of variables or characteristics and even a limited number of characteristics which are considered relevant in a given context may require separate and different explanations. What is perhaps unique is the particular pattern of characteristics or the values displayed by the variables under consideration. Philosophers of science have argued that in this respect there is no difference between history and the natural sciences (Hempel, 1965: 233; Nagel, 1961: 463 ff.; Gibson, 1960: 9; Popper, 1957: 77). "Laws do deal with what is common to many, but uniqueness does not imply that *nothing* is shared with other individuals, only that *not everything* is common to them" (Kaplan, 1964: 117).

It is possible to conceive even of the individual actor and his contribution to the event as a cluster of analytically distinct variables, and different criteria of relevance can be assigned to those personal characteristics which can be brought to bear on the analysis. This does not mean that one has to subscribe to an "actor-dispensability"-type of political theory; it merely indicates that even the actor need not be considered unique. He is unique only in the total configuration of his characteristics (biological, psychological, educational, occupational, etc.).

The different aspects of an event may lead to a number of different interpretations and explanations, each relevant in a specific context. This is possible because an act of political behavior can have different meanings, depending on the level of social or political organization in terms of which the event is analyzed, and on the level of generalization and abstraction at which it is interpreted by the investigator. Even an instance of individual behavior with no social interaction can have more than one valid explanation: a case of death can be explained as the result of poisoning or as a case of suicide (Kaplan, 1964: 329). Different sets of variables will be used for each explanation and each such set from one event lends itself to comparisons with other events in which these variables are present. It has been rightly pointed out (Gibson, 1960: 10) that even if one wanted to prove the uniqueness of an event, he could not do so by considering all its aspects simultaneously and would still have to analyze its component characteristics and compare them with those of other events. Thus, in terms of theoretically oriented conceptualizations, the "uniqueness" of events does not lead to the conclusion that comparison is an exercise in futility because generalizations in political analysis are "impossible."

The "uniqueness" argument is hardly more convincing on logical grounds. The claim that unique events, and only unique events, can be explained by relating them to their specific spatiotemporally determined antecedents and contexts implies that these specific antecedents and contexts are assigned the status of "explanation" because they are considered instances of a general—probabilistic or universal—law (Runciman, 1969: 10; Nagel, 1961: 550, 554). If we cannot assume reference to a general law, or at least to a number of recurring instances of the same relationship of which the investigator is aware, then the "explanatory status" of the relationship can be ascribed only to the investigator's special insight, understanding, or wisdom or, alternatively, the relationship has no "explanatory status" at all. It is true that some important scientific advances have resulted from the insights of exceptional minds; however, they became "important advances" only after the original insight had been substantiated and validated by recurring empirical evidence.

Nowhere is the need for identifying the constituent characteristics and components of an event more critical than in the study of "aggregative events" involving a large number of actors acting or interacting at different times. Such studies are on the borderline between history and political science, and the longer the period under consideration and the greater the complexity of the event, the greater the justification for considering it a sequence of individually identifiable events which require separate explanations. The logic of historical explanation lies outside the scope of this discussion; suffice it to say that the components of such complex events and the relationships between them are explained, implicitly or explicitly, according to patterns of probabilistic or genetic explanations and such explanations assume, implicitly or explicitly, the existence of regularities in human behavior (Nagel, 1961: 574). Historians, however, seldom make explicit statements on the logic of their explanations. Thus historical comparisons, generalizations, and theorizing are usually left to the philosophers of social and political history whose interest centers, by choice or by necessity, on long successions of events and broad social movements and processes of change.

The argument that men have freedom of choice and that, therefore, the search for "laws" governing their behavior is a hopeless enterprise need not preoccupy us unduly. As far as political behavior is concerned, this "freedom" is limited to the choices structured by the social and political systems. The duty of the social scientist, as Rustow has argued, is "to ascertain the margin of choice offered by man's social condition and to clarify the choices in that margin." This margin of choice does not contradict the possibility of formulating general relationships between the variables affecting political behavior; it is merely a corollary of the complexity of the network of "behavioral laws" which *structure* social and political behavior without ever *determining* it entirely (Nagel, 1961: 596 ff.; Kaplan, 1964: 121; Gibson, 1960: 23). One such "behavioral law" which limits the scope of randomness in human behavior is "purposive rationality" (Weber, 1947: 122).

Historicism, Evolutionism, Diffusion, and Tradition

Historicism is the trend, in political philosophy, which interprets social and political history in terms of "first principles" or "patterns" that underlie the course of history. Condorcet, Hegel, Comte, Marx, Spengler, and Toynbee are the most famous representatives of this approach. Evolutionism, such as Social Darwinism, is a particular type of historicism which posits a basic evolutionary principle in the development of societies. Developmental or evolutionary perspectives have recently been reemphasized in political science by students of the "developing" countries in Asia and Africa, by political anthropologists, and, in political philosophy, through the impact of the theologian-paleontologist Teilhard de Chardin (Thorson, 1970).

Although they deny the possibility of an empirical political science, historicists admit that there are numerous recurrent social conditions which can be observed within a "historical period" or within a given culture. Such conditions, however, are historically determined and do not persist from one period to another; hence, no long-term generalizations about uniformities in social behavior can be validly made. Evolutionists add that the very quest for basic uniformities in social behavior denies that societies develop, or that social developments can affect the regularities of social life. Adopting Toulmin's (1961) evolutionary theory of science (which concurs with Popper's [1959] view of science as the "survival of the fittest hypothesis"), Thorson (1970: 80-82) writes: "It is not scientific, but scientifically naive, to attempt to understand politics on the model of the nineteenth century physics. . . . genuine understanding involves taking time seriously as a fundamental aspect of reality. . . . Man is, above all, a biological organism and he is what he is because of and through the process of biological and cultural evolution." After criticizing Easton's concept of the political system as a truism, Thorson concludes that "universal generalizations are inevitably vacuous. . . . Stages or phases of political evolutions must be understood as primary and the structures and functions of political organization must be seen as related to the stage or phase of political development" (1970: 70, 83).

These basic positions of historicism and evolutionism deserve some comments. There are indeed important differences in social and political conditions between historical periods and cultural settings. This, however, does not necessarily imply that there can be no uniformities across different periods and settings. There are considerable differences between physical settings, and yet no one has claimed that there are no physical laws which hold true across such different settings (Popper, 1957: 77). Furthermore, the fact that social processes vary with their institutional settings and that the specific uniformities found to hold in one culture are not pervasive in all societies, does not preclude the possibility that these specific uniformities are specializations of relational structures invariant for all cultures. For the recognized differences in the ways different societies are organized and in the modes of behavior occurring in them may be the consequences, not of incommensurably dissimilar patterns of social relations in those societies, but simply of differences in the specific values of some set of variables that constitute the elementary components in a structure of connections common to all the societies [Nagel, 1961: 462].

Let us further consider the implications of the historicist and evolutionist arguments. Generalizations are possible, it is said, within historical periods or stages of development. Since no operational criteria for identifying the end of a period are supplied, the only method for ascertaining that a period is coming to an end would be the search for evidence that the prevailing "laws" which structure political behavior have begun to change. If I could find no better justification for comparing political behavior across systems and stages of development than the attempt to invalidate the prevailing generalizing theories and hypotheses, I would be quite prepared to accept this implication of the historicist-evolutionist argument.

Setting aside the issue of whether an adequate explanation of observed behavior, based on generally valid relationships between variables, can be translated into a prediction of future "events," let us continue to address ourselves to the argument that uniformities are, at best, system-specific and historically determined. Every generation learns some of the goal-orientations, attitudes, and behavioral styles of the preceding generation—through manifest and purposive or latent and involuntary processes of socialization. Culture is transmitted and learned; it is, in Thorson's metaphor, society's equivalent for the organism's genetic code. This, of course, is an argument supporting the limitation of generalizations to the boundaries of culture areas. However, one of the main goals of cultural anthropology has been the discovery of transcultural "laws," and it is the interpretation of cultural diversities in terms of similar societal functions which led to the adoption of functional analysis in sociology and political science. The undisputed fact that all cultures have a number of common characteristics despite their great differences in other respects is the basis of the political scientist's search for universal generalizations through cross-systemic comparisons. The list of common cultural characteristics—the so-called "cultural universals"—drawn up by Murdock (Berelson and Steiner, 1964: 647) consists of seventy-three items clearly related to biological, psychological, and social needs, the satisfaction of which enables man to survive in his interaction with the physical and social environment. Examples of social "cultural universals" are law, the division of labor, status differentiation, and trade.

Cultures develop and tend to grow in complexity; in this process, new cultural traits are either developed independently or adopted, through inter-action, from other cultures. Anthropologists agree that characteristics of social organization are less frequently borrowed or imitated than are cultural artifacts. Thus "monarchical and democratic societies, feudal or caste-divided ones . . . evolve [independently] over and over again" (Kroeber, 1948: 241).

Contemporary technology has contributed to the development of both more extensive and more intensive cross-cultural contacts, and geographical contiguity or migration have ceased to be prerequisites of cultural diffusion. The diffusion of forms of political behavior (e.g., of universal suffrage to societies with high proportions of illiterate adults), of political ideologies or ideological labels (e.g., of Communist parties to predominantly agrarian societies), and of patterns of organization—as a result of colonialism, foreign aid, or foreign intervention—are all well-known phenomena. One would there-fore have to assume that within-system uniformities—such as associations between sets of behavioral patterns or associations between behavioral patterns and socioeconomic characteristics—observed in different social, cultural, or political settings, can be ascribed to either independent de-velopment or to diffusion. How does this distinction affect comparative studies oriented toward the discovery of cross-systemically valid general-izations?

This methodological problem, first raised by Galton in 1889, has been intensively explored by cultural anthropologists (Naroll, 1970). The anthro-pologist faces the problem of dissociating "functional relationships, i.e., associations of traits arising out of the nature of human personality, society or culture," from "historical relationships, i.e., associations of traits spread through an area by borrowing or migration." Stated otherwise, not all cul-tures or systems in which a set of traits has been observed can be considered independent observations, and those cases in which the association of traits is primarily a result of diffusion are merely "artifacts of common historical circumstances." The correlation between traits reflecting in some units of observation a functional, and in others a historical relationship, is necessarily spurious.

In order to examine the relevance of diffusion in political analysis, let us consider briefly what characteristics of an item contribute to its cross-cultural diffusion. Anthropologists report that some cultural items are imitated or borrowed much more frequently than others. "Specific elements of culture . . . diffuse very widely at times and may be said to be always tending to diffuse: the wheel, for instance, smelting of metals, the crown as a symbol of royalty, battleships" (Kroeber, 1948: 241). We distinguish here two types of items: a group of artifacts or techniques which "show some intrinsic . . . recognizable superiority among existing forms" (Kroeber, 1948)—i.e., which are useful and represent an improvement over prevailing techniques, and another type of items (represented in the above statement by the royal crown) which are symbols of prestige and power. "In general . . . those traits that are objectively superior or that come from a more powerful or prestigious source are especially likely to be taken over" (Berelson and Steiner, 1964: 653). On the other hand, "the relations of elements among themselves . . . tend to change by internal growth rather than by external imitation. Of this sort are the relations of the classes and members of societies" (Kroeber, 1948: 241).

These summarizing statements of anthropological findings seem to suggest that a "borrowed" or otherwise "transmitted" political institution or form of behavior will not "establish roots" in the receiving society unless it is perceived by the borrowers as useful for a more effective achievement of their purposes (or satisfaction of their needs, including prestige), and unless it is congruent with their social position, which is determined by intrasystemic relations. Thus, the diffusion of political "culture traits"—to the extent that it is successful—is very unlikely to be a "historical artifact" which is not "functionally" (i.e., purposively or motivationally) related to other politically relevant variables. It is possible that a "borrowed" institution which has gained a foothold in the receiving system will ultimately serve purposes which differ from those for which it had been originally developed and subsequently "borrowed." The purpose and relevance of "borrowed" cultural items may change, but such changes are not particular to cases of diffusion. Independently developed items, with originally similar structures and functions, can also develop in dissimilar ways and acquire different meanings or serve different purposes while retaining some or most of their remaining identifying characteristics. It is probably true that there has been considerable diffusion in politics; this, however, does not invalidate generalizations based on cross-systemically observed regularities, provided equivalence of purpose or function can be demonstrated.

In contradistinction to diffusion, political traditions reflect the impact of events or personalities on the political orientations and behavior of a specific group, region, or nation. When this impact goes beyond the immediate consequences of the event, or the political lifetime of the personalities involved, and shapes attitudes that are transmitted to subsequent generations, it becomes a political tradition. Bonapartism, recently reactivated by the circumstances leading to the establishment of de Gaulle's Fifth Republic, has been a tradition characteristic of a certain segment of French society since the end of the eighteenth century. Similarly, the radicalism and anticlericalism of the Italian tenant farmers of Emilia, Umbria, and Tuscany originated in the eighteenth century, when the Church owned large land estates (Dogan, 1967: 148). A different type of political tradition characterizes the Italian province of Lucca, which votes overwhelmingly for the Christian-Democratic Party, although it is surrounded by a "red" belt; this enables it to maintain its individuality, which is explained by the fact that it once was an independent duchy. Such identification through differentiation has been reported by students of voting behavior in other countries (Scheuch, 1969: 133-155). There is a radical tradition among the small farmers (rather than tenants or laborers) in the West and Southwest of France, which originated in the distribution of land during the French Revolution. Another example is the finding that in southern and western Finland, the Communist vote correlates positively with the number of Communists killed in the civil war of 1918 (Allardt and Pesonen, 1967: 325-366). Major social upheavals create cleavages which may persist, locally or nationally, far beyond the relevance of the issues from which they originated, and powerful leaders sometimes leave "political legacies" which outlive even those of their successors who ignore or oppose them. The American Civil War, the Great Depression, and the Democratic coalition established by F. D. Roosevelt have created similar traditions in political attitudes and partisan identifications in the United States.

In most cases, such political traditions have observable social or geographical boundaries, and these boundaries help explain the continued persistence of such traditions. The survival of a political tradition which differs from that of its social or geographical environment cannot be explained by intergenerational socialization alone. Exposure to new problems and solutions, the diffusion of new ideas and a changing environment would gradually erode the value perspectives embedded in the tradition. When it is capable of surviving, one ought to look for a structural pattern which remains unimpaired by environmental changes. The radicalism of the small farmer in the Southwest of France is sustained by the fact that he cannot compete with the large landowner in his region, whose ability to modernize the processes of production reduces the small farmer's market. The fact that the land of the tenant farmer in Italy is not owned any more by the Papal State has not changed the economic and sociopsychological condition of the tenant. And the intensity of the feelings created by the civil war in Finland in 1918 could not have persisted if the areas involved had not remained islands of underdevelopment.

These interpretations suggest that the so-called "impact of the past" is to a large extent a cultural reinforcement of attitudes determined by persisting social, economic, or ecological constraints. Present attitudes are determined by, and expressed in terms of, these structural factors, but since the relative position of such groups in the social structure has not changed through time, culturally transmitted value perspectives and attitudes toward present problems reinforce each other. Similarly, the metaphor of "political legacies" can be restated in attitudinal and structural terms. Bonapartism, for example, can be conceptualized as personalized, centralized, and authoritarian government. In terms of attitudes, it reflects a mistrust of politics and politicians; as a process, it can be described as the mobilization of alienated or nonmobilized voters by a leader of the counter-elites.

If the persistence or reactivation of political traditions can be explained by variables and relationships pertaining to social and political structures, then a localized political tradition does not constitute—per se—an obstacle in the attempt to formulate general statements about the relationship between variables structuring political behavior. The analysis of political traditions also indicates the relevance of social, ecological, or organizational constraints and of the manner in which they affect political attitudes and behavior. Since such constraints may have observable social and geographical boundaries, the quest for general uniformities in behavior should be preceded by a consideration of the size and type of units of comparison which would most likely reflect such differences in social, ecological, or organizational constraints. This issue will be discussed in Chapter 3.

We have not encountered, so far, insuperable obstacles or unanswerable arguments against the possibility of constructing an empirical political science based on cross-systemic uniformities. Let us proceed, therefore, to explore the dimensions and spaces of a paradigm for cross-systemic comparisons. Chapter 3 will deal with the size of the unit of observation; Chapters 4 and 5 will describe the socioecological and perceptual spaces of the paradigm. In Chapter 6 the focus will shift from the paradigm to theories based on the most advanced area of empirical research: the study of voting behavior. Chapters 7, 8, and 9 represent attempts to formulate new elements for a general theory of political behavior, using economic reasoning and psychological theory. These new elements are intended to provide criteria for the evaluation of functional and substantive equivalence in the comparison of political behavior.

Chapter 3

DETERMINING UNITS OF COMPARISON

What Is Macro-Quantitative Analysis?

Postulating the possibility of a generalizing political science and accepting the methodological requirement that comparisons be conducted across systems does not imply a judgment on the type or size of systems which should serve as units of comparison. Should this judgment be made on theoretical or methodological grounds? Is it perhaps also a matter of access to data and data sources—i.e., a matter of convenience? Research reports seldom convey the reasons for the choice of a particular unit size, or information on the availability of alternative units in terms of the research problem under consideration. It has been shown in the preceding chapter that persisting differences in structural characteristics between environments are associated with "region"-specific political behavior. Whether such "regions" are treated as units of analysis or are submerged in a much larger unit should therefore be of some consequence for the theoretical interpretation of one's findings.

One increasingly visible trend in the "new comparative politics" reflects the choice of national political systems as units of quantitative analysis in cross-systemic comparisons. This chapter will attempt to examine the logical, theoretical, and methodological concomitants of this choice and their consequences for a theoretically oriented comparative approach. It will do so by emphasizing the logic of the very techniques used in macro-quantitative studies and by placing system-level data into a theoretical perspective.

It has often been said that the choice of the units of comparison depends largely on the type of problem the researcher is investigating. This is not a very illuminating truism. The choice of units of comparison is a somewhat more complex matter and involves three different questions:

(1) What is the most appropriate unit of analysis, if we wish to observe a given type of behavior (the dependent variable) in as broad a range of values as possible, in order to make statements of general validity or statements about the limits within which a generalization holds true? This is the problem of the type and size of the unit of analysis (social, organizational, ecological, or cultural unit) within which we wish to study the dependent variable.

(2) Given a specific unit of analysis, what other units at different levels of organization, should we observe and draw into the explanation of behavior within the unit of analysis, and under what conditions can we make inferences from observations at other levels? This is the problem of levels of observation and cross-level inferences.

(3) At what level of generalization, or what level of abstraction, do we wish to make statements about the dependent variable? This is the problem of levels of generalization or abstraction.

We shall be concerned here only with issues raised by the first two questions.

Some of these issues have been vividly debated in the controversy between *holism* and *methodological individualism*. Proponents of the holist approach have claimed that political "reality" occurs in wholes—complex units of interrelated components—more specifically, the nation-state, and that it can be understood only as a whole. The whole is *more* than the mere sum total of its parts and *more* than the mere sum total of the relationships existing at any moment between its parts. A group or society may keep much of its original character even if all of its original members are replaced by others. There is a group spirit, a group tradition; societies have needs and goals of their own which cannot be reduced to the needs and goals of their individual members. Both as a philosophical approach and as an analogy between social and biological theory, holism is opposed to the methodological individualism of behaviorism, according to which the only empirical unit of observation is man—the individual and his behavior.

Thus defined, the controversy can be easily traced back to the ancient and barren dispute between nominalism and realism (or idealism or essentialism). In these terms it has been interpreted by Karl Popper (1957: 17-26), who coined the term methodological individualism. The realist position implied that concepts such as state, government, values, or institutions "really" exist, above and beyond the concrete instances to which they are applied, not unlike Plato's ideas. For the methodological individualist these are, in Popper's words, "theoretical constructions" (analytical constructs in present-day parlance), models which we construct in order to interpret and explain certain experiences. And Popper adds that very often we mistake our theoretical models for concrete things. Sociological models have to be constructed in "nominalist" terms, that is to say, in terms of individuals, their attitudes, expectations, relations, and overt behavior (1957: 135-136). According to Popper, holistic thinking about both society and nature is not a high level or a late stage in the development of thought, but characteristic of a pre-scientific stage (1957: 76).

Behavioral political science has adopted the nominalist position.

> This does not mean that research is restricted to the individual person as the theoretical focus of investigation. . . . A group, an organization, a community . . . may be the focus of behavioral inquiry [but] groups, organizations, or nations have no independent status apart from the conduct of the individuals who are related by behaving towards each other in certain ways . . . institutions do not and cannot exist physically apart from the persons who inhabit them [Eulau, 1963: 14-15].

Thus, in answering the first question, the holist would claim that generalizations will hold true only within a given society, nation-state, or cultural area, which are also the appropriate units of analysis. For the behaviorist the choice of the unit of analysis has to be justified theoretically and empirically, but the *empirical unit of observation* (as opposed to both unit of analysis and level of observation) is the individual, whose behavior can be studied at different levels of social organization—which are the units of analysis. The type and limits of possible generalizations are open, empirically determinable, questions.

It has become fashionable in the social sciences to speak of a distinction between micro- and macro- analysis. The assumed similarity between the holist-individualist controversy, and the distinction between micro- and macro-politics, has sometimes been a source of confusion. The terms micro- and macro- have been used somewhat loosely, without an explicit distinction between units of analysis and levels of observation. For example, in his "Systematic Approaches to Comparative Politics," Merritt uses the term micro-politics for units of analysis, and macro-politics to indicate levels of observation. Micro-politics is "the study of the political behavior of individuals and small groups," whereas macro-politics is the study of the "interrelationships of structures and processes and their effects upon the behavior of the elements (individuals, groups, institutions)." The latter is also expected to "account for the findings produced empirically at the microtheoretical level" (Merritt, 1970: 5-6). In his attempt to clarify the difference between units of analysis and levels of observation, Eulau uses the terms micro- and macro- to denote levels of observation, and concludes consistently that for the political scientist micro-analysis consists in drawing a lower-level unit (of observation) into the explanation of behavior at a higher-level unit (of analysis). Macro-analysis implies the use of a higher-level unit (of observation) to explain behavior at a lower-level unit (of analysis). Consequently, micro- and macro- are not specific levels, but merely the poles of a continuum, denoting a direction and not a specific position on the continuum (Eulau, 1969: 17-18).

The term macro-analysis has also been applied to an increasingly visible trend in comparative politics, which cannot be classified within the holist-individualist dichotomy: this refers to macro-quantitative analysis. The *World Handbook of Social and Political Indicators* (Russett et al., 1964), the *Cross-Polity Survey* (Banks and Gregg, 1965), the various studies they have inspired, and other thematically or methodologically related works represent this approach. One of the common characteristics of these studies is the convergence of units of analysis and levels of observation: the nation-state. However, many such studies have also used data on the behavior of individuals within the nation-state and reconceptualized, measured, or evaluated such data, usually available in aggregates, as national system-attributes. The correlations between indicators of such system-attributes—across nations—have then been used either for the classification and ranking of nations on indices of specific interest (e.g., internal violence, economic development, democratization, or stability), or for testing causal models concerning the relationship between such indices and a number of structural and behavioral variables.

Macro-quantitative comparisons inquire into the conditions under which political systems exhibit certain attributes. "In macro-cross-national research the concern is for formulating empirical generalizations about whole political systems" (Gillespie, 1971: 14). The attributes of systems are analytical constructs referring to structural or behavioral characteristics: some complex constructs include both behavioral and structural components. Empirical indicators are sometimes grouped together into a more complex or more abstract category, which is either a composite summarizing measure, or a substantive concept at a higher level of abstraction. An example of a summarizing index is the "Total Magnitude of Civil Violence," a composite multistage measure combining indices of duration, pervasiveness, intensity, and amplitude of civil violence (Gurr and Ruttenberg, 1971). A nonadditive measure, based on patterns of rank orders of values on structural and behavioral variables is the Flanigan and Fogelman index of democratization, which includes succession to the principal executive office, political competition, electoral participation, and absence of suppression (Flanigan and Fogelman, 1967).

With whole systems as their units of analysis, macro-quantitative studies are often applied to the entire universe of existing nation-states and oriented toward a "grand theory" of politics, or generalizations at the highest level of abstraction. Quantitative cross-national comparison "is suited to gross discriminations among nations, but not to the micro-analysis that would account more precisely for the forms, timing and targets of specific occurrences ... since our immediate concern is the relevance of the theory for the most general case, this characteristic is less a limitation than micro-analysts might argue" (Gurr and Ruttenberg, 1971).

If macro-quantitative comparisons had been concerned only with gross discriminations (i.e., classifications, typologies), they could have enjoyed respectable status in the repertoire of traditional political science. Macro-quantitative analysis assumes, however, a "scientific posture." This posture has been severely criticized, primarily on logical grounds. Thus, according to Holt and Richardson (1970: 64), the approach is *atheoretical,* because "the very strategy of the approach tends to make it difficult, if not impossible, to provide a tight refutation of such a theory." It is true, of course, that the generalizations of macro-quantitative analyses cannot be nomothetic (Nagel, 1961: 63; Kaplan, 1964: 92), and since they cannot be nomothetic, their explanatory and predictive power has been questioned. Not less important than its logical status is the theoretical vulnerability of macro-quantitative analysis. Comparisons are limited to system-level data, but no assumptions are made about the structure, functions, and meanings of political behavior within systems; consequently, the macro-approach is deprived of criteria for evaluating its findings and its methodology, including the choice of macro-units of analysis.

The following are some of the most important methodological issues encountered in the comparison of aggregate data; some of the technical difficulties are not to be minimized either, but there is little of interest that can be added to what has already been written on the subject (see, for example, Merritt and Rokkan, 1966; Rokkan, 1968; Scheuch, 1966). These methodological issues have been discussed in the sociological literature, but until recently political science has not been particularly concerned with their implications. Yet even other social scientists will find it difficult to account for the fact that they thought they "discovered" the ecological fallacy with Robinson in the early 1950s, although Thorndike had already drawn attention to it in 1939 and a European sociologist had to remind us of an earlier heated controversy over problems of aggregation in economics (Scheuch, 1966: 136-137). At present, we have in the works of Blalock (1964), Alker (1964, 1965, 1969), Scheuch (1966), and Galtung (1967) several good introductions to the problem identified as the ecological fallacy or, more generally, as the "fallacies of cross-level inferences." It would perhaps be useful to distinguish between logical fallacies, their operational consequences, and explanations offered for these consequences, since even without accounting for the longitudinal or universal fallacies, the narrowly ecological fallacy seems to refer to a number of different, though not unrelated, problems. Let me add that these are general methodological issues, but their importance increases with the size of the units of analysis and that they are, therefore, particularly relevant in a discussion of macro-quantitative comparisons.

LOGICAL FALLACIES

The logical fallacy consists in making direct translations of properties or relationships from one level of observation to another when making such translations is an illogical inference from the observation. (This, I believe, is what Galtung [1967: 41] really had in mind when he claimed that the logical fallacy refers to translations rather than inferences). The logical fallacy involved in such illegitimate translations can refer to two different types of cases:

(a) Measuring the proportion of, say, foreign-born and the proportion of illiterates in a given population grouped in territorial units of the same type—say, counties—and correlating these measurements across counties will yield a correlation of, say, 0.50. Translating this finding to the individual level would result in saying that the correlation between being foreign-born and being illiterate is 0.50. The logical fallacy involved consists in assuming that the proportion of illiterates refers to the same individuals represented by the proportion of foreign-born, whereas both are statements about the entire population of each county, but may refer to different subsets of their population.

(b) A different type of logical fallacy is involved in the translation of structural or global characteristics of a group to the level of the group's individual members. This is a fallacy of the wrong level, but not an ecological or contextual fallacy. Perhaps the best example of the difference between this and the preceding type of logical non sequitur is that quoted by Lazarsfeld and by Galtung: the indecision of a hung jury does not mean that the members of the jury are indecisive.

In the case of the statement about the jury, the inference is absurd. In the statement about the correlation between being foreign-born and illiterate, the inference is not absurd, because there may or may not be some correlation between place of birth and illiteracy, but the translation is not valid, and the statement is probably highly inaccurate.

OPERATIONAL CONSEQUENCES

The single most important consequence of the ecological fallacy is related to levels of aggregation: the larger the units of aggregation, the more inflated the correlation coefficient between any pair of variables. In Robinson's example, the correlation between race and illiteracy in the United States, when data were grouped into nine large regions, was found to be 0.946; for state-level data, the correlation dropped to 0.773, and for individual-level correlations, to a mere 0.203. When Blalock analyzed a data set for 150 counties observed at the county level and grouped into fifteen groups of ten counties each according to geographic proximity, the correlation between the variables observed increased from 0.54 to 0.81, and when the counties were grouped according to the value of the dependent variable, the distortion was even larger (Blalock, 1964: 103).

EXPLANATIONS

Mathematical formulations for a calculus of the ecological fallacy have been based on the assumption of regional groupings of aggregate data. Of these formulations, the covariance theorem (Alker, 1965) is probably intuitively the simplest. The total (or universal) covariance of two variables x and y (C_{xy}) is the sum of a within-region covariance (calculated on regional means) WC_{xy} and a between-region (ecological) covariance (calculated on the universal mean) EC_{xy}:

$$C_{xy} = WC_{xy} + EC_{xy}$$

(WC_{xy} is a population-weighted sum over all regions of the covariance in terms of regional means; EC_{xy} is a population-weighted average product of regional deviations from the universal mean.)

Similarly, using regression analysis, Duncan et al. (1961: 66) have shown that the regression coefficient for the whole universe of data (B_{yx}) is equal to the average within-region regression coefficient (WB_{yx}) and the product of two terms: (a) the difference between ecological (between-region) and within-region regression coefficients ($EB_{yx} - WB_{yx}$) and (b) a term E^2_{xR}, which is the ratio of the between-region and universal variance of x.

$$B_{yx} = WB_{yx} + E^2_{xR} \ (EB_{yx} - WB_{yx})$$

(See also Alker, 1969.)

Finally, Robinson's original equation for correlational analysis of aggregated area data also implies terms reflecting within- and between-region correlations, as well as the above term E^2_{xR} and a similar term E^2_{yR} for y (Robinson, 1950).

The simplest verbal explanations have been offered by Blalock (1964) and Scheuch (1966). The term "region," in the mathematical formulations, does not stand for geographical proximity alone; it applies to any criterion for grouping the data. The general issue involved in the ecological fallacy "is really the relation of the criterion according to which units are grouped to the types of inference intended when using the results of aggregated units" (Scheuch, 1966: 154). This implies two considerations: (1) What outside variables, not accounted for and not correlated with *both* x and y, have an impact on the correlation, and (2) how does the distribution of values on such outside variables change as we increase the size of the unit for which data are aggregated (Blalock, 1964: 103-112). These considerations indicate that without accounting for the impact of outside variables and their regional distribution and range of values, the correlation or covariance between variables measured at the aggregate national system-level (which is the largest unit-size other than continents or cultural areas) is likely to be distorted, and no translation of findings can be legitimately made from the system-level to individual behavior. If it is impossible to *determine* individual-level relationships between variables from aggregate measures alone, is it, perhaps, possible to *estimate* individual-level relationships from aggregate data?

In an attempt to circumvent the difficulties posed by inference from aggregate to individual data through correlational analysis, Goodman (1953: 663) has proposed an alternative method based on regression analysis, and Stokes (1969: 62-83) has shown the possibilities and limitations of this method in applying it to the estimation of interparty transition-probabilities from time-series of aggregate election results. It will suffice, here, to refer briefly to the simplest version of this method.

The example refers to aggregates of individual characteristics (attributes and behavioral data). Let us assume that we know the proportion of blue-collar workers in the population of eligible voters in a number of countries, as well as the proportion of the Communist vote, as a percentage of the total vote for all parties, in each of these countries. Ignoring the problem of non-voters, can we infer from such aggregate data the individual-level relationship between being a blue-collar worker and voting for the Communist Party in each of these countries? Stated otherwise, can we estimate the percentage of blue-collar workers who voted Communist? Using percentage of blue-collar workers as values of x and percentage of Communist voters as values of y, we can plot these points, for each country, on a scatter diagram and obtain a regression line with an y intercept of a and a slope of b, represented by the equation

$$y = a + bx$$

If we denote by q the proportion of blue-collar workers, and by r the proportion of non-blue-collar workers, *who voted Communist,* we can write

$$y \text{ (Communist vote)} = qx + r(1 - x)$$

Solving for q and r in the above equations we find that r = a and q = a + b. Thus, the estimated percentage of blue-collar workers who voted Communist can be obtained directly from the values of a and b in the regression equation.

The limitation of this method consists in the explicit assumption that the proportion of Communist and non-Communist voters among blue-collar workers is the same, or almost the same, in all units (countries), irrespective of the marginal percentage of Communist voters or blue-collar workers. Ecological regression enables us to estimate the cell entries of a matrix cross-tabulating percentages of subcategories of two or more attributes or variables, knowing only the marginals of rows and columns, provided these percentages are fairly stable across units of analysis. The smaller the scattering around the regression line—i.e., the closer the coefficient of ecological correlation comes to 1.0—the stabler the cell entries across units.

Despite the ingenuity of this simple technique, it does not increase the relevance of macro-quantitative indicators. The purpose of cross-national comparison is to determine the relationship between variables across systems; we would use cross-systemic comparisons to determine whether or not the same proportion of blue-collar workers votes Communist in different countries. We are not interested in the actual cell entries, assuming that the proportion does not change across nations; had there been sufficient evidence to the effect that the proportion does not change, cross-national comparison would have been superfluous. From the viewpoint of a comparative analysis of political behavior, ecological regression puts the cart before the horse and is, therefore, of little avail.

So far, the reasoning has applied to the relationship between aggregate and individual-level relationships. What is the relationship between national system-level aggregates and the series of such measures obtained from the universe (or a subuniverse) of nation-states? Alker has shown that the logic of the covariance theorem applies also to the relationship between system-level data (Alker 1964, 1965, 1966).

Let us consider the universal fallacy. It consists in ascribing a relationship (correlation coefficients or regression slopes) calculated on national indicators for two (or more) variables across the universe of nations, to individual nations or groups of nations (regions). For example, the relationship between national voting levels (turnout) and the magnitude of government spending (as a percentage of the gross national product), calculated for a universe of twenty-six developed and underdeveloped nations, can be expressed by a regression line with a slope of 0.40 (for every increase of 1 unit in the level of government expenditure, the corresponding increase in the voting level is 0.40) and the coefficient of association ($\emptyset$) between the two variables, interpreted as a coefficient of correlation, would be 0.41. However, when the relationship was calculated for developed countries only, the slope decreased to 0.05 (i.e., disappeared almost completely) and the $\emptyset$ measure dropped from 0.41 to 0.05. For underdeveloped countries, the slope was obviously much steeper than the slope for the universal regression line; it increased to 0.70, with a corresponding increase in $\emptyset$ to 0.53 (Alker, 1965: 97). A similar example has been presented by Alker in his first analysis of the *World Handbook* data. The universal regression line, for forty-one countries, of scores on an index of achievement orientation developed by McClelland, and levels of national per capita GNP showed a negative slope of -0.55. Stated otherwise, as the national per capita GNP increased, the scores on the achievement orientation index decreased, a finding which either refutes the assumed relationship between achievement orientation and achievement or invalidates McClelland's measurement of this orientation. A decomposition of the series of data into regional regression lines showed positive slopes for Asian and African, as well as for Latin American countries, but a negative slope for European countries (Alker, 1964: 327). These observations indicate that (1) a low universal linear correlation may conceal a curvilinear relationship, and (2) a linear slope may change with changing values of an intervening variable (in the above examples: geographic regions and levels of per capita GNP). The nature of the intervening variable raises the question of the *longitudinal fallacy.*

When the relationship between x and y is observed in different subcategories of a controlled, third variable, a distinction must be made between subcategories of a nominal scale (e.g., continents, religions, ethnic origin) and segments of an interval scale (e.g., per capita GNP, education, etc.). When the "regions" are subcategories of a nominal scale, we can only show how much of the total covariance is explained by the variance within each subcategory and by the difference between subcategories. One does not assume that if and when an African nation will become a European nation, or Italians will become Swedes, they will also display the values of x and y presently observed in the European nation, or among Swedes. However, when the control variable is measured on an interval scale, are we not assuming, implicitly or explicitly, that if the present per capita GNP of region A will reach the present levels of per capita GNP of region B, it will also display the values of x and y presently observed in region B? Almost every "theory of development" is based on this assumption, which implies a leap from synchronically collected cross-sectional data to a diachronic, longitudinal inference. This is the longitudinal fallacy.

When we argue that an increase of 1 unit in the value of x will be associated with an increase of 0.40 units in y, we mean one of two things: (1)

whenever we shall encounter a case of $x_i + 1$ (i.e., an individual j for whom the value of x exceeds that of individual i by 1), its value of y will be approximately $y_i + 0.40$; these are the values predicted by a regression line. Or (2) if we raise the present value of x of individual i to $x + 1$, we shall find that his value of y has risen to approximately $y + 0.40$. It is this latter reasoning which is implied in the longitudinal fallacy, and it involves a questionable assumption of causality (Blalock, 1964: 39-40). When the number of cases is large and the goodness of fit is close, we can assume that only a small fraction in the variance of y is due to variables not drawn into the analysis, an assumption which would reduce the risk of committing the longitudinal fallacy. In cross-national comparisons of system-level data, however, the number of cases is small, the goodness of fit is rarely very high, and a number of presumably important variables (psychological, social, and cultural) are not accounted for. Therefore, the risk of committing the longitudinal fallacy in macro-quantitative comparisons is not negligible. So far, only the cluster of modernization variables has shown consistently high intercorrelations; their correlations with political variables, however, are moderate or weak. Thus higher education explains only fourteen percent of the variance in voting levels, and industrialization only nineteen percent in the variance of group violence (based on data from *World Handbook*). There is another, rather obvious, factor involved in the longitudinal fallacy. Synchronic data reflect a given, temporally defined state and distribution of knowledge. Longitudinal, developmental models cannot account for changes in the state and distribution of knowledge, but neither should they ignore the ability of nations to learn from the earlier experience of others. Planned development and "taking off" under circumstances in which the planners and rulers of a nation can benefit from the levels of development of modern polities, economies, and technologies, *can*–but not necessarily *will*–prevent some of the trend-reversals displayed by unplanned, "natural," and self-sustained patterns of development in the past.

All arguments, therefore, seem to point at the relative disadvantage and the methodological vulnerability of comparisons conducted at the national-system-level. At best, such comparisons can suggest hypotheses for further research at lower levels of analysis. *As far as within-system political behavior is concerned, system-level data are merely descriptions of the total, national environment.* One can, therefore, only pause and wonder at the recent expansion of the macro-quantitative literature with a scientific posture. Gurr has even coined a new term for this field—politimetrics—and used it as the title of a textbook on political science methods and techniques based on macro-quantitative data (Gurr, 1972). I could not agree more with Gurr when he states that "the investigator who plans to infer relationships among variables up or down levels of analysis from the level at which he actually measures the variables runs an increased risk of theoretical silliness and factual error." Yet, he also believes that the researcher often *wants to* or must risk these fallacies, and that "the important consideration is that he make the conceptual leap knowingly, and recognizing that some kinds of conclusions drawn from them can be truly fallacious" (1972: 35). An approach which admits the risk of theoretical silliness, without providing theoretical or methodological criteria for deciding when an inference is or is not "truly fallacious" deserves, perhaps, some reappraisal by its practitioners.

As a system-level description of the environment, macro-quantitative data include behavior, demographic and institutional structure, resources, outputs, and distributions. "Environment" is part of the very definition of social behavior, and political behavior would be meaningless if taken out of the context in which it occurs. The environmental or ecological "perspective" in the social sciences has been strongly advocated by Harold and Margaret Sprout (1965), and it is somewhat discomforting to believe that there was a need for this effort to "replace" man into his setting in our investigations. It is the way in which individuals perceive, interpret, or relate themselves to the environment which "affects" human values, attitudes, choices, and verbal and nonverbal behavior; and the Sprouts add cautiously and cautioning: environmental factors may limit human actions, irrespective of whether these factors have been perceived or taken into account by the actor.

If the perceived and interpreted environment "affects" human actions, it becomes imperative to operationalize the concept of environment. It is not sufficient to ask what kind of environmental factors—economic, social, cultural, physical, or any combination thereof—are relevant for any given attitude or act of behavior; one must also specify the spatial and organizational boundaries within which these factors have been perceived and interpreted, since it is the perceived structure of the environment which "affects" behavior. There are two elements in this statement which call for a spatial and configurational operationalization of the environment: (a) the actor's perception of the environment is spatially limited by his relative attachment to place and area of residence and work; presumably, this limitation is negatively correlated with education and exposure to the mass-media of communication; (b) the actor's needs, interests, and goals arise in relation to his life space, and there is a distance, both psychological (frequencies of attention and degree of salience) and physical, between the life space in which he moves, and the less immediate and only vaguely perceived "reality" of the total society, nation, or state.

Physical and psychological distance determine what is and what is not the perceived context of an action. This is a commonsense observation, but it has to bear on the selection of units of analysis in the comparative study of political behavior. With the possible exception of very small political units, such as Monaco or Luxemburg, the life space of the individual social actor does not extend to the boundaries of the national system. The individual lives and moves in his family, economic unit, neighborhood, local or regional branch of an occupational or political organization, a religious congregation, a city, a county. Society is organized functionally and territorially. The perceived environment of the actor does not consist of the categories and analytical measures reported in aggregate system-level data, but of spatially and functionally determined values of variables and relationships, and of the perceived changes therein. The environment consists of the spatial dispersion or concentration of values and other characteristics and the stable or changing location of individuals and groups with regard to such clusters of concentration or patterns of dispersion. This does not imply that the individual will not perceive the impact of neighboring environments (e.g., through trade and tourism), or of the central political decision-making processes, but he will be primarily interested in, or alert to, their impact on *his* environment and *his* position therein. How to determine the boundaries of the "relevant" environment is an empirical question; it requires, however, some theoretical model concerning the nature of the constraints which structure behavior in different areas of life.

Considering system-level aggregates and measures as description of the total environment leads to a more specific, and perhaps more useful, interpretation of "system attributes" in the analysis of political behavior. There is a class or category of political actors, for whom the total environment is indeed the frame of reference for political action. These are the political elites: national decision makers, elected or appointed, and political leaders who aspire to these positions. They are those concerned with the aggregation and integration of different interests, with the formulation and implementation of policies designed to change the distribution of incomes or levels of education, to raise or lower the level of economic activity, reduce the ratio of inhabitants per hospital bed, etc. Even when a policy-goal is intended to solve a "regional" problem, concerning a subset of the population or a specific territorial unit, policy-making is guided by considerations of the total environment (e.g., the budget) and of alternative uses of available resources to meet demands from other sectors of the environment. The total environment, and its constituent parts, are key factors in the analysis of political elite behavior. This is evident in the case of foreign policy and international relations, where the behavior of elites in other countries, and their environments, become extremely relevant. It also applies to domestic policies, but here the process is more fragmented and less visible as a whole.

For the voter, the local party militant, the union representative, the mayor, or even the regional legislator, the total environment—of which he may be aware as an interested citizen—is not perceived as a frame of reference for political action, with the exception of the infrequent occasions on which the citizen is called to participate in system-level decisions. It has also been shown that even in elections to the national legislatures, interests, loyalties, and issues defined in terms of the voter's perceived environment are sometimes more important in the electoral choice than national issues and policies. A behavioral approach to comparative politics must distinguish, therefore, between elite and mass behavior not only in terms of forms and types of behavior, or input and output, but also in terms of differences in the magnitude, structure, and complexity of the relevant environment.

Macro-quantitative comparisons are relevant in the study of international relations and a number of such comparisons have indeed been oriented toward the analysis of conflict and cooperation between nations (e.g., Deutsch, 1960; Rummel, 1963; Alker, 1964; Russett, 1967). One of the techniques frequently used in these, as well as in intrasystemic studies, is factor analysis. Let us examine the underlying logical assumptions in the application of factor analysis to macro-quantitative data.

Factor analysis was first devised in psychology. It was intended by its founders and developers (Spearman, Pearson, Thurstone) to provide mathematical models for the explanation of human abilities and behavior. More specifically, its principal objective was to attain a parsimonious description of observed data. Through factor analysis, the numerous variables observed in psychological tests could be reduced to a small number of underlying dimensions, which "explained" a large portion of the variance in clusters of observed variables. For example, twenty-four different psychological tests could be shown to reflect only five factors, the first three of which explained eighty-eight percent of the variance (Harman, 1967: 170). These factors were then interpreted by the investigator, according to the variables with which they correlated most, as representing an "underlying psychological dimension," such as verbal ability or orientation in spatial relations. Cattell was the first to substitute group characteristics (aggregate data) for individual-level observations in a factor analysis of cultural patterns (Cattell, 1949: 443-469). In 1960, Berry factor-analyzed forty-three economic and demographic national indicators across ninety-five countries in a study of economic development and found a "fundamental structure" of three basic dimensions, which he interpreted as (1) technological scale, (2) demographic scale, and (3) a group of poor trading nations (Berry, 1960: 78-107). In political science, factor analysis of macro-data was used by Rummel (1963, 1966) and Tanter (1965, 1966) for a study of the basic dimensions of conflict behavior, by Alker (1964) in a study of United Nations roll-calls and international conflict, by Russett (1967) for a typology of world regions; Banks and Gregg (1965) factor-analyzed the data of the *Cross-Polity Survey*, and Adelman and Morris (1965, 1967) used this technique to analyze the relationship between the

GNP and a number of social and political indicators in seventy-four countries. (This, of course, is only a partial list of relevant studies.)

The input in a factor analysis is a correlation matrix between each variable and every other variable in the set. The correlations are based on the observed values across the cases in the population (in the present context, national aggregates or central measures across a number of nation-states). The factor-analytic model assumes that the values of the variables in the set can be considered as determined by a set of linear equations; each equation relates one variable to the assumed common factors. Thus:

$$z_1 = a_{11}F_1 + a_{12}F_2 + a_{13}F_3 \ldots + a_{1m}F_m + d_1U_1$$

$$z_2 = a_{21}F_1 + a_{22}F_2 + a_{23}F_3 \ldots + a_{2m}F_m + d_2U_2$$

$$z_n = a_{n1}F_1 + a_{n2}F_2 + a_{n3}F_3 \ldots + a_{nm}F_m + d_nU_n$$

The z's are the variables measured in the data, $F_1, F_2 \ldots F_m$ are the common factors, the a's their respective coefficients, and the U term is the specific residual term. This set of equations is the *factor pattern,* and the a coefficients are interpreted as the contribution of each factor to the variance of the respective z.

The correlation of each variable with a given factor is its factor *loading.* Some variables show a much higher loading on some factors than on any other. This leads to the interpretation that a factor is structuring most of the variance of those variables, with which it is highly correlated. When the factors are assumed to be uncorrelated with each other (orthogonal), the value of the a's equals the value of the correlation between z and F. Since the factors are common to all variables, they are conceptualized as underlying dimensions structuring the variances of the entire set of variables.

The most obvious question one would like to ask is: what are these factors? The equations in the factor pattern are similar to regression equations of the type

$$y = a + b_1x_1 + b_2x_2$$

In a regression equation, however, the x_1, x_2, etc., stand for specific variables. For example:

$$y \text{ (voting turnout)} = a + b_1x_1 \text{ (level of education)} +$$

$$b_2x_2 \text{ (party competitiveness)}.$$

In a factor pattern, however, the F's are hypothetical constructs, dimensions with no observable empirical referents. The psychologist, who inquired into the "structure" of intelligence or ability tests, was not looking for empirically identifiable dimensions. He studied the structure of thinking processes, and was satisfied to observe a factorial structure, even if it could be shown to exist only in the logic of his mathematical analysis of correlations between the variables to which his tests referred. The mathematical analysis also indicated that there was no single "correct" factorial solution, that any correlation matrix could yield a number of factorial solutions, depending on the further assumptions one made about the relationship between the factors themselves. A simple geometrical proof indicates that the angle between two vectors, which represents the correlation between two variables, does not depend on the position of the coordinate axes (the factors) that define the plane on which the vectors are located. In a multidimensional space, the factors can be "rotated" into many positions.

Although the logic of factor analysis does not provide criteria for a single correct solution, this does not imply that, of the many possible sets of underlying factors, one is not more meaningful—i.e., does not approximate the actual structure of the clusters of variables—somewhat better than any other set. The psychologist prefers one set of factors to another without reference to the correlations between the variables (which remain unchanged), but by interpreting the meaning he assigns to the variables with high loadings on a given factor. When he labels a factor "orientation in space" or "verbal ability," he generalizes the meaning of a set of observed variables or characteristics of behavior. What he assumes, therefore, is that the factor "verbal ability" organizes the observed behavior in a consistent, meaningful way. In psychology, "ability" is a characteristic imputed to the mental or psychic organization of the tested individuals. The factor is conceived as an *organizing principle* of behavior.

Consider now the position of the political scientist identifying the extracted factors in his analysis of correlations between system attributes across nations. Let us look first at a few examples. In their factor analysis of the *Cross-Polity Survey* data, Gregg and Banks (1965: 555-578) used sixty-eight political system indicators to analyze relationships within the political domain itself. (The fact that in this study polychotomous characteristics were assigned interval values for correlation purposes does not affect the problem of factor identification and the authors report that despite their scoring technique there is close correspondence between their factors and those identified in three other independent studies.) The first factor extracted was interpreted as "access to political channels." The following matrix shows the variables with the highest positive and negative loadings on this factor.

Factor		*Factor*	
Loading	*Variable*	*Loading*	*Variable*
.94	Electoral system	−.58	East European area grouping
.93	Constitutional regime	−.70	Elitism
.92	Group opposition	−.71	Communist system
.87	Status of legislature	−.75	Role of police
.86	Horizontal power distribution	−.77	One-party system
.85	Representativeness	−.77	Military supportive
.80	Press freedom	−.81	Totalitarian regime
.73	Military neutral	−.82	Status of executive
.68	Articulation by parties	−.83	Articulation by institutional
.63	Articulation by associational		groups
	groups		

The second factor extracted was labeled "structural differentiation," and some of the variables with high positive loadings on this factor were: Political modernization (.76), Articulation by associational groups (.54), Bicameral legislatures (.51); among the variables with high negative loadings were: Postcolonial bureaucracy (−.92), Developmental ideological orientation (−.83), Articulation by nonassociational groups (−.58) and Aggregation by executive (−.48). The third factor was labeled "consensus" and it displayed high loadings for Government stability (.89), Stability of party system (.84), Advanced Western regional grouping (.66), Latin American grouping (−.59), Military interventive (−.60), and Domestic killed (−.66).

Factor analyses by Rummel (1963, 1966), Tanter (1966), and Bwy (1968), intended to identify the underlying dimensions of violent domestic conflict, have pointed at two basic factors with high loadings for two different sets of indicators of violent behavior: anomic violence and organized violence. Factor analysis has also been used in studies pooling behavioral and structural indicators describing the social, economic, cultural, or physical environment. It will be useful, however, to postpone consideration of analyses involving mixed indicators until we shall have clarified the theoretical status of factors extracted from behavioral indicators.

Factors extracted from psychological tests have been interpreted as principles of mental or psychic organization manifested in the behavior recorded by these tests. The factors identified in the analysis of political data—e.g., access to political channels, structural differentiation, organized violence, etc., are also underlying principles of organization. The political indicators, however, are aggregates of individual behavior, and aggregates, societies or nations have no mental or psychic organization. If these underlying principles of organization cannot be imputed to the mind or personality of a nation, do they exist only in the mind of the factor analyst, or do they have empirical referents?

At first sight, it would seem that the organizing dimensions of aggregate indicators of political behavior *do* have direct empirical referents: the principles of political organization of the observed nation-states, articulated and formalized in the verbal and nonverbal behavior of decision-making elites. Their empirical referents would be constitutions and laws, the ideologies, platforms, and beliefs of these elites, recorded in documents and speeches, laws, administrative regulations, policy directives, etc. One may wish to pursue this line of argument and consider factor loadings as a measure of the congruence between actual behavior and the respective principles of political organization. Those who would tend to subscribe to this interpretation should be reminded, however, that it does not escape the fallacy inherent in all comparisons of macro-level data. The entries in the correlation matrix are measures of correlation between pairs of variables across the entire universe of nations, or a subset thereof. A cluster of variables with high loadings on a given factor is a cross-national grouping of variables, and the factor is a cross-nationally observed principle of organization. In brief, the factors are still overarching, generalizing concepts, with no empirical referents, although they may be helpful in pointing at hypotheses about correlations, and causal relationships, within nations. In the so-called Q-technique of factor analysis, which is based on correlations between pairs of nations across the entire set of variables, the factor loadings indicate similarity of profiles on a number of variables, but the variables remain undifferentiated in the "pool," and no interpretation of the factors can be shown to correspond to an empirical referent.

Despite the indeterminacy of factorial solutions, the logic of factor analysis lends support to the intuitive—or metatheoretical—concept of a political *system* as an organized pattern of behavior structured by sets of goal-oriented and policy-implementing directives. *The factor analysis of individual-level measurements of behavioral variables, within nations, could point at the degree to which actual behavior is consistent with the professed principles of organization or with some of the rarely tested assumptions of political ideologies.* (For a discussion of the various dimensions of political participation revealed by a factor analysis of individual-level data, see Chapter 6.)

Let us now consider factor analyses of macro-data involving political and nonpolitical indicators. To what extent do the methodological difficulties arising in the factor analysis of behavioral data apply to mixed data sets? When one considers only indicators of the physical environment, such as area, geographical location, climate, or natural resources (although the latter involve the intervention of man, and therefore differences in levels of technology and distribution of benefits), one is unlikely to encounter any of the fallacies occurring in inferences from behavioral indicators. For the purposes of political analysis, area, climate, etc., can be considered as unchanging attributes of an environment common to some, or all, subsets of a population. If differences in physical characteristics are associated with differences in principles of political organization (for example, centralization with small units and federalism or decentralization with large units), the physical variables should cluster together with those indicating political organization, or *total* GNP (Russett, 1967: 20-21). More often, however, political indicators have been correlated with demographic, economic, technological, and socio-cultural data. Three types of problems can be encountered in this kind of comparisons.

First, some of these indicators clearly refer to different subsets of the population.

Second, measures of global properties or central tendencies are not always as relevant as the distribution of a given characteristic among subsets of the population. Per capita GNP is a classic example of this type of problems. As an overall average of economic activity and development, it does not reveal the distribution of economic participation and rewards; patterns of inequality (measured, for example, by the Lorenz curve or the Gini index) are certainly as relevant for political analysis as the overall measure of "development." Ohlin has pointed at several other weaknesses of the per capita GNP measure (Ohlin, 1968). As an overall measure of economic development, per capita GNP displays high correlations with indices of modernization and industrialization (Russett et al., 1964: 277). Per capita GNP explains approximately sixty-five percent of the variance in these indices. This has been confirmed by a factor analysis of per capita GNP and twenty-two social and political variables across seventy-four "less-developed" countries (Adelman and Morris, 1965). The interest of this study resides in the finding that one part of the variance in per capita GNP was found to be associated with indicators of modernization (size of agricultural sector, literacy, type of family organization, mass communication) on a factor labeled "urbanization and industrialization," while another part of the variance was associated with indicators of political differentiation (effectiveness of democratic institutions, parties, labor movements, political strength of the military, administrative efficiency, and centralization) on a factor labeled "political westernization." Social and political stability loaded highly on a separate factor, on which the loading of per capita GNP was only 0.12. These findings suggest that the cross-national correlation of these macro-indicators conceals or confounds one of the following possible relationships:

(a) at lower levels of development, the GNP is associated with social modernization, whereas at higher levels, it is associated with political westernization;

(b) at all levels of economic development, the GNP is more strongly associated with social modernization than with political westernization;

(c) there is reciprocal causality among economic, social, and political development;

(d) economic, social, and political development alike are merely reflections of different degrees of change in attitudes toward modernization, of functional specialization or integrating mechanisms.

For reasons related to the fact that no analysis of covariance (or correlation or factor analysis) can "rigorously demonstrate" causal relationships, Adelman and Morris support the more eclectic view reflected in alternative d. For the purpose of the present discussion, this is also evidence for the type of difficulties encountered in comparing system-level central tendencies and aggregate behavioral data across nations. One may add that even the variable "annual growth of per capita GNP" has not displayed any theoretically interesting correlations with national indicators of political behavior (Russett et al., 1964: 277).

Third, measurements of central tendencies are not only uninformative; they can also be misleading. Take government expenditure as a percentage of GNP: its relationship to political behavior will depend on both the social and economic criteria of taxation, and on the purposes of the expenditure (quite apart from the responsibility and responsiveness of government). Both the system of taxation and the social, political, or military goals of government expenditures have to be interpreted in a within-system context. This is the problem of the dimension of *meanings* on which the comparison is drawn, a problem encountered in all comparisons of human behavior.

The preceding examination of macro-quantitative studies has suggested that system-level data are essential in the analysis of the behavior of national elites and that factor analyses of system-level data can provide a framework for estimating the degree to which the implementation of policy decisions has achieved the stated goals of such policies. However, as far as mass behavior is concerned, macro-quantitative comparisons are fraught with risks of fallacious inferences and *cannot* provide criteria or remedies for the elimination of such risks as a consequence of the fact that subsystemic constraints resulting in within-system variance—i.e., some of the factors explaining actual behavior—are not brought to bear on the analysis. Chapters 4 and 5 will present a paradigm for multilevel analysis and cross-level comparisons, designed to yield both cross-systemic generalizations and an assessment of the conditions under which they hold true.

Chapter 4

THE SOCIOECOLOGICAL SPACE

Having explored the limitations of comparisons conducted exclusively at the level of national systems, we shall now inquire into the justifications for cross-level comparisons. The single most important reason for conducting comparisons across levels of social organization is the social, organizational, ecological structure of political systems.

"The systems with which we ordinarily deal, such as societies, nations and cultures, are organized in terms of several levels of components and the interactions within these systems are not limited to any particular level but cut across these levels." If we accept this statement, we immediately realize that cross-level analysis is a general requirement and not one which distinguishes between "comparative" and other types of studies. (The above quotation is from Przeworski and Teune [1970: 12]. These authors believe, however, that "comparative" studies are those in which the influence of larger systems upon the characteristics of units within them is examined at some stage of the analysis; yet, they also add that "all studies that are comparative are cross-systemic" [1970: 74].) The requirement for cross-level analysis derives from the general assumptions one makes about the properties and structure of political systems. Political behavior always occurs in or between systems, but this statement is vacuous unless we add that systems consist of partly overlapping environments within environments, of partly overlapping organizations within organizations, with different levels of integration. Political analysis

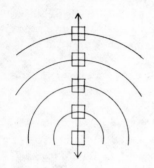

1. **cross-level analysis**

   Example: comparing the political participation of members of a neighborhood group in local activity with their participation in city, county, state and national politics.

   Line of comparison: vertical

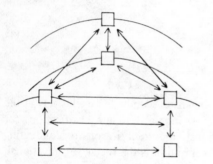

2. **cross-systemic and cross-level analysis**
   (a) with common levels of integration.

   Example: comparing voting behavior in two cities with their respective behavior in county, state and national elections.

   Lines of comparison: vertical and horizontal

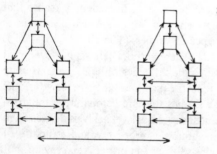

3. **cross-systemic and cross-level analysis**
   (b) *without common levels of integration between systems, with common levels of integration within systems.*

   Example: comparing the voting behavior of urban minority groups in two nations, with their voting behavior in regional and national elections.

   Lines of comparison: vertical and horizontal

Figure 1.

must address itself to these levels and areas of constraints. However, a cross-level analysis which is not cross-systemic is really only a case study. Although national political systems have been the single most frequently used unit of comparison, cross-national studies are not the only type of cross-systemic studies. Yet, whatever the level of organization chosen for the comparison, the analysis must proceed at two or more levels.

Thus, cross-systemic comparisons consist of the study of mass and elite behavior, structured by different areas and levels of integration—*across sets of such environmental and organizational constraints*—either within or between nations. Considering levels of integration as a vertical dimension, and "parallel" sets of such levels as a horizontal dimension, political behavior can be studied according to the three models of analysis shown in Figure 1.

The above models have been described only in terms of political units. At each level, the relevant environment also includes social, economic, ecological, and other components. There is, therefore, at each level on the vertical line, a horizontal interaction between political and nonpolitical components. With the exception of the physical environment, these nonpolitical components are sometimes also parts of vertically integrated subsystems (e.g., local or regional branches of national economic, professional or ethnic organizations).

The term "vertical" is not intended to convey a hierarchical relationship between levels, although such a hierarchy may in fact exist. "Vertical" refers to levels of *inclusion* and levels of *integration*. Inclusion simply means that a smaller unit is included in a larger one; integration refers to the extent to which the diversity between the smaller units is reflected, reduced, or eliminated at the "higher" level of organization. The integration of the various local units at the regional level can be achieved by a hierarchical relationship of authority, by processes of selective aggregation of opinions and interests, or by a deliberate separation of spheres of activity, which merely transposes the integration between the various local units and the regional unit to an even higher level of organization.

For each unit at a given level, the relevant environment includes lower- and higher-level units of the same kind, and the remaining socioecological components at its own level. This environment constitutes the behavioral frame of reference at the unit level. The economy of a region, the organization of its educational or health systems, its ethnic or religious subgroups, as well as many other items can be perceived as the politically relevant environment. Sometimes the salient factor in the environment is the dependence of one of its components on higher-level decision-making: for example, employment in a regionally concentrated industry which depends heavily on supplies to, or subsidies from, the central government. In other instances, a seaport, or the intersection of important lines of communication, may determine the economic and occupational structure of an area. Political behavior is embedded in a variety of social, economic, and cultural environments. The totality of these environments constitutes the *socioecological space* of political behavior. The structure of this space consists of levels of inclusion and integration, and these levels can be identified by the constraints which they impose on political behavior. Such constraints may originate at both lower and higher levels of integration. This is the justification for cross-level analysis in the socioecological space.

The environments perceived by political actors as relevant to a given problem constitute the frame of reference for their interpretation of the problem and for their goal-oriented behavior. It is the task of the analyst to identify the relevant environment, the boundaries of which need not coincide with administrative or otherwise convenient lines of demarcation. The purpose of cross-level analysis is to identify the "rules of composition" according to which the constraints imposed by the environment and various levels of organization determine behavior at the level under consideration, and the rules of composition according to which the resultant behavior in all units at a given level is integrated at a higher level. These compositional patterns have often been neglected in political science. This can be explained by the frequent holistic emphasis in traditional political science and by the concentration on single-level analysis in early empirical research. On the other hand, voting studies—which developed from aggregate ecological analysis— have benefited from the double advantage that the ecological units of analysis are determined by the boundaries of electoral districts, and that the rules of composition are simple arithmetic operations involving numbers of votes. Far less progress has been made in disentangling the compositional patterns of the determinants of voting trends. The task of cross-level analysis is to examine the patterns of composition which account for the fact that "the whole is not merely the sum of its parts," and cross-systemic analysis addresses itself to the conditions under which regularities in the evolution of such patterns prevail. (For a different interpretation of the paradigm of "progressive inclusiveness," allowing for the "translation" of individual- and group-level findings into statements about national societies, see Hopkins and Wallerstein [1967: 25-58].)

The relevance of intermediate levels of integration, and of rules of composition, has been presented, so far, as an assumption about the structure of the socioecological space, and in terms of the need to identify the boundaries within which individuals, groups, and organizations perceive their goals and toward which they direct their goal-oriented behavior. This approach can also be supported on *methodological* grounds. Is it not the explanation of the ecological fallacy which indicates the compositional nature of the relationship between variables? The covariance theorem clearly reflects the impact of the subcategories of a (regional) control variable on the (national) total covariance of two variables. Cross-level analysis reveals the impact of such regional constraints. The term "region," in this context, stands for different kinds of subnational units: ecological, administrative, political, economic, demographic, etc. With rare exceptions, political scientists have not applied the available analytical tools to the empirical study of cross-level compositional effects. Yet, as Stokes has shown some time ago, national components accounted for only thirty-two percent of the variance in the direction of party vote, whereas congressional districts and statewide components accounted for sixty-eight percent (Stokes, 1965: 61-85).

The need for multilevel, contextual analysis has been noted by a relatively small group of political scientists and sociologists with a comparative and methodological orientation. The first to have drawn attention to systematic cross-level analysis was Stein Rokkan.

In "The Comparative Study of Political Participation" (1962: 47-90), Rokkan points to the fact that in national election studies the structural context of micro-behavior is regularly overlooked or deliberately disregarded.

> Even in highly centralized systems there will be marked local differences in the range and character of the alternatives presented to the citizens on polling days, not just because of the variations in the group appeals of the party candidates, but even more because of the variations in the extent of local resistance to partisan conflict. Even highly disciplined national party organizations are not able to present the same alternatives to the citizens in all constituencies, let alone at all levels of government.

Quoting, for example, from his study (with H. Valen, 1960, 1970) of voting turnout in Norwegian communes, he reports that if fewer parties present themselves at local than at national elections in a given commune, turnout will be low also at the national elections, but if the same range of alternatives is presented at both levels of elections, turnout will be average or high. After noting the need for comparative quantitative analysis of the impact of macro-forces on micro-behavior, at different levels of organization—only partly satisfied in American voting studies by the focus on state-to-state differences in suffrage requirements and county-to-county differences in the structure of the party system—Rokkan proposes a model for cross-level comparisons of micro-data. A "second-order" comparison would analyze individual behavior (e.g., voting turnout) in terms of one of the following levels of constraint: (a) national-level constraints (e.g., electoral system); (b) local constraints (e.g., the local competitiveness of the party system); (c) the collectivity significant for the citizen (e.g., social or cultural constraints); and (d) other micro-level characteristic roles (e.g., marital status). A "third-order" comparison would study individual behavior in terms of *both* national and local constraints, or environmental political and sociocultural constraints, etc. An example of the latter type would be a study of the variability of educational differences in political participation as a function of the degree of partisanship in local politics. Such studies can be conducted across nations, with the additional advantages of increasing the number of cases and the range of variability. Although Rokkan deals only with research *designs* for the study of *citizen* participation—i.e., he is not concerned with elite behavior and with the cross-level rules of composition which could be discussed only in the context of research findings—this essay is still the single most useful introduction to the problems of cross-level analysis, which political scientists have not ventured to approach too often. (For explicit and implicit micro-macro studies, see Eulau [1969].)

Douglas Price has forcefully argued the case for the study of subnational structural constraints (1968: 133):

The simple fact is that neither total individual association nor the aggregate (ecological) association guarantees discovery of the politically important question, which is of within-group individual association. From data on within-group individual behavior one can easily determine both total individual association (a simple matter of pooling the data) and the ecological association (by computing the group means and comparing them). But there is no necessity for within-group individual associations to accord with ecological association, or with overall individual association. [To require a national sample consisting of state subsamples is an important step] if survey analysis is to move beyond studying individuals in terms of purely individual characteristics and begin to explore the effects of structural characteristics and the specific linkages to office holders.

One of the theoretically most interesting studies with an explicit emphasis on the relevance of subnational environments is Juan Linz's analysis of "The Eight Spains" (with de Miguel, 1966: 267-319). Referring to the comparative study of development, they write:

It would seem that many societies we call semideveloped on the basis of a number of national indices are really a mixture of developed and underdeveloped sectors (or regions), and that their peculiar problems result from that imbalance. It would seem that in some cases, particularly in Latin America, much of the difficulty lies in the further diffusion of modern elements from some regions to others, the modernization of some sectors while others are already highly modernized but suffer under strains created by the lag in others. Overall internation comparisons would not help much to clarify such problems.

Linz and Miguel distinguish between two types of subnational units for comparative analysis.

In one type, using indicators for one or preferably several variables, we select certain cutting points to characterize units as "industrialized," "religious," or by combining such dimensions, as "developed" ... the selection of one or another set of cutting points will lead us to include several dispersed units (provinces, cities) in a common type without regard for their geographical continuity, historical or administrative links, and, what is more interesting, without consciousness of common interests or solidarity among those composing them. Another possibility is to take actual social units, perceived by participants and observers as having distinctive characteristics, such as institutions, traditions, climate of opinion, social integration, power structure, etc. ... Ideally, the "operationally" defined units based on systematic indicators should coincide to a certain degree with actual social units perceived as "real" by the participants [For an earlier conceptualization of analytical regions see Shevsky and Bell, 1955.]

The first procedure has been used by the authors for a typology of analytical regions according to criteria of social structure. The provinces of Spain were then plotted in the space defined by two such criteria and the scattering subdivided into seven units, each containing a cluster of not necessarily adjacent provinces. These analytical regions, characterized by different configurations of social structure, provide the units for contextual analysis, on the assumption that it is the interaction between an individual's sociodemographic characteristics and his environment which affects his attitudes.

Another study of regional imbalances is Erik Allardt's study of the social sources of Finnish Communism (1964: 49-72; 1966: 337-348), which indicates that variations in a given type of political behavior (e.g., the amount of radicalism) can be explained by different social and economic factors in different parts of the same country. Allardt found that Communism was strong both in (a) industrialized, developed areas, where very strong political traditions prevent interaction between individuals from different groups; these areas were also characterized by a rigid class structure, absence of insecurity, and little migration; and (b) in rural and undeveloped areas, where political traditions were weak, insecurity great, development rapid, and migration considerable.

These studies represent a new trend in "ecological analysis" by substituting "real" (e.g., perceived) or analytical regions for the nominal, geographical, or administrative regions of earlier, more traditional studies. Obviously, not all interpretations in terms of natural or historical regions have become obsolete, but unevenly distributed processes of modernization have shifted the contextual relevance of "traditional" regions in political analysis. Nowhere has the actual process of the shifting relevance of traditional regions over a relatively short period of time been shown more clearly than in Mattei Dogan's analysis of social conditions and political behavior in Italy (1967: 184 ff.), which demonstrates that while internal migrations are directed toward the north of Italy, Communism moves toward the south, and while Italy is displaying considerable industrialization, Communism is becoming increasingly rural. More recently, Dogan has used analytical regions in order to distinguish between the impact of social and religious factors which could not be easily separated in observations based on the traditional regions in French electoral studies (1969: 285-298). In a secondary analysis of the Almond and Verba *Civic Culture* data, Muller has attempted to distinguish between regional differences in political efficacy, involvement, and competence scores by using natural, geographic regions. Although he found statistically significant differences in some cases in all countries except the United Kingdom, one may assume that analytical regions would have been far more discriminating units of comparison, and the author admits that the (natural) region "is a surrogate variable" which may reflect industrialization, income, education, political history, and tradition in various combinations (Muller, 1970: 792-809). Cross-state comparisons of American legislators and legislative behavior (e.g., Wahlke, Eulau et al., 1962) or policy outcomes (e.g., Dye, 1966; Sharkansky, 1967) have used contextual interpretations of lower-level data, but display, in many cases, a greater emphasis on cross-systemic than on cross-level analysis. The possibility of combining individual (survey) and aggregate (census) data— and avoiding both the ecological and the individualistic fallacies—has channelled the attention of contextually and comparatively oriented analysts from problems of techniques to problems of theory and method, involving assumptions about the structural constraints of political behavior. Recent examples of such preoccupations can be found in Linz's observations on the research design and findings of his studies of Spain (Linz, 1969: 91-131) and Erwin Scheuch's report on some theoretical implications of his comparative contextual studies of voting behavior in Germany (Scheuch, 1969: 133-155).

The conceptualization of group properties in terms of the characteristics of group members, and their relationships, has been explored by Paul Lazarsfeld over twenty years ago, and restated several times (Lazarsfeld and Barton, 1951: 187; Lazarsfeld, 1958: 117, 1961: 422; Lazarsfeld and Menzel, 1961). Group properties can be (a) analytical, when they are obtained by performing some mathematical operation upon some property of each single member (e.g., the standard deviation of incomes); (b) structural, when they are obtained by performing some operation on data about the relations of each member to some or all of the others (e.g., sociometric measures of cohesion) and (c) global, when they cannot be derived from information based on members, their properties, or relations (e.g., constitutions). Each of these group properties can be a source of environmental constraint, and the contextual impact on individual behavior will depend on the individual's position (on the relevant dimension) relative to the distribution of positions in the group (Blau, 1960: 178-193).

Thus, in addition to the purposes of multilevel analysis, the inclusion of a contextual (ecological, environmental) dimension in the analysis of political behavior commits the researcher to a position with two further theoretical implications:

(1) Political behavior, as purposive behavior, cannot be understood and explained in spatiotemporal categories alone; it assumes a perceptual space, in which the socioecological space is perceived, interpreted, and evaluated by the actor, his environment, and the investigator.

(2) *Dealing with both structural characteristics and individual positions in relation to the critical structural variables (i.e., individual differences in the relationship between objective and subjective environment), the "language" of comparison across different environments will require new conceptualizations, summarizing individual characteristics as a function of the critical contextual variable, since the relationship between individual characteristics (e.g., socioeconomic, cultural) and political attitudes and behavior is now assumed to vary between contextual settings.*

These purposes and implications of contextual analysis are already apparent in the "new ecological approach."

We note the beginning of a realization that in many of our observations on the level of individual actors we do not really take seriously the fact that there is something like social structure. . . . The inclination to equate observations of individual attributes with the state of the polity . . . is, however, due not merely to a particular blindness of empirical researchers, but also to a gap in theorizing [Scheuch, 1969: 143].

Scheuch believes that *cross-level theorizing is more relevant than relating two or more variables at the same level of reality* and recommends that social science theories, which maintain a dependency between the state of a higher-order collectivity and the characteristics of the units within the collectivity, should *specify the processes of interchange between system levels.*

Linz is concerned with the variation in the meanings of the social, economic, or demographic characteristics commonly used in political analysis.

Persons in apparently the same "objective" situation—in terms of occupation, skill, income, education, social origin, religion, etc.—will think differently about their position and react to it differently depending on the social context. Context is defined by attributes such as whether those so placed are in a majority or in a minority in their community, whether they work in large or small plants, whether they are present in different proportions, and whether they interact or are isolated [1969: 107-108]. Basic social positions have a different subjective meaning in different contexts [1969: 119].

Social, economic, and demographic characteristics have always been used as control variables, because they have been considered as shorthand indicators of specific—though changing—group interests. Attitudes and interests, however, are generated in perceived environments, and environments differ in social composition and homogeneity; social characteristics of individuals are, therefore, merely *indicators of within-region differences* in attitudes or interests and *cannot be assumed to be equivalent across regions.* Consequently, the use of assumedly equivalent sociodemographic control variables in the analysis of nationwide samples can be misleading.

Linz quotes several findings to illustrate that unidimensionally described occupations are associated with different beliefs and attitudes in varying environments. Analyzing beliefs about modernization among seven occupational groups and controlling for the level of economic development of the environment (per capita income in provinces), he found, for example, that in middle- and high-income provinces the same proportion of farmers and white-collar workers believed that rapid success in life was due to "luck," whereas in low-income provinces the proportion of farmers holding the same belief was almost three times higher than that of white-collar workers. Furthermore, among farmers, the proportion of those who believed that success was due to "hard work" or "intelligence" (separately recorded responses) was twice as high in high-income as in low-income provinces, whereas white-collar workers did not display any significant differences in this respect. Similarly, the subjective class identification of farm laborers varied sharply between low-income and high-income provinces, while that of white-collar workers did not.

Between-region comparisons of beliefs or attitudes toward abstract questions, such as "success in life," do not involve more than one level of integration. The analysis becomes more complex when regional samples are compared in terms of attitudes or overt behavior related to national political issues. The latter type of analysis would require two levels of classification: (a) regions would have to be identified in terms of the variables most relevant to the national issue under consideration (and ranked accordingly), and

(b) categories of respondents would have to be defined in terms of those properties which most sharply determine, or describe, their position in the within-region distribution of the characteristic according to which regions have been classified under (a).

The following (imaginary and simplified) example illustrates the problem of comparisons using different levels of integration: one national-level variable, three regional, contextual variables, and two individual-level variables. A general election is scheduled in a country with a two-party system. According to an earlier opinion poll, the single most important issue is an item of proposed legislation concerning workers' unemployment benefits. The economic structure of the country displays considerable between-region heterogeneity, and the strategists of the party supporting the bill want to obtain an estimate of potential voting support. In order to adjust their campaign to the assumedly varying attitudes of different economic and occupational categories of voters, they decide to conduct a survey and have the choice between a survey addressing itself to separate subsamples of undimensionally defined categories of occupational groups, and one designed to determine how the variables relevant to the voter's choice are likely to be structured and to interact in the various configurations of socioeconomic regions. The risks involved in drawing conclusions from the first type of survey are illustrated by the following description of the regional, contextual variables.

Since only salary- and wage-earners would benefit from the proposed legislation, the ratio of potential beneficiaries to non-beneficiaries can serve as a convenient criterion for the ranking and classification of regions. However, not all potential beneficiaries are likely to support the bill, since they would have to bear one part of the costs of the program by means of a pro-rata deduction from their salaries. Furthermore, even low-income workers may oppose the program, if they have secure jobs in prosperous industries. Regions, however, differ in the degree of prosperity and, therefore, job security, prevailing in industries with a high concentration of low-income jobs, as opposed to those with a high proportion of skilled labor and college-trained personnel. With a regional sample, the analysts can study the impact and interaction of the individual-level variables "income" and "education," the regional variables "industrial structure" and "job security," and the social context variable "proportion of eligible beneficiaries." The example shows that unidimensionally defined occupational or income categories are not very helpful in the cross-regional comparison, because they are differently related to "industrial structure," "job security," and "proportion of beneficiaries," which, in turn, vary between regions. In reality, the situation would be more complex, because, for example, opportunities for occupational or geographical mobility, or propensity to save, could act as intervening variables. It is possible, however, to reduce the complexity of the design by abandoning the unidimensional conceptualization of socioeconomic categories and by combining them, together with the contextual variable "job security," into a summarizing variable (or topological points) indicating subjective positions, or distances, or net rewards, from the national-level variable—i.e., unemployment benefits. The example also suggests that even clusters of variables, which have been found to be highly intercorrelated at the national-system level, such as the modernization or urbanization syndromes, are likely to be misleading. The scattering of positional indicators represents a measurement of the subjective environment and can be compared across objective environments defined, ranked, or classified in terms of the same dimension whose interaction with individual-level variables is reflected by the positional indicators and their regional groupings. (For a discussion of the measurement of subjective environments in terms of objective environments, see Czudnowski [1968] and Scheuch [1969].)

Before we explore in somewhat more detail in the following chapter the dimensions of the perceptual space of political inquiry, one further issue concerning the approach discussed in this chapter will retain our attention. Seeking cross-systemic generalizations, comparative analysis has to account for the specific impact of particular social, political, and cultural systems on the relationship between structural and behavioral variables. According to Przeworski and Teune, "the crux of the problem lies in the status of the proper names of social systems within general theory" and "the goal of comparative research is to substitute names of variables for the names of social systems, such as Ghana, the United States, Africa or Asia" (1970: 8-10).

> Names of nations . . . are residua of variables that influence the phenomenon being explained but have not yet been considered . . . such concepts as "culture," "nation," "society," and "political system" [should be] treated as residua of variables, which can be incorporated into a general theory . . . we can attempt to replace these names by variables [1970: 29].

This is an important argument, relevant to the very purpose of comparative research. However, from the viewpoint of multilevel contextual analysis, it applies only to "global," system-level characteristics, such as "the constitution" or the "impact of Gaullism on French politics." System-level attributes which are statements about the characteristics of—or relations between —the component subunits or individuals ("analytic" and "structural" group properties) are not evenly distributed among all members or groups of a society. If proper names do not stand for variables which have the same values, meanings, and impact in all subnational contexts, there is no advantage in conceptualizing them (e.g., "French political culture") as system-level attributes. If the primary units of analysis are regions, no composite system-level residua need to be considered, and whatever regional "traditions" are encountered can be operationalized in terms of the attributes or variables observed within the region. Natural regions may have proper names, and if these names stand for a particular scale of values or pattern of behavior, such patterns would have to be accounted for in any case as parts of the relevant environment. At the system level, "French political culture" stands for a variety of structural constraints, dispersed across provinces and social strata. At the regional level, "political tradition" has clearly identifiable empirical referents, which are part of the relevant environment even if they are merely characteristics of a particular subgroup, such as "peasant radicalism" or "militant secularism." For *analytical* regions defined in terms of specifically relevant clusters of variables, such as "the structure of rural property" or "percentage of labor force employed in industry," the impact of social or political traditions from different natural regions would probably constitute a residual error term, or—if the impact is additive and unidirectional—an independent variable which would have to be accounted for irrespective of its "proper name status" in the natural region.

Thus, the problem of "proper name attributes" is reduced to global sys-tem-level characteristics, such as the structure of national decision-making processes or the number of organized political alternatives. These types of constraints have been the central focus of institutionally oriented political science. Since they involve quite explicit structural arrangements, the impact of these constraints on political behavior can be studied empirically. Behav-iorally oriented political scientists have been interested primarily in single-level, or within-institution behavior (e.g., voting, legislative roll calls, judicial behavior). Some progress has been made in cross-level analyses of representa-tion and legislative behavior (e.g., McClosky et al., 1960; Miller and Stokes, 1963; Boynton et al., 1969). Few empirical studies, however, have been con-cerned with cross-level comparisons of the impact of global properties. Yet, these are precisely the rules of composition according to which behavior at lower levels is integrated into behavior at higher levels of organization. A cross-systemic study of global properties would be a study of cross-level rules of composition. An interesting case study, which attempts to examine rules of composition by combining constituency, electoral laws, party system, and legislative behavior and interpreting the relationship between these variables in terms of coalition-building and competing ideologies, is Howard Rosenthal's study of French candidate selection and electoral politics (Rosen-thal, 1969a, 1969b; Rosenthal and Sen, 1969).

It is true, however, that some of the areas to which the limitations of global systemic properties refer are those of the informal processes of execu-tive decision-making. These areas are not very accessible to the researcher, and when they become researchable, they can only be explored from the sources, and with the methods, available to the historian—i.e., from documents and more or less incomplete or arbitrary recollections. Global properties of political systems can also be studied comparatively across a number of successive case histories—i.e., longitudinally—which again places them within the limitations of historical research. These seem to be factual, rather than theoretical obstacles in the empirical study of the impact of system-level constraints. In more researchable areas, however, such as cross-sytemic studies of party systems, a greater theoretical sophistication, based on less parochial conceptualizations, should not prove to be impossible (Scarrow, 1969: 77-101; Golembiewski et al., 1969: 358-388).

Having stated the case for the choice of natural or analytical regions as units of comparison and emphasized the need for cross-level comparisons, we shall proceed to examine, in Chapter 5, the perceptual dimensions involved in the study of political behavior. This will lead us to the problem of "equivalence of meaning."

THE PERCEPTUAL SPACE

Perceptual Dimensions and the

Problem of Equivalence

In the introduction to his "Theory of Social and Economic Organization," Max Weber stated, over half a century ago, that the meaning of social action consists in its relation to an intended purpose. Comparing social action involves, therefore, the comparison of subjective purposes or goals. Yet, while purposes of action derive their meanings from the actor's frame of reference, the consequences of action acquire their meanings in the perceptual spaces of those affected by the action. A social science, however, requires general concepts for the formulation of generalizing propositions about behavior. In order to translate the subjective meanings of political behavior into general concepts and propositions, comparative analysis requires both metatheoretical assumptions and rules of interpretation. In this chapter, an attempt will be made to clarify some of the issues involved in this requirement.

Most social scientists would agree that social behavior has either purposes or consequences, or both; stated otherwise, social behavior can be defined as (1) behavior through which an actor intends to affect the environment (including his own position in the environment); (2) or as behavior which is considered to have affected the environment; (3) or as behavior for which both conditions (1) and (2) have been satisfied. It is possible that this view merely reflects a bias of the Western philosophical tradition and that according to some deterministic or fatalistic cosmology man is only fulfilling the will of some metaphysical entity. However, since empirical social science has grown within the Western philosophical tradition and it accepts the evidence that man has been capable of changing his environment as proof of his ability to engage in purposeful behavior (irrespective of how one evaluates the consequences thereof), there is no need to defend this position any further here. Political behavior, as a subset of social behavior, has generally been considered as purposive, regardless of whether government and politics were defined as authoritative allocations of values or as processes of conflict resolution. The fact that political behavior occurs in a cultural context of values, norms, customs, and habits limits its randomness or arbitrariness, but does not eliminate its goal-orientations, and there is little doubt that culturally determined components of political behavior have consequences for the relevant environments.

Speaking of purposes and consequences of behavior, we notice a shift of emphasis from the act itself to what Abraham Kaplan has called the *action*— i.e., the meaning of the act. Furthermore, the terms "purpose" and "goal" merely stand for *intended consequences,* and "consequence" is meant to convey *actual consequence,* whether intended or not. In these initial distinctions I am following, with a minor change, the conceptualization of the relationships among personality, social system, and culture proposed by Melford Spiro (Spiro, 1961: 107). Spiro makes a further distinction between "actual consequences for the actor or for society." Substituting *observed consequences* for "actual consequences," one may add that since the concept of consequence denotes a factual judgment and an evaluation, it is also necessary to ask who has observed these consequences, who is evaluating them, and what or whose criteria of evaluation does he adopt?

Going beyond the Weberian definition, the purposiveness of political behavior is interpreted here as having meanings in terms of both intended and observed consequences. The concept of "meaning" requires a brief clarification. Psychologists, linguists, and philosophers of science have offered a number of different definitions and "theories" of meaning (Osgood et al., 1957: 4-9; Brodbeck, 1963: 309-324). Most of these definitions refer to semantics and to the cultural variability of meanings; here we are not concerned with semantics, but with the meaning of behavior, which may or may not include verbal behavior. The meaning of an act is what the act "stands for" or represents in a perceptual space. For the actor, it is what the act stands for in terms of the consequences intended by the actor. It is a combination of what May Brodbeck calls significance (meaning$_2$) and psychological meaning (meaning$_4$), in which significance is related to the actor's intentions. This is a subjective meaning of action. The act, however, has observed consequences. The affected environment may view the act from the viewpoint of the actor's intention, but it will most probably consider it also from the viewpoint of the consequences observed and interpreted by the environment. This, therefore, is another subjective meaning of the action. The two meanings may or may not coincide. Furthermore, not every member of the actor's environment will necessarily agree with a particular interpretation of the observed consequence; there can be, therefore, several subjective interpretations of the observed consequences by different members of the environment. When all members of the environment agree on the observed consequences of an action, there is intersubjective agreement on the meaning of these consequences; the actor, however, may still persist in his own interpretation of the consequences (although, facing agreement in the environment on a different interpretation, he may either accept it and subsequently attempt to redress the balance by an additional act, or experience the frustration of being unable to do so).

The parenthetical comments, at the end of the preceding paragraph, have been added not only in order to show that the smallest unit of political behavior which is of interest to the investigator includes both intended and observed consequences, but primarily in order to emphasize that the description of the action has tacitly assumed *three* perspectives in the perceptual space. The perspectives of the actor and of the environment have actually been reconstructed by the investigator. In evaluating the possible consequences of differences between subjective interpretations, it is necessary to specify whether or not the actors are aware of such disagreements. The investigator has a perspective of his or her own, a vantage point that is located outside the space in which the behavior takes place, and his rules of interpretation are not structured by the intentions and expectations of the actors involved. Behavioral scientists who engage in experimentation are more careful than political scientists in making the necessary distinction between the perceptual spaces of the actors and that of the investigator or in stating explicitly what are observed and what are inferred relationships. There are risks involved when the distinction between these perspectives is treated as a tacit assumption. I think this is precisely what Heinz Eulau had in mind when he wrote: "What I did in presenting this example is to smuggle in my theoretical standpoint as an observer" (Eulau, 1969: 11). The investigator's perspective rests on specific assumptions, and if it is only tacitly assumed, there are risks of "smuggling in" and "smuggling out" something that ought to be present at all times. Take, for example, the following statement from a discussion of contextual analysis: "The social context can affect the attitudes of people consciously or without their awareness ... the fact itself—

independently of the awareness of it—that a great majority or a small minority in a community (or organization) holds the same opinions will affect the social relations of those holding them and their . . . degree of conviction, resistance to change, etc." The statement moves back and forth from observations to inferences. Where there is awareness of the impact of the social context, the investigator describes what he has observed; where no such awareness exists, the investigator is making inferences for purposes of explanation. The important issue, of course, is whether the awareness of the social context has an *additional* impact on attitudes and behavior, especially when the attitudes under consideration are directed at those contextual factors by which they are assumedly affected.

The position of the investigator of social behavior has been the subject of a long controversy concerning the status of explanation in the social sciences. It was claimed that the social scientist has to "understand" the action—i.e., to share the state of mind of the actors—and that this was a method of observation appropriate only to the study of man. By the same token, however, no explanation based on "understanding" which relied on introspection, identification, or common cultural experiences could be of any scientific worth. We can dispose of this argument, despite its epistemological ramifications, with the observation that "understanding" the meaning of other people's actions is not an impediment, but a facilitating factor, because it directs the investigator to the type of evidence he has to seek in order to validate his hypothesis based on "understanding." In this respect, the social scientist is in a much better position than the natural scientist, because the latter cannot seek hypotheses for the explanation of natural phenomena or chemical reactions in his experiences as a member of human society. Stated otherwise, understanding is no substitute for—only a guide to—empirical evidence. Some of the problems particular to the social sciences are related to the validity and reliability of the evidence, especially since so large a part of the evidence consists of verbal behavior; none of these problems, however, can be solved through the "understanding" of the investigator. (For an early and a recent discussion of this problem, see LaPiere [1934] and Phillips [1971].)

For a more accurate description of what is involved in the observation of behavior in the socioecological space from various perspectives, it is also necessary to consider the different levels of inclusion and integration. With which of these different observed consequences is the investigator concerned? This question, sometimes discussed under the misleading heading of "levels of interpretation," relates the perceptual to the socioecological space. If we add a time dimension, the *mapping sentence* of political inquiry can be formulated as follows:

who (characteristics of the actor)

in what situation (environment, circumstances)

does what (behavior)

for what purpose (intended consequences, for whom, at what level of
social and organizational integration)

with what consequences (observed consequences, for whom, at what level
and whose criteria of evaluation)

at what time.

Any act of political behavior—a candidacy for political office, an administrative or judicial decision, a televised interview, or the threat of a strike by
postal employees—is intended to bring about some change in a specific environment. This does not mean, however, that its consequences can be observed
only in the environment to which the intention of change refers. The candidacy of a black Democrat of relatively high socioeconomic status for the
mayoralty of a city with a large black minority may cause a split not only in
the black vote, but also in the local Democratic Party and in the labor unions,
the former preferring a working-class-oriented white, the latter a working-
class-oriented black. The election of a Socialist mayor in a West German city
may change the budgetary allocations for urban development made by a
state legislature controlled by a Christian-Democratic majority. Conversely,
the lasting coalition in the Israeli national cabinet between the National
Religious Party and the larger and dominant Labor Party determines the
N.R.P.'s policy of avoiding coalitions with other parties at the municipal
level, even when its local electoral support has been much larger than that
of the Labor Party; and when a British M.P. votes against the party line in
the House of Commons, the party organization in his constituency is in
trouble. The purpose of *cross-level analysis* is to account for the relationship
between consequences observed from the perspective of different levels of
organization, inclusion, or integration, and to relate them to the intentions
of the actors.

There is a further distinction to be made in the analysis of intentions and
consequences of political behavior. This refers to a characteristic which political behavior does not share with other areas of social behavior. Politics
consists of all actions intended to affect, or affecting, the authoritative
decision-making process and its outcome. By definition, therefore, all political goals are *public* goals. (The term "public," as opposed to "private," is
used here with a sociological connotation and conveys reference to any group
or category larger than the kinship group of the actor.) This means that the
overtly professed intended consequences of a political act are necessarily
public consequences. The political actor, however, also attaches a *private*

meaning to his action—i.e., he also seeks a private goal. Such private goals may be a consequence of achieving the public goal, or they may consist of the very action of seeking the public goal. In both cases, they may be instrumental, expressive, or acceptance goals—i.e., they may be sought as *means* for an ulterior goal, as *"consummatory"* goals or as *symbols of acceptance* by some informal group or formal organization. It is common knowledge that many political actors also pursue private goals, such as status, personal influence, or material benefits; ideological goal orientations, however, are generally interpreted only in terms of a public, community-oriented goal. This is, at best, an oversimplification. The actor shares his ideological orientation with many others, some of which may not be less intensely committed to the goal than the actor himself, yet only he has chosen, accepted, or felt the need to participate, through overt behavior, in the goal-achievement process. Participation, as a goal per se, can be achieved even if the intended public consequence has not materialized.

We must distinguish, therefore, between private and public intended consequences. In politics, however, only the intended public consequence is overtly professed. Some private goals of political action are legitimate, or tolerated, in some societies and illegitimate in others. Yet, no private goal is overtly professed even it it is socially or culturally acceptable, because the private consequences of an act are not relevant to those who share the actor's public goal orientation. A candidate is not likely to draw additional support if he admits that he wishes to enhance his prestige, that he likes the game of politics, or that he expects some direct or indirect material benefit. Private goals may or may not be legitimate, but they will remain covert because they are irrelevant to the achievement of the intended public consequences; yet, for the actors concerned, such private goals are highly relevant, and the investigator will have to include them in his attempt to explain the action.

In this respect, the study of political behavior differs considerably from that of other types of social behavior. In economic behavior, the relevant goals are overtly professed and socially acceptable: the income- or profit-seeking activities of individuals or firms, which are not guided by intended public consequences, as well as the public-oriented economic decisions of governments, national banks, and various economic organizations. The political analyst has the far more difficult task of incorporating covert private and overt public goals as variables in his substantive or formal theorizing. This observation is particularly relevant in the comparative study of elites in such areas as recruitment, role performance in office, or coalition-building.

We have now reached a stage in which the paradigm of political behavior includes intended and unintended consequences, private, public, overt, and covert goals, the perspectives of actors and of affected members of the environment at different levels of the socioecological space and referring to any area of life in which an issue is being channelled into the political process. Given the complexity of this paradigm, can we hope to discover cross-systemic behavioral regularities? Is the adoption of a position which incorporates system-theory and what may be termed a "phenomenological behaviorism" not a self-defeating enterprise?

Critics of this approach will claim that despite the diversity of subjective interpretations, human beings do not display an unlimited variation in their political behavior. Scott Greer, who contrasts the subjectivity of individual experience and the "coerciveness of the definition of the situation," believes that the phenomenological position

> leads, in practice, to an extremely awkward framework for inquiry . . . there is a high degree of uniformity in any society's life, produced by outside constraints without much attention to individual variation. One may note the regularity with which most automobile drivers stay on the designated side of the street. Regardless of what this means to them (fear of dangerous accidents, of police, of penalties, habit, a "compulsive personality," public spirit) their behavior *en masse* is highly predictable [Greer, 1969b: 59].

As far as it goes, the argument is basically sound; but how far does it go? When personal safety, fear of sanctions, and social conformity all lead to the choice of the same alternative, it is hardly surprising that the resultant behavior is highly predictable; in such behavior, there is no "puzzle" for the social scientist to solve and he is likely to be more interested in deviant cases. It is true, of course, as Greer adds in another passage (1969b: 110), that communication tends to force agreement in the way men perceive social events through the emergence of general concepts, and these concepts tend to standardize men, and even their senses. In any cultural area, men share many beliefs and values which tend to reduce the variation in the interpretation of events, and some beliefs have been found to be held across cultural boundaries. (H. A. Thelen has distinguished among three types of control pressures which account for uniformities in human behavior: [1] Environmental pressures, or "task requirements in relation to needs"; [2] shared values and expectations; and [3] rule enforcement; see Katz and Kahn, 1966: 36.) The need for political decisions occurs, however, in situations in which uniformity is not predictable as a result of shared beliefs or habits; in such situations, there is no real choice, whereas political behavior generally implies a choice between competing claims, alternative uses of scarce resources, or both.

Two further observations are necessary to clarify the issue. First, whatever the constraints which tend to reduce the variation in behavior, the political actor's perspective of his action is not as irrelevant as the driver's reasons for

accepting to use only one side of the street, because political behavior is con-
tinuously oriented toward a restructuring of the patterns of constraints which
affect behavior in all areas of life. How one views these constraints is not a
negligible component of behavior, even if the available alternatives for restructuring the environment are severely limited, because they are all objects
of political action. Second, a nonphenomenological behaviorism in political
science is self-defeating because it excludes precisely those components of
behavior which are the subject matter of empirical political theory. A theory
of political behavior has to explain the relationship between needs, goals and
the behavior which channels goal-seeking into the political process. Areas of
life in which there is almost no constraint on behavioral variability are unlikely to become politically relevant. When there are only a limited number
of behavioral alternatives, it is obvious that any of the available alternatives
can attract different individuals for different reasons. Majorities are often
based on coalitions of widely different interests; decisions are often possible
only because the proposed alternative is the second-best choice for a number
of participants, whose first choices did not receive sufficient support. The
very concept of "preferences," which lies at the roots of political behavior
and analysis, denotes a judgment of meanings. Observing only regularities
in behavior, without attaching meanings to behavior, is very similar to what
political scientists of the institutional "persuasion" have been doing most
of the time.

In cross-systemic analysis, this dimension of meanings is a crucial concern.
As Verba has recently put it: "If the problem of comparability of measures
taken from two different social systems derives from the fact that the measures are embedded in different structural and cultural contexts, the solution
to the problem lies in trying to maintain the contextual grounding of the
measures when making comparisons" (Verba, 1969: 79). This "contextual
grounding," the manner in which behavior is "embedded" in different contexts, is precisely the meaning of that behavior, structured in the perceptual
space by intended and observed consequences related to objects of orientation in the socioecological space. (For one of the earliest discussions of
contexts and meanings in political science, see Lasswell, 1948: 217-222.)

Comparing political behavior involves comparing actions with meanings.
The structure of the perceptual space suggests that any given action may
have a number of somewhat different meanings even in its own context;
neither identity nor dissimilarity of meanings can be assumed, but must be
investigated empirically. One must specify the dimension of meaning to
which the comparison refers before establishing equivalence. But how does
one establish equivalence of meanings? Nominal identity or similarity may
be misleading. Cultural anthropologists and sociologists, using functional
analysis, have defined equivalence as "functional." When different actions,
patterns of behavior, or institutions perform the same function in their

respective systems, they are considered equivalent across systems. Yet Verba rightly complains that "there is more reference in the literature to the importance of funtional equivalence than there are clear definitions of what exactly a functional equivalent is or how you know one when you see it." He then explains that since different items can be appropriate indicators of the same variable in different settings, "one must begin with fairly general hypotheses or theories before one searches for equivalent measures. Before one compares voting rates, for example, one ought to consider the underlying dimension for which voting is relevant [which], in turn, means considering the underlying theory of politics ... for which the study of voting is relevant" (Verba, 1971: 314-315).

Thus, establishing equivalence, which is a rule of interpretation, depends on a theory of politics. The methodology of equivalence depends on the assumptions one makes about the subjective, environmental, and systemic meanings of political behavior. No problem of equivalence can be decided on logical or methodological grounds alone; it is therefore unlikely that the same methodology of equivalence will apply in different areas of social behavior. In political science, the problem is compounded by the fact that there is no agreement on an "underlying theory of politics"—i.e., unlike economics, political science is still in a "preparadigmatic stage" (Bendix and Lipset, 1957: 79-98; Mitchell, 1969: 101-136; Holt and Richardson, 1970: 27).

As the mapping sentence for the conduct of political inquiry suggests, there are several analytical dimensions on which equivalence may be sought. The actor's characteristics and his location in the relevant environment are structural properties of the object of investigation. Comparing actors, samples, environments, we would seek their *equivalence in structural terms*. Differentiating between subjective, environmental, and systemic consequences of an action would lead us to seek *equivalence of perspectives*. The time dimension may require *equivalence in chronological or developmental time*. Most cross-systemic comparisons have focused on formally similar types of political participation, on attitudes toward similar objects of orientation, and on intrasystemic relationships between structural and behavioral components. Whether or not such formal similarities are required depends on the *functional*—i.e., *means-ends-results* relationship between the *action and the actor's purpose and its consequences*. Similar goals can be sought, or similar consequences can be obtained, through different actions. More complex problems of equivalence arise when both actions and goals (but not consequences), or actions and consequences (but not goals) differ between systems. Ideally, a functional equivalence assumes control for the structure of the environment; in practice, however, these are more or less adequate approximations. Formulating a means-ends-results relationship always implies

a decision concerning the perspectives from which the action and its consequences have been viewed.

No criteria for the equivalence of two functional relationships can be
established without a general paradigm, or metatheory, of politics, from
which specific theories (or hypotheses), as well as methodological rules of
interpretation, can be derived. The most systematic attempt to explore
the problem of criteria for equivalence in comparative social inquiry has
been made in *The Logic of Comparative Social Inquiry* (Przeworski and
Teune, 1970; hereafter *The Logic*). The remainder of this chapter will examine the proposals put forward by the authors of *The Logic*.

Przeworski and Teune are concerned with the conceptual, cross-systemic
equivalence of different indicators, especially in the case when no *common,
cross-systemic* criterion can be found. Conceptual equivalence implies, of
course, equivalence of meanings, but since no distinction is made between
perceptual dimensions, the investigator's perspective is equated with both
the actor's and the environment's perspectives. Since the cross-systemic
validity of such data cannot be inferred from a common criterion, the
authors of *The Logic* suggest as a substitute criterion the similarity, across
systems, of the within-system intercorrelations between indicators. They
"strongly emphasize" that this procedure for testing equivalence is "meaningful" only in the context of explicit theoretical assumptions concerning
the dimensions of the general property to be examined and the behavior
of specific indicators. The establishment of equivalence can be considered
as consisting of (1) the application of rules of interpretation relevant to the
area of behavior under consideration, and (2) a quantitative evaluation of
the so interpreted indicators. Przeworski and Teune seem to suggest that
both the rules of interpretation and the criteria of measurement-equivalence
can be derived from the theoretical assumptions one makes about the property under consideration and about the "behavior" of specific indicators of
this property in different systems. They also believe that if different indicators, in different systems, are similarily intercorrelated within their respective systems and there is a theoretical ground to believe that they should,
they can be considered as equivalent. One may ask, however, how to proceed
in the following situation: If one hypothesizes that the indicators chosen
will behave in a certain manner in different systems, but the evidence does
not confirm the hypothesis, does that mean that the hypothesis concerning
the behavior of indicators is invalid, or has he perhaps chosen inadequate
indicators in some systems? What guidance does the rule of interpretation
offered in *The Logic* provide? Let us examine the methodological background
of the issue in somewhat more detail.

Comparison is the first step beyond description. It seeks to establish
whether any specific property, or set of properties, is present in the units of

comparison and, if the property is measurable, to specify the distribution of its magnitude between the units. The problem of equivalence arises when the property cannot be directly observed and measured, and its presence, or the measurement of its magnitude, must be inferred from other observations that have been chosen as indicators of the property. If indicators cannot be identical, as they are in physical measurement, they have to be equivalent— i.e., we require some rules which would help us establish that different indicators are evidence of the same property. When we wish to generalize beyond unique actors and events, we conceptualize properties or variables which we then seek to identify or measure in a number of cases. Thus, the difficulty of establishing equivalence of indicators will increase as we enlarge the domain of the concept (the number of different overt manifestations in which we assume its presence) and as we increase the diversity of settings (cultural, political, etc.) in which these manifestations assumedly occur. Cross-systemic comparisons are, by definition, comparisons across different settings; the difficulty of establishing the equivalence of indicators depends, therefore, directly on the level of generalization and abstraction at which we conceptualize our variables or analytical constructs. Such conceptualizations require rules of interpretation, or correspondence, which enable us to relate our observations to the property or variable under consideration.

Paul Lazarsfeld has argued that "indicators can at best have only an inferential relation to the underlying factor sought" and are therefore only probabilistically related to the intended classification.

> Whether a man is liberal, whether he has status in the community, whether an army has morale, or whether an educational system is a success—none of these questions can ever be answered unequivocally and absolutely, because morale or status cannot be measured with the degree of agreement and precision with which weight or length of an object can be measured [Lazarsfeld, 1959: 61].

Consequently, the many indicators we can find for a concept are never perfectly correlated. But "if we have a reasonable collection of indicator items, then for most purposes it does not matter much which subset we use to form our index. This is true so long as our aim is to find statistical relations among a number of variables, not the correct classification of each case." Social strata, for example, have sharply contrasting attitudes toward economic and political issues. To test these relationships, it does not really matter which of a number of alternative sets of indicators for socioeconomic strata we use (income, education, occupational status, etc.), since the correlation between different indicators of strata and any particular attitude is about the same. This is the "doctrine" of the *interchangeability of indices*.

But Lazarsfeld also emphasized that "it is not the relation of the indices to one another which is the crucial problem, but their relation to outside variables"; it is this relation to an "outside variable" which validates the interchangeability of indices.

The authors of *The Logic* have attempted to adapt the interchangeability of indices to cross-systemic comparisons. They are aware of the fact that common indicators may have different meanings in different settings and that a given concept may require different indicators in different settings (1970: 92). They propose to use the separate indicators in each system as a subset of the universe of indicators for that concept. Some of these indicators may be common to all systems. Those of the common indicators which are highly intercorrelated, both within systems and for the pooled populations, can be considered as common and identical. If insufficient common and identical indicators are available, system-specific indicators which correlate highly with the identical indicators are considered as equivalent across systems. When no common identical indicators can be found, the similarity in the structure of the sets of system-specific indicators—i.e., the pattern of correlations within systems, compared across systems, can serve as a criterion of equivalence (1970: 91-131).

According to this view, when no common identical indicators can be found, the validity of the measurements is established in terms of each social system, and the cross-systemic reliability of the measurements establishes the equivalence of measurements for the inference from different observations to the common concept. But if the cross-systemic similarity in the within-system structure of sets of *different* indicators is considered as reliability of measurement on the same dimension, are we not assuming, a priori, that the underlying concept or property is similarly patterned in different systems? If we assume that the property can be inferred from sets of different but similarly intercorrelated indicators, then the cross-systemic reliability is also assumed a priori and the inference from reliability to equivalence is spurious. If we do not know how different indicators will behave in different systems—and the entire purpose of the comparison is to explore the behavior of indicators—then cross-systemic similarity of systemic intercorrelations of different indicators cannot validate the choice of indicators and their equivalence on the dimension they assumedly represent. For Lazarsfeld, even within-system proof of equivalence resides in similar correlations of different sets of indicators with a specific "outside variable." In cross-systemic comparisons, when no common identical indicators are available, similarly intercorrelated system-specific indicators may very well refer to entirely different dimensions. The risk involved in this procedure is very similar to that resulting from a violation of the first rule of comparability: the members of a set of units are comparable if and only if (a) there exists a variable V common to each of them, and (b) the meaning of V is the same for all of them (Zelditch, 1971: 273). The authors of *The Logic* impute the choice of indicators to the theoretical assumptions of the investigator, but the expected similarity in the behavior of different sets of indicators of the same dimension is also a theoretical assumption. However, no specific theory can validate a methodology; rules of interpretation are independent of any specific theory, otherwise they could not be used to demonstrate the validity of the theory.

The above statement may appear to contradict Clyde Coombs' argument that "in selecting a method of analysis (an experimenter) is selecting a theory about behavior. The data are either asked to satisfy or forced to satisfy the theory" (Coombs, 1953: 524). The contradiction, however, is merely semantic. What for Coombs are "methods" of measurement, I would classify as the techniques of measurement. Rules of interpretation, however, are not techniques; they determine the status of techniques for data gathering or data analysis within the paradigmatic framework from which these rules have been derived. "A paradigm is a body not only of concepts and laws, but also and more importantly of methodological principles and strategies, definitions of problems and *criteria of their acceptable solution,* instrumentation and applications, standards of relevance, and an ordering of aims" (Zelditch, 1971: 277; italics added).

The interpretation of cross-systemic similarities in the structure of indicators as a substitute for cross-systemic equivalence has been applied by Przeworski and Teune in a comparative study of values in politics. An example from this study (Przeworski and Teune, 1967: 551-568), in which the authors examine the domain of the concepts "social harmony," "material progress," and "selflessness" across four countries, indicates that they interpret *any* positive correlation pattern between indicators as "similarity of structures." Psychometric theory is generally very lenient concerning the magnitude of interitem correlations required to justify the pooling of item scores (Scott, 1969: 249). In this example, the authors propose a scale on which a system-specific item in country A, ranging in correlations with the cross-national set of identical indicators from .03 to .18, and a system-specific item in country B, with corresponding correlations ranging from .18 to .53, are considered equivalent. Acceptance of any of these items assigns the same score on the scale. A cumulative scale, on which items are ranked according to item popularity, could have provided a more discriminating measurement, but it is possible that the items chosen did not display scalability. This, of course, raises the question of unidimensionality. The authors of *The Logic* accept the possibility of multidimensional concepts and suggest that if system-specific indicators can be assigned to each dimension, a factor analysis should reveal similar clusterings of indicator loadings on the hypothesized factors.

This is an imaginative but indeterminate solution, because of both the indeterminacy of factor solutions and the hypothetical status of factors as principles of organization which require empirical validation (see Chapter 3).

Przeworski and Teune have greatly contributed to the clarification of the methodological problems encountered in the search for cross-systemic equivalence. They must be credited for extending Lazarsfeld's "theory" of the interchangeability of indices to the field of cross-systemic comparisons. Two out of the three procedures for establishing equivalence proposed in *The Logic* remain within the logical framework of Lazarsfeld's methodology; the third, attempting to escape the constraints of this framework, is necessarily vulnerable.

Kenneth Janda has proposed a "means and variance" comparison of standardized scores of indicators across cultural systems as a means of detecting system interference and as a step for establishing cross-systemic equivalence. Janda's proposal is much more in line with the accepted norms of methodological conservatism. Using only common indicators (of party institutionalization in three cultural areas), he argues that even for common indicators the comparable "means and variance test" is only a good detector of systemic effects, but not a good criterion for judging conceptual equivalence. "The final, and by all means the most crucial test of conceptual equivalence" consists in comparing the relationship of the measured variable to other variables both across and within systems and establishing whether such relationships exist in theoretically interpretable ways. This, of course, is Lazarsfeld's original requirement for correlations with an "outside variable" (Janda, 1971).

Thus, any demonstration of equivalence of meanings must be consistent with the logic of comparison and proof (represented, in this context, by Lazarsfeld's "theory" of the interchangeability of indices). This logic is independent of any specific theory of social behavior. The identification of relevant indicators of conceptual equivalence depends, however, on a metatheoretical (or paradigmatic) framework which is sufficiently general to allow for cross-level and cross-systemic propositions and yet sufficiently operational to provide rules of interpretation for inferences from observations of subjective meanings to general concepts and propositions.

No such general paradigm, or metatheory, is available in political science. Middle-range empirical theories have focused on specific levels in the socio-ecological and political structures, and cross-level and cross-systemic comparisons are the exception rather than the rule. Furthermore, although forms and norms of individual behavior and institutional procedures provide a useful focus of inquiry in the search for uniformities, it is unlikely that *general* theorizing in political science can proceed without incorporating a model of meanings: motives, purposes, and observed consequences. In a truly Weberian sense, even forms, norms, and procedures are "meaningless" unless they can be related to intended (and observed) consequences.

The following chapter reviews the major theories in the most frequently researched area of political behavior: voting. Voting studies are a pluralistic universe precisely because, in the absence of a general paradigm, the various partial paradigms remain isolated, and knowledge does not become cumulative. Yet this partial knowledge sheds some light on the search for a general paradigm for political science.

Chapter 6

THEORIZING IN A PREPARADIGMATIC
DISCIPLINE: In Search for a Theory of Voting

Having delineated in the preceding chapters some of the building blocks for a paradigm of comparative political analysis, it will be useful to pause for a necessarily fragmentary but fairly representative illustration of empirical theorizing in the current preparadigmatic stage of the discipline. The area chosen for this illustration is the study of voting behavior. Although an attempt has been made to present a somewhat detailed and yet comprehensive discussion, this is not a substantive survey of findings, but a review of theoretical approaches; research findings will be cited only for the purpose of documenting the analysis of the different theories of voting.

This chapter will serve as a link between the methodological perspective reflected in the first part of this book and the subsequent search for new approaches to a general theory of political behavior more likely to satisfy two major desiderata of any useful paradigm: equivalence of meanings across settings and time, and—as a consequence thereof—the cumulativeness of knowledge.

Empirical research has been conducted primarily in the area of citizens' attitudes, opinions, preferences, and voting behavior. The available information on elite behavior—which is far less accessible to empirical research—does not easily lend itself to cross-systemic generalizations, and cross-level elite studies are still primarily an item on the research agenda of political science. An attempt to discuss the major theoretical approaches in the search for a general theory of political behavior must focus, therefore, on the area of mass behavior, in which a large number of increasingly sophisticated studies have accumulated in the last twenty-five years. Even in this area, however, there is a paucity of cross-systemic studies and, as a consequence thereof, an understandable reluctance to advance beyond low-level or middle-range generalizations derived from national case-studies. Given the political relevance of opinion surveys and voting studies, the costs of large-scale cross-national research, and the "technological lag" which had separated European from American political science for some time, it is not difficult to understand why even theoretically oriented scholars have often conceptualized the determinants of voting behavior in terms of system-specific variables.

In addition to these factual difficulties, one must also note the theoretical limitations inherent in the micro-analytical approach to the study of voting. The individual vote is only an imperfect social action: it does not elicit interaction and has no observable consequences (Czudnowski, 1968: 886; Sartori, 1969: 82). Converse has described the act of voting as "a prime behavioral outlet for class consciousness" (Converse, 1958: 388-399). Note how he carefully avoids committing himself to anything more specific than "behavioral outlet." In an attempt to provide a theoretical framework for the relation between class and party in the analysis of voting, Eulau perceived voting as *role behavior* (Eulau, 1962: 87-90). He therefore pointed at the difficulty of using the concept of class identification in connection with voting behavior. A role implies a relationship between at least two actors, predicated on a set of mutual expectations. Identification theory cannot account for this two-way perspective of a role, since there is no feedback. Eulau therefore proposed to substitute "awareness of class roles" for class-identification, since awareness of class roles presupposes a set of demands and expectations in relation to another class, a "generalized other." At this initial point of the discussion, let us merely note Eulau's attempt to introduce an interaction-oriented interpretation of the social psychology of voting. From yet another perspective, the vote has direction, but no intensity. Attitudes or preferences may vary in intensity, but not the vote itself. A voter who repeatedly supports a given party is not necessarily a *strong,* but merely a consistent, persistent, or loyal supporter of that party. Finally, only at the aggregate level do votes have observable consequences. The individual vote is an imperfect case of social action. In *The Psychology of Voting,* Lipset, Lazarsfeld, Barton, and Linz have emphasized at least two of these "imperfections": "It does not cost anything to vote, in sharp contrast to buying and to most other actions that require some sacrifice of time, or at least of some other desirable alternative" and "the visibility of consequences of the voting act is obviously very slight, and the voters are very much aware of this fact" (Lipset et al., 1954: 1164).

It is not surprising, therefore, that the study of voting behavior has been approached with the conceptual and methodological tools of *social psychology*. This approach was also particularly adequate for the analysis of voting in the United States, where "party identification" has been found to be the single most important variable determining voting preferences. Party identification is a psychological attachment which can persist without formal party membership, and even without a consistent record of party support (Campbell et al., 1960: 121). This is now a well-documented finding (Campbell et al., 1954; Campbell and Stokes, 1959; Goldberg, 1966) and the stability of partisan identifications has been conceptualized in Converse's calculus of a "normal vote" (Converse, 1966). Long-term party loyalties are not an exclusively American phenomenon, and one would assume that the interesting variables in the cluster referred to as party identification would be stability and content, and the relationship between them. American voting studies have revealed, however, that for a considerable proportion of the American electorate, partisan identifications "seem to be rather contentless commitments" (Sears, 1969: 359) which can be overcome by such short-term "forces" as the candidate's personality or religion.

The authors of *The American Voter* have reported that only 3.5 percent of the 1956 voters had an "ideological level" of conceptualizing their political perceptions, and a further twelve percent a near-ideological level; thirty-four percent perceived differences between parties in terms of group benefits, eleven percent had only "shallow" group benefit perceptions, and forty percent perceived no issue content, or only vague "nature-of-times" differences. A measure of the association between these "levels of conceptualization" and what has been termed the "strength" of partisan identification could have cast some light on the contents-dimension of party identification. Although the measure of this association has not been reported, the authors of *The American Voter* believe that "among people of relatively impoverished attitude who yet have a sense of partisan loyalty, partisan identification has a more direct influence on behavior than it has among people with a well-elaborated view of what their choice concerns" (Campbell et al., 1960: 136). Yet, they also report that at lower "levels of conceptualization" the rate of defection from Democratic identification is considerably higher than at the more consistent and systematic "ideological" level of conceptualization (Campbell et al., 1960: 264). Converse has explored this seeming contradiction (1966) by using a measure of involvement (defined as motivation to attend to information about political matters) as a substitute for levels of conceptualization. His findings, for 1952 data, suggest a curvilinear relationship between the party identification-vote correlation and the number of mass media respondents monitored for political information. The identification-vote correlation is higher at the zero-level of media exposure and decreases until the two-media level is reached; at successively higher levels of media exposure, the correlation increases. Although Converse's hypothesis of higher partisan stability at the zero-level of media exposure is plausible, Dreyer has recently shown that it is not supported by data for the five post-1952 elections (Dreyer, 1971-1972). Dreyer's findings also indicate that at all levels of media exposure, the correlation of party identification and party vote consistently decreases for every presidential election held after 1956.

Thus, party identification per se—without involvement and information—seems to have become a relatively weak indicator of party vote (the correlations for 1960, 1964, and 1968 were .24, .21, and .34, respectively). If attitudes toward issues and candidates, though "colored" by party identification, are necessary to bring about a closer correspondence between identification and vote—i.e., if party identification has little content of behavioral consequence, what is the meaning of a subjectively or otherwise assigned *intensity* dimension of party identification? The rationale for an intensity dimension of attitudinal variables resides in the behavioral differences associated with varying degrees of intensity; but when such behavioral differences are ascribed to other variables (involvement, information, etc.), what is the residual justification for the distinction between "weak" and "strong" identifiers?

We are thus left with a single dimension of both theoretical and practical interest: stability. Characteristic of the stability of American partisan identifications is their intergenerational longevity, associated with the role of the family as an agent of early political socialization. Although the frequency of "strong" identifiers increases with age and with the duration of a specific identification, and although "young people not only vote less ... but appear less securely bound to the existing party system" (Campbell et al., 1960: 162-163, 497), one of the most persistent findings of American voting and socialization studies in the last twenty-five to thirty years has been the intergenerational similarity of partisan orientations. One can even notice an increase in this similarity in the 1950s (Hyman, 1959: 77; Campbell et al., 1960: 147). The lowering of the voting age should cast some further light on these relationships.

There is nothing surprising in the parental transmission of party identifications; in many areas of life, attitudes are developed in pre-adult socialization processes. What is significant is the low frequency of deviations from partisan identifications through experiences in adult life. Adolescence is the period in which the individual first encounters strong influences outside the family and proceeds to define his or her adult roles; thereafter, a marriage, a new job, or a change in neighborhood may create pressures under which he is likely to adopt new political identifications. Most observers agree, however, that—at least until the mid-sixties—the average citizen's "awareness of political events [had been] limited and his concern with ideological problems ... only rudimentary.... Only an event of extraordinary intensity can arouse any significant part of the electorate to the point that its established political loyalties are shaken" (Campbell et al., 1960: 151). The two events which patterned the distribution of regional and socioeconomic partisan attachments in the 1940s, 1950s, and early 1960s were the Civil War and the Great Depression. At the time of this writing, it is difficult to estimate how these loyalties will survive the Vietnam crisis, racial integration, the political mobilization of women and youth, Watergate, and the unemployment and inflation of the mid-seventies.

There seems to be little doubt, however, that "stability," the major characteristic of an almost contentless party identification, has been only a corollary of the low salience of American politics in the absence of a major national crisis. As such, the stability of party identifications and the extent to which it is being translated into voting behavior at any given time are *residual variables*. Their magnitude depends on the strength and direction of changes introduced by "short-term forces" and the question of whether or not a change is only a short-term force becomes meaningful only in a longitudinal, historical perspective. It is likely that cultural norms of incremental rather than radical change, and structural characteristics of the American party system, have prevented social change from being translated into new political alternatives (see, e.g., Burnham and Sprague, 1970). This is reflected in the choice of party identification to represent a long-term trend of stability in voting behavior; this choice, however, also relegates attitudes involving social change and political issues to the continuous status of noncumulative short-term forces (Kessel, 1972: 464).

During the decade which followed the publication of *The American Voter*, the conceptualizations and analyses of this study, and its companion volume of 1966, remained the accepted doctrine. Since 1969, however, a new "cohort" of voting analysts has attempted to bring evidence in support of an issue-oriented tendency in the American electorate, with special reference to the 1964 and 1968 presidential elections. In the meantime, the concept of party identification, as a determinant of voting behavior, had been applied in cross-national comparisons. Let us examine first some of these comparative studies before we return to the more recent developments in American electoral analysis.

The concept of party identification has not been very helpful in cross-national comparisons. In a study of party identification in Norway and the United States, party membership, with its European connotation of organizational and ideological commitment, has been mistakenly assumed to be the equivalent of party identification in the United States (Campbell and Valen, 1966: 250), and in a comparison between the German *Bundesrepublik* and the United States, the American "strong identifier" was equated with *Uberzeugter Anhänger* (convinced follower) and "weak identification" with "preference for a given party at a given time" (Zohlnhofer, 1965: 132). It is not surprising, therefore, that according to the findings of these studies, strong partisan identifications are considerably less frequent in Norway and Germany than in the United States (25%, 25%, and 36%, respectively). How ambiguous these findings are likely to be can perhaps be estimated from Rokkan's comparison of participation in Norway and the United States (Rokkan, 1970: 376-383), although his data refer to overt behavior rather than psychological identifications. Campbell and Valen were, of course, aware of the fact that "the Norwegian parties are considerably more ideological and class related in their appeals to the electorate than are the American parties," that they "are likely to recruit from a narrower range within the electorate" and "to exert a stronger influence on the political atitudes and behavior of their members than do the American parties." Consequently, the authors expect to find strong differences between identifiers in the two countries, but these differences are ascribed to the party systems and do not weaken the authors' confidence "that we are indeed measuring the same phenomenon" (1966: 253). As evidence for cross-systemic equivalence, the authors use two structural criteria: the correlation of strength of identification with age and with the frequency of voting. Both validating criteria are somewhat problematic: weakening sight, for example, is also correlated with age, which does not make it an indicator of party identification; and given the documented differences in functions, styles, and clientele between the Norwegian and the American party systems, the cross-systemic equivalence of the second validating criterion—i.e., voting—has yet to be established.

Written several years later, Zohlnhofer's study of party identification in Germany and the United States reflects a more cautious approach. It admits that the measuring instruments are comparable only "in principle," and that the cross-national "comparability of relationships between variables is meaningful only if the variables refer to structures of basically comparable social and political *relevance*" (1965: 127; my translation, italics added). The author then explicitly takes this comparable relevance in Germany and the United States as a given parameter, into which he does not inquire. As was to be expected, his findings confirm the differences between party identifiers that were found in the comparison between Norway and the United States. They are then explained historically (political crisis and military defeat in Germany, as opposed to stability in the United States), by the different structure of parties and party systems, and by the cabinet system of government which enables the German voter to impute responsibility for political decisions to the ruling party or coalition. As a consequence thereof, "party identification" is found to have a far greater group—and status-based incidence—and to be based on considerably greater emotional as well as cognitive programmatic considerations, in Germany than in the United States. The author concludes that although party preference and vote are rooted, in Germany, in the same recent historical experiences, *it is the voting decision which determines party identification.* This, of course, contradicts the causal and temporal sequence in the interpretation of American data, where party identification has been considered the main determinant of the vote.

These studies reveal, therefore, that the use of party identification as an independent, explanatory variable in a general theory of voting is unlikely to be very helpful. Furthermore, "party" is a multidimensional construct, and the cross-systemic equivalence of parties must be established on the dimension on which the comparison is drawn.

At this point in the discussion, one should add that even for the authors of *The American Voter* the causal priority assigned to partisan attachments is only an emphasis, and "not a simple and sovereign principle of political behavior" (1960: 292). In a recent response to Burnham's criticism that the sociopsychological model of the American electorate developed in *The American Voter* is "inherently static, without historical depth and . . . as weak in its sociological dimensions as it is strong in its social psychology" (1974a: 1019), Converse rightly denies that the model was intended to be "entirely generalizable to all times and places" (1974: 1026). As stated earlier in this section, Converse's "concept of a normal vote" is, by definition, a short-term model and does not lend itself to the analysis of long-term changes without the introduction of additional variables. The Burnham-Converse controversy (Burnham, 1965, 1974a, 1974b; Converse, 1972, 1974) focused on the steady decrease in voter turnout and increase in partisan indifference in the American electorate between the 1890s and the 1920s, in the face of strong shifts in the demographic composition of the electorate which should have been exerting pressures in the opposite direction (if the sociopsychological model based on data of the 1950s could be applied to that period). Converse believes that these "anomalies" can be explained by changes in electoral legislation and the subsequent changes in the composition and behavior of the electorate, whereas Burnham argues that the model based on findings of the 1950s can be applied neither to the sociological context nor to the salience of politics of an earlier period.

Leaving aside the issue of the adequacy of the available data for inferences about past individual-level behavior, the controversy has been presented as a clash between analytical models. In empirical social science, clashes between models can be resolved only by comparing the amount of variance they explain across settings and time. Given the nature of the presently available data, it is doubtful whether the controversy can be resolved in a convincing manner, as far as past behavior is concerned. Yet it seems that the controversy does not involve mutually exclusive models, let alone paradigms, and that the well developed sociopsychological model will survive—with the necessary adjustments for adapting a middle-range to a higher-level theory— within the broader, contextual, and multidimensional, but not yet fully developed, model proposed by Burnham and delineated, in paradigmatic terms, in the preceding three chapters of this book.

Recent attempts to reappraise the findings of *The American Voter* in the context of the 1960s are related to the "rediscovery" of issue-voting. Evidence from a number of independent studies of 1964 and 1968 election survey data seems to indicate that since the Eisenhower years there has been an increase in the "ideological awareness"—or "issue sensitivity"—of the entire American electorate (see, for example, Field and Anderson [1969], Pierce [1970], and Pomper [1972]; for 1964 case studies, see Stokes [1966], Kessel [1968], Burnham [1968], and RePass [1971]; for 1968 studies, see Converse et al. [1969], Kirkpatrick and Jones [1970], Pomper [1969], and Boyd [1972]). At the time of this writing, the best assessment of these findings and interpretations, and of the methodological and theoretical problems involved, can be found in the June 1972 symposium on issue-voting in the *American Political Science Review*. In addition to some more specific and subtle problems, on which the participants in the symposium have taken positions, they also confirm the importance of three broader issues raised at various points in this book: (1) the limitations of a single-level analysis of voting (Pomper, 1972: 427), which are closely related to the problem of noncontextual analysis and the use of national cross-sectional samples; (2) the residual nature of the partisan identification variable, as evidenced by the very "rediscovery" of issue-voting in the "turbulent decade of the 1960s"; (3) the issue of the time dimension in the assessment of long-term and short-term forces which may conform with, deviate from, or actually bring about a change in the "normal" distribution of partisan identifications and electoral choice (Kessel, 1972: 464).

How does this recent literature on issue voting contribute to the search for a theory of voting? It is perhaps too early for a systematic appraisal at a time when the available evidence is still based on surveys and models not designed to separate issue-orientations from other determinants of voting, and it has been legitimately questioned whether the covariation of perceived proximity on issues and voting behavior can be taken as evidence of "policy voting." Brody and Page (1972: 457-458), suggest three possible situations or processes: (a) the voter's policy position and perception of the candidates' positions are independent of each other; (b) the voter's issue position yields to, or forms around, the perceived position of the favored candidate ("persuasion"); and (c) the voter "projects" his own position onto the favored candidate. Yet, for a differentiation between policy-voting and habitual behavior determined by party identification, how important is it to distinguish between an independently made voting decision and a vote resulting from persuasion, if the latter is also policy-determined (i.e., independent of the candidate's party affiliation or personal appeal)? For a theory of voting, it is far more important to distinguish between an issue-determined and a non-issue-determined preference for a candidate. This can be achieved through panel studies, where it is easier to study the stability or change in the voter's orientations toward candidates and issues.

The single most important advantage of a policy-voting analysis is the ability to relate the prevailing micro-psychological models of voting to both the substance and the processes of political decision-making. The increased issue awareness of the American electorate has prompted voting analysts to reappraise the role of a "contentless" partisan identification as a determinant of voting behavior. Pomper, for example, has shown that policy positions and awareness of party differences on six selected issues have consistently covaried with "strength" of party identification, and he believes that these findings "clearly accord with the concept and significance of party identification" (1972: 419). For the authors of *The American Voter,* however, awareness of party differences was associated with involvement and levels of conceptualization, but not with "strength" of partisan identification. Yet, if it is true that partisan attachments are associated with issue orientations, then we are dealing with two different attitudes: one which is habitual and relatively contentless, and another which is associated with issue orientations. It would hardly help conceptual clarity to use the same concept for a "lagging indicator" reflecting party loyalties in terms of the issue-stands of an earlier period, and for a partisan attachment associated with, or supported by, orientations to the current issues of the 1960s and 1970s, when there is sufficient clarity about the difference between the processes involved.

The Theory of Group-Voting

The rationale for a group-oriented analysis is in the general hypothesis that individuals sharing a group characteristic also share specific interests, or at least similar orientations toward issues or candidates. The authors of *The American Voter* have developed a very closely reasoned model differentiating between distinctive voting behavior which is group-oriented or group-determined, and distinctive voting behavior resulting from the similarity in life situations and responses among members of a specific social category or group, who act and react independently of each other and without the mediation of the group. The latter case obviously applies to sociological categories (sex, age groups, income groups, etc.), but the distinction between the two patterns is not as easily apparent when we consider, for example, racial, ethnic, or religious "groups." Let us exclude from the present discussion the impact of formal organizations (e.g., labor unions), since this clearly involves overt organizational efforts to influence the partisan choice of the memberships.

According to the triangular model of Campbell et al. (1960: 299), what actors perceive as group norms will influence their partisan choice as a positive function of the strength of their group identification and of the group's political salience. The latter variable can be reformulated as measuring the *relative* political salience of some group-related issue or candidate—i.e., relative to that of other issue- or candidate-orientations of the voter, which are not perceived as related to the group. Of the three variables involved—group identification, political salience, and group standards or norms—"it is the group standards that are psychologically real and are responsible for influence when it occurs" (1960: 296). One may add that group identification is only an intervening modifier of adherence to group norms, and that the political salience of the group is subject to short-term variation, since it "usually depends on the most transient objects of political orientation: the candidates and the issues." Furthermore, "high salience alone does not create an unanimous group response" (1960: 318). Finally, group norms sometimes persist even when there is no apparent salience. The analyst has to address himself, therefore, primarily to the development, communication, and perception of group standards for partisan choice, remembering that a large proportion of voters (49% in 1956) conceptualized issues and partisanship in terms of group conflict or group benefit.

The distinctiveness of a "group's" partisan choice may occur in one of three possible situations:

(a) when group norms are articulated by visible leaders or spokesmen of the group (this includes candidacies of minority-group members);

(b) when no visible leadership articulates group norms for partisan choice, but such norms develop, are communicated and reinforced as a consequence of interaction between the members of the group;

(c) when there is no evidence of either visible leadership or group interaction. This may refer to culturally transmitted or individually acquired psychological reference groups, or to cases of similarity in life situations, without psychological reference groups and group standards.

Situations of type (a) combine party identification and group interest hypotheses. Evidence for situations of type (b) can be found in voting studies based on specific communities (e.g., Berelson et al., 1954), or among union member households and workers in unionized workshops. Type (c) refers to studies based on cross-sectional national samples and involves the need for evidence of a psychological reference group and norm. It is this type which deserves some methodological observations.

In order to establish the net impact of the group-factor in the distinctiveness of the group vote, students of voting behavior have compared, for example, the Catholic, Black, or Jewish vote with that of control groups matched with the test group on several important socioeconomic characteristics or aspects of life situation. If, after removing the effects of the specific distribution of socioeconomic characteristics in the test group, a group-specific bias in voting is still apparent, it is attributed to a group norm. Yet, in the absence of evidence for leadership cues, group interaction, or psychological group reference, the hypothesized group norm has to be demonstrated. Alford has pointed out that when one refers to "the typical voting preference of Catholics, workers or Negroes, he merely makes a statistical statement," and "the conditions which cause a particular Catholic worker to vote left are not the same as those which cause 70 percent of Catholic workers to vote left" (Alford, 1963: 90). The former are personal phenomena, the latter socially and historically determined political phenomena. Alford thus draws attention to the need for separate explanations at the micro-level and at the level of aggregate data. More accurately, perhaps, the analyst has only aggregate data on cases in a sample, but by attributing the distinctiveness of the vote to a group norm, he is making statements about individuals by drawing into the explanation hypotheses from a different level of observation: the development, articulation, and transmission of the norm.

It has also been shown that the distinctiveness of the vote increases with the strength of group identification; furthermore, the frequence of high group identifications (i.e., group cohesiveness) is assumed to depend on the type of groups and settings involved; "a prime determinant may simply be the degree to which group members feel set apart from other people by virtue of social barriers" (Campbell et al., 1960: 310). The need to include contextual variables (e.g., social barriers) and the actor's perception thereof in the interpretation of degrees of group identification is congruent with a sociopsychological approach; yet, by using aggregate cross-sectional data, how much do we know about the context which assumedly establishes differences in group identification? Furthermore, if there are social barriers, it is assumed that the individual perceived them as related to his race, ethnic origin, or religion; but for the actor, *his* race, ethnic origin, or religion are social and psychological realities irrespective of the psychological reality of the group. What this analysis suggests is that, controlling for perceived issue salience to the group, two interpretations of ethnic or religious voting patterns observed on aggregate cross-sectional data are possible:

(1) Ethnic or religious characteristics are data of the same type as age, sex, education, or income and create life situations which determine a distinctive tendency toward partisan choice. When no evidence of perceived contexts or group norms is available, the analysis is socio-logical, rather than psychosociological.

(2) The observed distinctness and continuity of partisan choice among individuals sharing certain ethnic or religious characteristics can be explained at the party-identification level, without introducing group membership as a psychological variable.

Needless to say, these interpretations which reflect the constraints of non-contextual aggregate data are theoretically poorer than contextual theories of group voting.

Class Voting

Even for Karl Marx, the relevance of "social class" for political behavior was a function of the "class consciousness" of its members. Although there are objective and empirically observable differences in wealth or income, in education and life-styles between occupational and status categories, the "reality" of classes as determinants of behavior is psychological. Some formal organizations, such as labor unions and political parties, may lend objective reality to the representation of class interests, but even unions, which are only partial class organizations, seldom include all individuals who would qualify for membership, and political parties find it inopportune to limit their recruitment and appeal to an operationally definable "class." Not less important is the fact that, although social classes are a universal phenomenon, a particular class is always system-specific; it is defined as a relative position in a stratification system, measured on one or several relevant dimensions, whereas ethnic, racial, or religious identities are independent of system char-acteristics. Finally, whether we consider class as an objective or a subjective stratum, it consists of a cluster of variables or dimensions of identification; these generally display positive intercorrelations, but any decision about cutting points which would constitute the boundaries between objective classes is necessarily arbitrary, and the equivalence of classes across systems is, at best, an equivalence of rank orders.

Voting studies have used both objective and subjective indicators of class membership. Some studies have introduced the additional distinction between "subjective location in the status hierarchy" and "awareness" of location in this hierarchy (Campbell et al., 1960: 333-380; Eulau, 1962). The authors of *The American Voter* have reported that "awareness of class . . . behaves as a variable of the group identification type," and that "it is distinct from the traditional concept of class consciousness in that it includes a lower register of class feeling" (1960: 344). This view is supported by Sartori (1969: 83), who suggests that status awareness denotes status sensitivity, whereas class consciousness is an ideological commitment. He adds, however, that both status and class are conceptually muddled (which is true, because they are multidimensional constructs, and each dimension seems to have its own critical thresholds), and that the relationship among subjective awareness, ideological commitment, and objective conditions may vary not only as a function of the gap between the steps on the stratification ladder (and, therefore, of mobility), but also along a semantic dimension—i.e., whether "worker" and "middle class" are considered "good" or "bad" words. Obviously Sartori refers to differences in political culture and not merely to semantics.

Converse (1958) and Campbell et al. (1960: 347) conclude from their analysis of American voting behavior in the 1950s that the role of social class in political behavior is fluctuating and depends on the degree of status polarization at any given time. Status polarization is defined as the degree to which upper- and lower-status groups in a society have taken up mutually antagonistic value positions, and therefore reflects the intensity of class identification. Polarization seems to have fluctuated in the United States in connection with events in the economic order, but has influenced voting behavior primarily among those who are involved and are capable of a sophisticated conceptualization of politics. Stated otherwise, when parties do not take explicitly antagonistic stands on economic and policy issues, the less-involved and the less-informed voter will not make a partisan choice according to his status position. In 1956, the correlation of subjective status and vote, among voters who perceived party differences and were aware of their status position, was only 0.24.

In the first major cross-national and theoretically oriented review of voting studies, Lipset et al. used five sociopsychological variables and intraclass communication for a classification of *objective* class characteristics associated with voting regularities within lower-income groups (1954, II: 1124-1175). The data covered elections in the Anglo-American democracies, continental Europe, Scandinavia, as well as India, Japan, and other more recently established democracies. The analysis suggests that it is possible to identify environmental structures in which individuals with specific sociodemographic characteristics develop voting patterns indicating a class awareness in partisan choice—e.g., miners, lumbermen, commercial farmers, fishermen, European workers in large plants situated in large cities, low-status minority groups, etc.

One should add, of course, that in the period preceding the use of survey research, the interpretation of voting behavior was based exclusively on objective class indicators, without testing the underlying hypothesis that by and large objective characteristics are fairly reliable indicators of psychological group or class orientations.

Is it possible to dismiss the distinction between subjective class orientations and objective indicators of class, in the study of political behavior, as relevant only to the history of our methods and techniques, and to claim that with the development of psychometric tools and the availability of resources for survey research, the objective, "shorthand" approach to class voting is of no further interest to political science (although it remains the main tool available to the historian)? The conceptual framework of *The American Voter,* the typology of socioecological indicators of fairly stable voting patterns developed by Lipset et al., the findings of a recent comparison between American and British survey data, as well as the literature on social mobility and voting seem to indicate that the distinction between subjective and objective class indicators is still of theoretical interest, although it presents some methodological difficulties.

Campbell et al. have shown that the polarization of sociopolitical attitudes increases class-determined partisan choice. Using occupation as an objective indicator of class, they also found, however, that in the United States the relationship between occupational status and subjective status is not very high. They hypothesized that a social structure which allows for, or promotes, class misidentifications, lowers the potential of that society for status polarization and, consequently, for a stronger or more frequent class orientation in voting behavior (1960: 370-377). The potential for polarization in the United States is low, because the population is distributed along the entire continuum of status ranks, with many intermediate ranks which promote status misidentification through the proximity of, and interaction between, ranks. Thus, the pattern according to which subjective class identifications diverge from objective class is an indicator of flexibility or rigidity in the social stratification system: the closer the "fit" between subjective and objective class, the greater the rigidity of social stratification and the likelihood of a persistent pattern of polarization and class vote. Objective class indicators should therefore be a better predictor of voting behavior in less "open" societies, while subjective class should be a better predictor in less rigid social systems.

Thompson has presented evidence which shows the extent to which this theorizing is borne out by a comparison of British and American voting behavior (Thompson, 1970: 139-151). According to this study, subjective class accounted for four times as much of the variation in Democratic Party preferences in the United States (1964) as was explained by objective class, and twice as much as was explained by subjective class in Britain (1967), whereas objective class accounted for twice as much of the variation in Labor Party preferences as did subjective class, and for four times as much as was explained by objective class in the United States. The evidence points in the expected direction, but shows only a moderate impact of both subjective and objective class, with only about fifteen percent of the variation explained by the former in the United States and by the latter in Britain. Thompson's multivariate analysis also showed, however, that both in Britain and in the United States, the political orientation of the respondent's father, at the time the respondent was growing up, was the single most powerful explanatory variable, accounting for over thirty-seven percent in the variation of Labor and Democratic Party preferences. This, undoubtedly, points at the importance of parental socialization in a theory of voting for relatively stable societies.

A more detailed analysis, by political generations, would reveal perhaps that the parental impact is related to specific events, crises, etc. It is possible, for example, that the modal case of parental influence, in a sample interviewed in the mid-sixties, is located in the years following the Great Depression. The socializing impact of "father's political orientation" could therefore be a function of external events and of the manner in which such events affected the family. Furthermore, one would have to inquire into the role the respective parties were able to play in the crisis period. It is therefore possible that "father's political orientation" is primarily an indicator of *partisan* socialization in some cases, and primarily an indicator of the respondent's identification with his *class of origin* in other cases, and the distribution of these two types of cases would presumably vary considerably between Britain and the United States. Such hypotheses would require a more refined operationalization of the cluster of variables subsumed under "parental socialization."

Some of the difficulties encountered in cross-systemic comparisons of class voting are a consequence of the fact that "class" is a generalized, subjective and relational, and therefore indeterminate analytical construct. Moreover, attempts to compare subjective and objective class indicators— which yielded the concept of "misidentifiers"—have often tended to oversimplify the ordinal scales on which such comparisons have been made and to blur our understanding of the relationship between class and vote. Thompson has shown, for example, that if the distinction between manual and non-manual workers is used as a cutting point between objective classes, forty-four percent of the assumedly middle-class nonmanual workers (in the Butler and Stokes British data) view themselves as working class (Thompson's own data show only 34%). Is there a rationale for a cutting point which leaves almost one-half of the upper stratum subjectively identified with the lower stratum?

Thompson suggests that the discrepancy between subjective class perceptions and partisan choice could be explained by "unconscious needs and feelings" which override conscious class perceptions. Finally, Thompson cites Runciman's search for what the misperceiving white-collar Britishers have in mind when they define themselves as "working class." It appears that they consider themselves as "ordinary people," an image assumedly intended to distinguish them from the "privileged" classes, the traditional social and political elites. The nonprivileged classes, however, also included large segments of the middle class, and one cannot ignore the fact that the Labor Party deliberately shed its image of a doctrinaire class party under its recent more pragmatic leadership.

The use of objective indicators for a theory of class voting cannot proceed from the convenient but untenable position that political polarization in a two-party system reflects, or appeals to, a social polarization in a dichotomized stratification system with two, and only two, social classes. By forcing respondents into the Procrustean bed of a class dichotomy (and the use of "upper class" as a third possible choice of subjective identification often runs counter to strong cultural prejudices), the researcher creates misidentifiers as an artifact of his or her instrument. Objective class indicators could perhaps be used as indices of subjective class, provided subjectively meaningful distinctions were introduced into the broader objective classification. It is only with a more discriminating and subjectively validated classification of objective status and class positions that a more rewarding testing of the class voting hypothesis can be expected. Even then, however, one has to allow, in addition to mobility along the social ladder, for realignments of status and class categories in terms of the available spectrum of political parties.

As a corrollary of class-oriented interpretations of voting, social scientists have endeavored to shed more light on the role of class identification by studying the political behavior of the socially mobile. The discussion of status polarization has already pointed at the limitations imposed on the comparative study of mobility by the use of dichotomic social "scales" to match the Left-Right, or two-party, parameters. Even a more complex—i.e., more realistic—ladder of social strata does not imply, however, that objective increments in status or income are linear in any social system, let alone across different systems. Given the multidimensionality of status ladders, Lenski has introduced a distinction between inconsistencies *within* ascribed *or* achieved status characteristics, and those *between* achieved *and* ascribed status. He suggests that both types of inconsistencies lead to increased support for Left-wing parties, but that the latter type of discrepancies has a more frequent impact on political orientations than the former. Using religion as an indicator of ascribed status and middle or working class as categories of achieved status in an analysis of survey data from four Anglo-American democracies, Lenski has brought evidence in support of his "theory" (Lenski, 1967: 298-301). However, in a multivariate analysis of attribute data (father's class, sex, present class, and education), Thompson found "virtually no support" for Lenski's hypotheses of status-inconsistency interactions in Britain and in the United States (1970: 160).

Lopreato's study, "Social Mobility and Political Outlooks in Italy" (1967), introduces both objective and subjective distinctions between layers within the new class of upward mobiles. Positions in the middle class vary according to consumption patterns (measured by the number of consumer items owned), according to occupational role-profiles (managerial or decision-making roles, as opposed to more supervised, "routine," nonmanual occupations) and to the degree to which the upwardly mobile perceive that they have gained social recognition of their economic and occupational achievements by the "established" members of their new class. Lopreato's Italian data show that, although consumption patterns and occupational profiles have some impact on differential political choice among "newcomers" and between "newcomers" and "old-timers," the single most discriminating variable in the distribution of partisan choice is the perception of interclass restrictions.

This line of approach is worth pursuing. The theoretically interesting question is not whether the distribution of leftist and rightist votes among middle-class Europeans of working-class origin, compared to that of their class of origin and of their new class peers, displays a different pattern from that which has been observed among American middle-class voters of working-class origin. Rather, in order to explain such differences (assuming that indeed such differences exist), one would like to inquire into the conditions which bring about the political acculturation of the upwardly mobile into the dominant partisan identification of their new class peers. Controlling for styles of consumption and occupational profiles, is political acculturation impaired by residential segregation or differentiation, by occupational clienteles (for example, for lawyers or physicians), by perceived ideological cleavages in the larger society, or rather by stages in the life cycle or by personality traits? What proportion of the presently unexplained variance in political acculturation can be explained by such factors, and what model explains them best? If transculturally applicable operationalizations of such factors could be arrived at, they might help in establishing a bridge between theories of voting and theories of development or change.

After expressing his dissatisfaction with the available theoretical formulations and empirical evidence, Barber seems to begin his own contribution to a theory of social mobility and voting (in his *Social Mobility and Voting Behavior,* 1970) at the point at which Lopreato had left it: "For both the upwardly and the downwardly mobiles, political loyalties and attitudes tend to change in the direction appropriate to their new status, resulting in politi-cal behavior *intermediate* between that typical of their old status and that typical of their new status" (1970: 36). Barber has no difficulty in present-ing "evidence" for this statement from 1952, 1956, and 1960 American electoral surveys, but he does not deal with the theoretical question of who will and who will not cross party lines. What is an intermediate position in political behavior that one could assign to the socially mobile? Between voting Democratic or Republican, an intermediate position would imply one of the following possibilities: (a) an oscillating partisan choice, varying from one election to the other; (b) a split-ticket vote; and (c) abstention. To inquire into the first possibility, one would need panel data for a number of successive elections; for the second, data for electoral choices at several levels of office. Barber has not used either type of data. As for the third possibility, it has been simply excluded from Barber's analysis. Instead, "intermediate" refers to the percentage of an aggregate of mobiles, in a national sample, voting Democratic or Republican, compared to the respec-tive percentages in the aggregate of non-mobiles in the sample. Of what interest are these aggregate measurements for a theoretical statement relating voting behavior to social mobility?

Voting studies based on objective class indicators, without controls for the divergence between objective and subjective perspectives—i.e., without contextual interpretations at the individual level—are primarily macro-socio-logical, as opposed to psychosociological. They lead to descriptions of central tendencies in the aggregate behavior of members of economic classes and other social categories and groups. When no individual-level contextual data are available, explanatory hypotheses are formulated by reference to macro-environments: systemic political variables, social structures, and history. Individuals, however, do not live and interact in systemwide environments, and even the most plausible structurally or historically oriented hypotheses about class voting require validation at the micro-level. As a result of these difficulties, sociological studies of class voting can yield only broad-scale generalizations and agendae for individual- and cross-level research. Alford's comparative study of class voting in four Anglo-American democracies is an excellent example of a conscious effort to emphasize the theoretical limita-tions of a macro-sociological analysis of political behavior.

After demonstrating the differences in "class voting" (defined in terms of the difference in the support given by voters in manual occupations to the major Right- and Left-wing parties) between Britain, Australia, the United States, and Canada, Alford discusses a number of "possible causes" which might account for these differences. Thus, where class voting is higher, (1) parties might more consistently represent class interests, (2) or more con-sistently appeal to class interests, (3) or simply possess the historical loyalties of certain classes. Other possible hypotheses refer to differences in the rate of economic growth, urbanization, the relative size of the middle class, educational opportunities, the rate of upward and downward social mobility, the gap between the wages of skilled and unskilled workers, the presence or absence of an open "frontier" as an escape from intense class struggle, and the impact of regional and religious factors. Although macro-data for some of these hypotheses display cross-systemic consistency in the ranking of the four countries and their respective levels of "class voting," the author emphasizes that none of these macro-sociological hypotheses can be tested with the type of data at his disposal. These "gross characterizations" (Alford, 1963: 122) of the possible causes of class voting are, therefore, merely an agenda for individual- and cross-level research.

Economic and occupational class is the single most widely used variable in macro-sociological voting studies, but the underlying theoretical framework views voting behavior as associated with all politically relevant social cleavages. One of the major themes of such studies is the cross-cutting or cumulative effects of economic and noneconomic cleavages. The most ambitious statement of the theoretical framework for a macro-sociological and historical analysis of voting has been formulated by Lipset and Rokkan (1967). It focuses on the historical sequence of social, cultural, and political cleavages in the development of the party systems in eleven European democracies (center-periphery, state-church, land-industry, owner-worker), on the extent of their overlap, their persistence, and the time lags in their translation into political options. The model is followed by a series of national case studies. This is an impressive framework for cross-level, longitudinal, and cross-systemic comparisons, a systematic analysis of the history of modern party systems, designed to identify the structural constraints of individual and group behavior "within the limits set by the past and the present configuration of [the] polity." Rokkan is aware of the fact that this historical model of nation-building is not a theory, but a "typology of the macro-contexts of political behavior," and he believes that "we have to live with comparisons of unique configurations, but can make headway . . . by . . . tackling the tasks of identifying the critical dimensions of variation" and invariance across historically given systems (Rokkan, 1970: 139).

Yet, the relationship between social cleavages, party systems, and voter alignments is precisely a question with which a sociological theory of voting would be concerned, and the multilevel longitudinal dimension, which enables Rokkan to point out that the party systems of the 1960s still reflect the cleavage structures of the 1920s is indicative of the need to draw cross-level comparisons into the analysis. It follows from Rokkan's model that (1) the available voting alternatives are set by political elites, and classes, ethnic, religious, and regional groups "align" themselves along these alternatives;

(2) there is a time lag in the adjustment of party systems to rapidly changing social structures, and, therefore, (3) a sociological theory of voting would have to distinguish between voting behavior which reflects the congruence, and that which reflects the incongruence between party system and social cleavage. The congruent vote would be an act of purposive behavior, the incongruent an act of loyalty, traditional attachment, or trust.

It is true, of course, that configurations described in terms of the historical layers of nation-building in Western Europe do not lend themselves to universal generalizations; but, as Rokkan himself points out, identifying cross-systemic variances is likely to lead to those invariances in the relationship between structural and behavioral variables, to which a theory of voting is assumed to address itself.

Many of the case studies brought together under the Lipset-Rokkan model demonstrate that the configurational approach does not necessarily apply only to national, "total," configurations. Applied at the regional level—for natural or analytical regions—"configuration" simply means the behaviorally relevant socioecological structure, and can be extremely useful in empirical theorizing, as shown by contextual and interaction hypotheses of voting behavior.

Class, Social Interaction, and Contextual Voting Analysis

It has been pointed out that group norms, as determinants of partisan choice, are either articulated by the group leadership or developed, transmitted, and reinforced through social interaction between the members of the group. The interaction thesis has been a major theme in the study of influence, small group behavior, and communication. Voting studies have examined the effects of *assumed* interactions on partisan choice, and the findings indicate that voters are likely to have friends and co-workers of the same political preference, that the political homogeneity in personal associations is positively correlated with the frequency of voting support for a given party, and that when the voter's immediate personal environment is split in political preference, he is more likely to vote in line with the majority of the larger community (Berelson et al., 1954: 88-117). Furthermore, Lipset and his associates (1954: 1140) have reported that where occupational groups tend to be identical with the social community (i.e., in socially isolated occupations, such as fishermen, miners, forestry workers), the social structure is favorable to intragroup communication and unfavorable to cross-class communication. Thus, off-the-job contacts reinforce on-the-job contacts and occupationally salient attitudes.

Voting studies have placed greater emphasis on the structure of the environment than on the behavioral dimension of interaction analysis; only recently has there been a somewhat more systematic effort to explore the impact of different patterns of interaction on electoral choices. A study by Soares and Hamblin (1967) revealed that whereas a linear multiple regression, using five contextual socioeconomic indicators, explained only forty-five percent of the variance in the vote for the radical Left in Chile, a multivariate power function of the same indicators (i.e., a multiple regression using logarithmic transformations of these indicators) raised the explained variance to eighty-one percent. Soares and Hamblin had no solid theoretical justification for believing that the vote for the radical Left was a power function of environmental socioeconomic indices, but the curve-fitting was so compelling that they were willing to assume that the vote for the radical Left, as an expression of aggressive alienation, followed the power function pattern of the relationship between stimuli and *nonvoluntary* responses. The multiplier effect was then explained as an "interaction" between aggregate measures, such as percentage in high school or college (measuring class polarization), percentage divorced (measuring anomie), and percentage in mining industries (measuring industrial development). Disclaimers notwithstanding, this seems to be a fairly simple case of the ecological fallacy.

The theoretical puzzle at which this study had pointed prompted Burnham and Sprague (1970) to test the multiplicative model on American voting data. Using a political and four socioeconomic predictor variables (aggregate county-level data) and presidential election returns from Pennsylvania for 1960-1968, they found that there was very little difference in total explanatory power between the additive and the multiplicative models, as far as the vote for Democratic candidates was concerned. However, the relative magnitude of the partial correlations for three of the five variables did change considerably, suggesting that theoretical interpretations would depend on the model chosen. But which of the two models is to be preferred, and on what grounds? A tentative answer to this question is provided by the finding that, for the same data set, the multiplicative model improved the explained variance in the Wallace vote from seven to twenty-seven percent. The authors interpret this deviation from the additive model as reflecting the difference between the relatively stable social infrastructure of the established parties and a radical grass-roots movement (the non-Southern Wallace vote) which cuts across social structure and party alignments. The established parties are based on different ethnocultural alignments, but differ only marginally in terms of major policy outcomes, whereas the radical Wallace vote reflects a protest against the lack of responsiveness of the major parties to the issues of a rapidly changing socioeconomic reality. But why does a protest movement imply a multiplicative, interactive model?

Burnham and Sprague suggest that racial hostility and economic threat account for the alienation from the party system and for the act of aggressive hostility expressed in the Wallace vote. Of the five predictor variables used in the analysis of the Pennsylvania vote for Wallace, only two displayed a considerable increase in the partial R^2 of the multiplicative model: percentage "nonwhite" and percentage "foreign parents." Furthermore, the Wallace penetration seemed to have been greater in blue-collar than in middle-class areas. The authors conclude that at the aggregate level of analysis, the radicalization of economic threat and racial hostility displays a multiplicative impact on voting behavior, along the lines suggested by Soares and Hamblin.

One may ask, however, whether it is really necessary to assume a quasi-involuntary response model to account for the interaction with contextual variables. It may be equally, if not more, plausible to assume that the additive model applies to voting behavior which is not contextually determined and does not imply interactions at the *individual* level. The vote for the Democratic Party can be determined by an ethnocultural group's past or present party identification, irrespective of interactions with other minority or majority groups. However, when factors such as racial hostility or economic threat become predominant determinants of voting decisions, one must assume that feelings of hostility and threat are a function of an interaction with some other individuals or groups, who represent, symbolize, or are perceived as objects of hostility or sources of threat. Therefore, the larger the proportion of non-whites or first-generation Americans perceived as sources of threat, the greater the opportunity for individual interaction between the "threatened" and the "threatening." A behavioral tendency determined by contextual interaction (e.g., a protest vote) is therefore necessarily some function of the number of possible interactions—i.e., of the product of the proportion of "threatened" and the proportion of "threatening" in the politically relevant environment. The probability (in contradistinction to the possibility) of an encounter between "threatening" and "threatened" voters and of its impact on voting decisions, the influence of the media and of formal and informal communications among the "threatened," are likely to be additional elements in the calculus of an interaction-theory of voting, presumably with second-order multiplicative effects (interactions of interactions).

The thesis of an individual-level interaction has been explored by Przeworski and Soares (1971) in a study which departs from the aggregate-level interpretation of the Soares and Hamblin analysis. By gradually increasing the complexity of the interaction model, the authors propose nine interaction theories of group voting. Of the many methodological observations made in this study, two are particularly relevant to the present discussion:

(a) When only narrow ranges of the independent variables can be observed, a linear prediction will usually provide a good fit. However,
a short segment of any smooth curve can be approximated by a
straight line. Thus, theoretically unmotivated curve-fitting may lead
to results which are meaningless, unless the full range of the independent variables has been observed (1971: 66).

(b) Since predictions generated by different interaction models refer
only to the central tendency, several competing theories may simultaneously provide good fit. When such theories provide equally good
fit and absorb the same number of degrees of freedom, the radical
empiricist guidelines for basing evaluations of theories on the tests
of fit do not take us very far. The fact that some function fits significantly to some observations is not particularly significant for a systematic knowledge of politics. Consistency with other things we know
ultimately becomes the decisive criterion for a temporary acceptance
of a particular theory (1971: 67). (For earlier discussions of the theoretical interpretation of statistical interaction see Blalock, 1966,
1967a, 1967b; Boyd, 1969.)

The Organizational Hypothesis

In his incisive critique of the sociology of voting, Sartori has questioned
the independent status of a class-theory of voting. "Class is an ideology,"
but (quoting Barnes, 1966: 522) "no idea has ever made much headway
without an organization behind it . . . wherever ideologies seem to be important in politics, they have a firm organizational basis." What we are really
investigating, via class behavior, is the impact of an organizational variable:
the influence of party and trade-union control (Sartori, 1969: 84-85).

Evidence for the organizational hypothesis can be found in Liepelt's comparative study of party support in Germany and Austria (Liepelt, 1971:
183-202). Using the so-called "tree technique" (Sonquist and Morgan, 1964)
for ordering and dichotomizing variables, Liepelt demonstrates that 20.2 percent of the initial variance in preferences for the Socialist Party in Germany
and 21.4 percent of the variance in Austria, can be explained by variables
which "reflect ties to large scale organizations that integrate the individual
or groups of individuals into the partisan arrangements of the political community. . . . These are the Catholic church . . . and the organized Labor
movement." Arian has performed a similar analysis of 1969 Israeli election
data and found that the largest proportion in the variance of voting decisions
was explained by "membership in the Federation of Labor *(Histadrut)*" and
"religious observance." Somewhat suspicious of the purely organizational
impact of the Histadrut, the author prefers to consider it a "social network,"
which he defines as involving either organizational affiliation or a behavioral

pattern, since affiliation and behavior are "not necessarily related" (Arian, 1973). Yet, if behavior is not necessarily related to membership, we are probably dealing, in this case, with a predominant subculture within the Histadrut, or with an ideological identification; this would also make the analysis more compatible with "religious observance" as the second most important predictor variable, and Arian himself has demonstrated that the partial organizational overlap of the two subcultures does not establish the predominance of the organizational over the cultural factors. Organizational membership has also been found to be a major voting determinant in an ecological correlation analysis of Italian voting and census data (Capecchi and Galli, 1969: 235).

The British data presented by Butler and Stokes (1969) show a thirty-one percent difference in the support for Labor between union and nonunion families; subjective class identifications account, however, for a difference of fifty percent in support for Labor between middle- and working-class voters (1969: 76, 155). The Butler and Stokes study reveals a number of different patterns in the relationship between socialization, class self-image, unionization, and party preference, in which the organizational hypothesis survives only in fully unionized workplaces; furthermore, in industries such as mining, shipbuilding, printing, and dock labor, where recruitment has been largely hereditary and union membership compulsory, the impact of unionization overlaps, at least partly, with intergenerational socialization.

Measures of association between organizational *membership* and party preference are not likely to be very reliable indicators of the strength of organizational impact. Butler and Stokes have dealt with this problem by controlling for voluntary as opposed to compulsory membership, and for the degree of unionization of workplaces; in Israel, party preference was found to be associated with a "social network," or participation in a subculture, rather than with formal organizational membership, and all this raises some second thoughts on the interpretation of the German and Austrian data. More important, however, than the adequacy of any specific indicators is the theoretical implication of the organizational hypothesis. To the extent that voting decisions can be shown to be part of an interaction between individuals and an organization, there would be *direct* evidence for a social-interaction theory of voting.

Sociopsychological and Political Determinants. The Theoretical Status of Voting as Participatory Behavior

A frequent characteristic of sociopsychological and sociological approaches to the study of voting is their tendency to overlook the fact that in the relationship between class or status and vote, both the social structure and the party system are independent variables. We have seen how Rokkan or Burnham and Sprague have explicitly avoided this fallacy. Thompson's comparison of British and American data on party-preference provides some evidence for the differential impact of sociopsychological and political variables in two different political systems. Using a multivariate technique for attribute data, Thompson demonstrated that after accounting for the impact of father's politics, father's class, respondent's subjective and objective class, educational level, and sex, all but 2.7 percent of the variance in preferences for the British Labor Party could be explained. The study also showed, however, that these sociopsychological variables could not account for a 23.4 percent "random shock" (unexplained variance) *against* Labor preference. In the United States, there was a 27.6 percent random shock *in favor* of Democratic preference, with only a 9.2 percent random shock against Democratic preference. This analysis suggests that the impact of political stimuli—i.e., voting behavior which is left unexplained by sociopsychological variables, will increase with the social heterogeneity (or decrease with the class orientation) in the political appeal of the parties. Yet, the extent to which the party system reflects the structure of society and the extent to which parties choose to adapt their appeal, at any given time, to the prevailing social cleavages, are political variables which are independent of the social structure per se.

By positing that voting can be the expression of loyalty, or of instrumental, expressive, or normative political orientations, and by exploring different partial theories of voting, the Butler and Stokes (1969) analysis of the British electorate is of greater interest to the comparativist than many earlier European and American election studies. Furthermore, this study is concerned with electoral choices as a link in the political process; it relates party preferences, and changes therein, not only to the ways in which parties and leaders align themselves on issues, but also to valued goals and government output. "There is . . . little doubt that, whatever the degree of its ignorance or confusion, the [British] electorate attempts to use the ballot to achieve things it cares about" (1969: 31). Adopting a macro-perspective, the authors consider voting (in general elections) as the second most frequent "form of political behavior," outnumbered only by "following campaigns" via mass media or by conversation (1969: 25). This is the traditional view of voting as one of several steps on an assumedly unidimensional ladder of political participation or involvement (Milbrath, 1965). Sufficient evidence has been adduced in this chapter to challenge the view that voting (let alone other forms of political participation) is a unidimensional form of behavior. Participation is an important concept in democratic theory, but it is only a formal, classificatory, or organizing concept. Pappi has criticized the so-called "index of political participation" because it fails to distinguish between (a) political action, (b) politically oriented action (e.g., writing to a legislator, signing a petition), and (c) the prequisites of (a) and (b), such as "following political news in the media." He suggests that these different types of activities may have "structurally different meanings," referring presumably to consequences at different levels and in different types of social and political organization. Quoting Habermas et al. (1961: 15), he adds that when participation is not considered within a specific situation, when one does not inquire into its contents and meaning, it becomes some kind of goal per se. Although Pappi examines primarily the system-level meaning of electoral behavior, he clearly indicates the need for a multilevel interpretation of the concept of participation (Pappi, 1970: 42-47).

Since the act of voting can be the result of different sociopsychological and political processes, it can have different objective and subjective meanings. Among the latter, neither expressive nor normative orientations toward the act of voting (e.g., citizen duty) can be conceived as intended to affect the environment, or the voter's own position therein. There are, of course, additional difficulties with the theoretical status of the act of voting: voters do not initiate the act, neither do they determine the candidates and issues on which the electoral contest is fought (Verba et al., 1971: 16). Furthermore, different voters may support the same party for different reasons. Proponents of an economic theory of government and politics have pointed at the costs attached to the benefit of a vote taken simultaneously on a whole set of issues, rather than separately on each issue. There is sufficient indication that voting does not share the characteristics of other "forms of political participation." So far, however, the line of argument has been primarily theoretical. Verba, Nie, and Kim have to be credited for supplying the first empirical evidence for this hypothesis.

In a study of the dimensions of participation in Austria, India, Japan, Nigeria, and the United States, these authors factor-analyzed indicators of citizen participation and found that voting was only weakly related to campaigning, cooperative activity, and citizen-initiated contacts with government officials. Commenting on their "principal component analysis" of the U.S. data, in which the first component was interpreted as a common dimension of "propensity for political activity," they write: "The second component unambiguously points to the uniqueness of voting when compared to other political acts . . . the three voting variables display high positive loadings ranging from .6 to .7, while all of the other ten activities have weak negative loadings" (1971: 25-26). The data in each of the five countries revealed the same structure for the four types of participation. The correlations between voting and each of the other indicators were significantly lower than the correlations between campaigning and communal activity, and nowhere did the correlation between voting and contacting government officials exceed the .09 level (1971: 42). The authors conclude that "the weak relation of voting to other acts and to general political involvement should make one pause before voting is taken as a cross-nationally valid indicator of political mobilization" (1971: 64).

This study also provides empirical evidence for the relevance of the distinction made earlier in this book between private and public purposes of political behavior. Citizen-initiated contacts are expected to result in a particularized benefit (as opposed to some general collective outcome, or a vote oriented toward a number of simultaneously posed public issues), and contacts with a personalized referent constitute a separate dimension of participation which displays no significant positive, or a weak negative, correlation with cooperative activities or contacting with a social or community referent. "Particularized contacting is engaged in with little general concern for political matters . . . and recruitment to such activity does not seem to depend upon those mobilization processes associated with a standard socio-economic model" (1971: 64). Verba and his associates suggest that there may be other processes by which individuals come to participate than the standard socio-economic one, including the "group consciousness" model, the "personal relevance of government" model and the "partisan mobilized" model. Of course, the "partisan mobilized" model comes closest to Sartori's organizational hypothesis. (For a path analysis of participation based on the socio-economic model, see Nie et al., 1969: 361-378; 808-832.)

In a further elaboration of their analysis of participation, Verba and Nie (1972) have constructed a typology of political acts based on the following dimensions:

(1) empirical modes of participation (voting, campaigning, cooperative action, and contacting government officials);

(2) gratifications (political outcomes, side benefits—social, material or symbolic);

(3) referents of gratification (the individual or his family, some group, or the entire community or nation).

Voting may be expected to provide group or community benefits, as well as any of three types of side benefits. However, there is also a category of voting which is not attached to any expectation of gratification.

These distinctions are extremely useful in clearing the ground and pointing to the direction in which the search for a general theory of political behavior could proceed. With the exception of the organizational (or mobilization) hypothesis, all partial theories have considered voting as an act of individual behavior. Yet, by definition, voting is an instance of collective action. This raises the question of the relationship between individual determinants of voting and the intended consequences of the collective act. The major contribution of the Verba and Nie conceptualizations resides in the consideration of *both* the personal and public intended consequences of political behavior. It provides an empirically grounded conceptual framework which may help establish a link with normative theories of a rational calculus of collective action. The distinction between individual and collective action, and between individual and collective goals, may seem trivial; after all, no one has claimed that voting and campaigning, or contacting government officials and cooperating with other citizens are equivalent forms of political behavior. Yet, the relationship between intended individual consequences and observed collective consequences is critical, because it assigns different meanings, at different levels of imputation, to the same empirical behavior and helps establish equivalences across different empirical forms of behavior.

Chapter 7

FUNCTIONAL EQUIVALENCE

Theoretical Introduction—Exchange

Theory, Politics and Public Goods

Although the preceding chapters have taken us through a discussion of a variety of methodological and substantive issues, the underlying purpose of the discussion can be summarized in the following two statements: (1) If the comparative analysis of political behavior is to yield a *cumulatively* growing understanding of politics expressed in empirical generalizations or logically universal statements, it must seek to establish cross-systemic criteria of equivalence, allowing for operationalization at different levels of organization with appropriate imputations of meaning to the actors involved and the relevant environments. (2) Such criteria of equivalence are predicated on the acceptance of a general paradigm or metatheory of politics, which ought to be sufficiently abstract to cumulatively incorporate the findings of cross-systemic and cross-level comparisons, and yet sufficiently operational to allow for unambiguous rules for the interpretation of empirical observations. The various partial theories of voting reviewed in Chapter 6 have illustrated some of the difficulties resulting from low- or middle-range theorizing in the absence of a general paradigm or metatheory.

The remainder of this book consists of a search for criteria of equivalence capable of satisfying the above requirements. The proposed criteria necessarily reflect the choice of a paradigm, even if it has not been fully articulated. More specifically, the proposed criteria reflect two separate but complementary building blocks of a paradigm in which politics is defined as a *particular type of purposive collective action.*

We shall therefore attempt to answer three basic questions:

(1) What are the characteristics of the particular type of purposive collective action which enable us to identify it as political in contradistinction to other types of purposive action?

(2) Given the adherence of empirical political science to *methodological individualism,* but also the definition of politics as *collective* action with purposiveness as one of its distinctive characteristics, what criteria of functional equivalence (i.e., in terms of purposiveness) will account for both the individual and the collective level of meanings of political action?

(3) Since purposiveness refers to a means-ends relationship, but any "end" —i.e., goal or value can become the object of political action, is there a set of criteria for identifying *substantive* equivalence of political action across cultures, systems, and stages of economic and technological development?

It is clearly easier to formulate these questions than to provide satisfactory answers; yet, the search for a general paradigm must begin somewhere. The suggested answers are necessarily prolegomenous and merely intended to explore the possibility of parsimoniously "organizing" the greatly diversified universe of political phenomena along dimensions of stable and unequivocal meanings. This chapter will explore the first of the above questions by examining the only available attempt to subsume politics under a general metatheory: the reductionist position of some political economists and exchange theorists who consider politics an exchange phenomenon which can be analyzed with the concepts and propositions of economic theory. The second and third question will be examined in Chapters 8 and 9, respectively.

The two major foci for the imputation of meanings to political behavior in the socioecological space are the individual and the collectivity, irrespective of the level of organization at which the collectivity is identified (e.g., neighborhood, city, county, state, or nation). Although the relationship between the individual and the collectivity has been one of the central themes in political philosophy, the first proposals for a theory of collective political behavior have been made by economists and students of public finance and public choice. The works of Arrow (1951), Baumol (1967), Black (1958), Buchanan (1968), Downs (1957), Musgrave (1959), Olson (1965), Riker (1962), Samuelson (1955, 1958), and Tullock (1970) (to list only some of the best-known examples) have injected a new conceptual framework into political analysis by using economic models to bridge the gap between individual rationality and collective decision-making. These models attempt to combine an individualistic conception of the collectivity with a macro-theory of individual behavior.

In a challenging essay on "the shape of political theory to come," political scientist William Mitchell has complained about the paucity of political scientists in the interdisciplinary fields of political sociology and political economy, and about the omission, in political sociology, of any concern with governments, public policy determinations, and their consequences for the citizenry (Mitchell, 1969: 103, 107). (Whether political sociology is an interdisciplinary field or part and parcel of political science is an idle question which carries some of the overtones of traditional parochialism in the social sciences.) His complaint is justified; it is not less true, however, that even some of the most distinguished innovative attempts to apply economic reasoning to the "calculus" of political behavior and decision-making sometimes display an astonishing disregard for the undisputed characteristics of governmental and political processes.

The adoption of principles and models drawn from economic science in political analysis seems to have been based on the assumption that there is a fundamental similarity between economic and political motivations and that politics is essentially an exchange process. Although the phenomenon of power in social interaction has been usefully conceptualized in terms of exchange theory (Blau, 1964), relationships of authority and legitimacy defy the conceptual framework of economic and social exchange analysis, and authority and legitimacy have always been key concepts in the very definition of government and politics. Waldman has recently attempted to formulate an individualistic "social contract" theory of politics by interpreting legitimate authority in terms of exchange. In addition to the satisfaction of certain values, including security from threat, citizens "expect that what they get from the polity will be a just return for their contributions to it." If these expectations are not met, "they are less likely to accord it legitimacy and may engage in . . . acts of aggression against it" (Waldman, 1972: 90). The most consistent part of Waldman's analysis focuses, however, on power and social structure, rather than authority, and legitimacy is described as a cost/benefit calculus. The major difficulty consists, of course, in the interpretation of authority, which is a collective public good, in terms of an individualistic concept of exchange.

Political scientists can therefore be expected to take the position that although there may be considerable exchange (i.e., economic behavior) at certain stages of the political process, the distinctive characteristics of this process involve authority and legitimacy, which cannot be reduced to exchange relationships. Political economists would argue that authority is merely institutionalized power, that institutionalization is not a specifically political phenomenon (although one may add that it is not an economic phenomenon either) and that, consequently, political behavior, involving the exercise of power, can be explained in economic and exchange terms. It is with the contention of the political economists that politics is essentially an exchange phenomenon that I wish to take issue, because it obscures the contribution that economic reasoning can make to the advancement of empirical political theory. This will require a brief introduction to the concepts used in the arguments of the political economists.

The economy is generally viewed as a market in which individuals and firms exchange their products. Both partners in a transaction, the seller and the buyer, are assumed to derive a benefit from the exchange. Exchange is a corollary of the division of labor; they are functionally interdependent components of a mechanism through which individuals satisfy their needs and seek to increase their benefits. *Homo economicus* is a benefit-maximizer or satisficer through production and exchange. Even classical political economy conceded, however, that in addition to protection from violence and invasion, and the administration of justice, there were certain "goods" which only governments could supply. According to Adam Smith, the sovereign has the "duty of erecting and maintaining certain public works and certain public institutions, which it can never be for the interest of any individual . . . to erect and maintain, because the profit could never repay the expense to any individual . . . though it may frequently do much more than repay it to a great society." The supply of public goods was thus conceived as a process through which certain activities were placed under the authority of government because they could not be provided by the motivations and exchange mechanisms of the market. Baumol has retraced this argument in the writings of successive schools of European economic thought. Whether in terms of Pigou's concept of the divergence between private and social product (in contemporary terminology, the theory of externalities) or in terms of the attempts to construct a theory of the demand and supply of public goods, the allocation of resources through the political process has generally been considered as an *alternative* to the allocative mechanisms of market exchange (Baumol, 1967).

With the increasing importance of welfare-economics and welfare-politics, the economic properties of public goods have become a subject of growing theoretical interest. The public goods of the laissez faire state displayed two major characteristics: (1) jointness of supply, or indivisibility—i.e., the consumption of a unit of the public good by individual A did not decrease the supply available for individuals B, C, . . . N, and (2) non-exclusiveness—i.e., no individual could be excluded from the consumption of a public good.

Roads, bridges, and police protection are classic examples of such goods. Comparable examples from contemporary welfare-states are public education, national health, and other such social services. Economists therefore focused their attention on the economic problems of the supply of public goods, since there was no analogue to the model of the exchange market, in which consumers could reveal their real demand for such goods.

At this point it becomes necessary to draw attention to the fact that some political economists continue to refer to goods displaying the above characteristics as "public goods," whereas others have rightly pointed out that these characteristics merely denote collective rather than individual *consumption*. One should also add that collective consumption is not necessarily related to the supply of such goods by public authorities. The "consumption" of radio or television programs of privately owned stations is as indivisible as that of a public highway. Such goods should therefore be referred to as *collective goods*. When one continues to refer indiscriminately to "public goods," one will have to observe that some of the goods supplied by public authorities are indeed highly divisible (e.g., subsidies, allocations of material resources owned or controlled by the government), an observation which contradicts the meaning originally attached to the term "public goods."

Margolis and Samuelson have pointed out that the criteria for the supply of public goods are not always economic and include considerations such as the redistribution of incomes, paternalistic or nationalistic policies, and the many situations in which private interest can be expected to deviate from social interest (Margolis, 1955; Samuelson, 1955). Other economists (e.g., Breton, 1966) have introduced political participation as a variable in their model of the demand for public goods. These (and similar) preoccupations have led to three conceptually different approaches: (1) those which have applied *economic reasoning* to areas of behavior conceptualized in traditional, and substantively autonomous, political terms (e.g., Downs, 1957); (2) those which have considered public finance as a field which combines mutually independent economic and sociopolitical criteria for decision-making; and (3) those which interpret politics as exchange behavior—i.e., in terms of *economic theory* (e.g., Curry and Wade, 1968). Some recent proponents of the "new political economy" have combined these approaches, though not all have fully articulated their underlying assumptions.

In *The Calculus of Consent,* Buchanan and Tullock (1962: 19) introduced the economic model of the political system in somewhat ambiguous terms:

Both the economic relation and the political relation represent cooperation on the part of two or more individuals. The market and State are both devices through which cooperation is organized and made possible.

Men cooperate through exchange of goods and services in organized markets, and such cooperation implies mutual gain. . . . At base political or collective action under the individualistic view of the State is much the same. Two or more individuals find it mutually advantageous to join forces to accomplish certain common purposes. In a very real sense, they "exchange" inputs in the securing of the commonly shared output.

The argument is not very convincing. Exchange implies cooperation, but cooperation does not necessarily imply exchange. "Joining forces" does not mean "exchanging inputs," and if "exchange" refers to the transformation of inputs into outputs, the model comes closer to the cost/benefit analysis of a firm than to a market theory of exchange.

In his agenda for the "new political economy," Mitchell (1969) seems to accept the cost/benefit interpretation of politics and attempts to incorporate it into a broadly conceived model which also allows, however, for nonmarket controls and for the system-adaptation and stabilization efforts of political institutions. Buchanan's *Demand and Supply of Public Goods* (1968) departs from the exchange model and emphasizes "publicness" as a distinct characteristic of *organization* in the supply or distribution of goods and services. Tullock, in *Private Wants and Public Means* (1970), explicitly subscribes to a corporation theory of the state. Property, contract, and the state are externality-reducing institutions. (Externalities are the positive or negative effects of an activity, or agreement, on third parties which are either not compensated for their losses or not made to share the cost of the benefits which they derive from the activity of others.) The difference between government and a corporation, according to Tullock, is merely a difference in power and "the difference between this organization [the government] and a general contract is less than one might suppose" (1970: 53). Tullock does not understand why political scientists believe that "government is not, like the market, simply a mechanism to obtain our preferences" (1970: 108-111). When he associates political science with the doctrine that "the government is supposed to do things that are good for the individual, not things that the individual wants," he obviously criticizes only elitist ideologies and I have no quarrel with his position on this issue. But even majority rule does not make government necessarily a "benefit-maximizing" institution. However, since Tullock also admits that government intervention is justified to enforce such noneconomic values as justice or social equality (1970: 171, 191) and that the institutions of property and contract depend on the law enforcement function of the state, one must assume that he has merely overstated his case. Such disagreements notwithstanding, Tullock's thought-provoking applications of economic reasoning to problems of choice between public and private decision-making are clearly indicative of an approach which political science cannot afford to ignore.

Curry and Wade (1968) seem to believe that the contradiction resulting from the indiscriminate use of the term "public goods" can be resolved by simply denying the existence of collective, indivisible goods. They argue that since parks, highways, or military forces vary in size, they must be divisible. Indivisibility, however, as a characteristic of collective goods, does not refer to size, but to conditions of distribution and consumption. Both quantity and quality of a collective good can vary without affecting its indivisibility in terms of distribution and consumption.

A serious shortcoming of the market-exchange model of politics consists in the inability of the model to go beyond processes *preceding* the decision-making stage. Blau, who has interpreted even compliance with authority as an exchange phenomenon (i.e., exchange for social approval) allows for a distinction between the actions of institutionalized authority and the exchange of benefits between individuals: "The organization of collective effort replaces the free competition for and exchange of benefits among individuals by normatively regulated transactions" (Blau, 1964: 216). Political decision-making is not an exchange transaction, whatever the exchanges which have preceded it. Vote-trading in legislative behavior is an exchange transaction, but it is part of the process of coalition-building and not of decision-making itself. Narrowly viewed, vote-trading is an exchange of commitments to support specific items in a decision-making process. *In this exchange, no public goods are involved.* If one considers the actual distribution of benefits which is a consequence of the decision, it becomes apparent that *at this stage no exchange occurs.* The benefits received by the vote-trading parties are supplied by a public authority, and the necessary resources are drawn from the common funds of the collectivity. Stated otherwise, the parties not participating in the vote-trading coalition share the costs of providing the benefits to the winning coalition. This is the problem of the externalities created by vote-trading under majority voting.

Some students of collective decision-making have claimed that since legislative vote-trading enables minority groups to obtain the support of the majority for issues of high preference for the minority which would have been ignored otherwise, vote-trading is an integral part of the democratic mechanisms of decision-making. Economists have added that it is a device for increasing the overall welfare of the community by its redistributive effects beyond the limitations imposed by majority-voting (Buchanan and Tullock, 1962: 186; Baumol, 1967: 45). Others, however, have pointed at the externalities generated by vote-trading (Rothenberg, 1969) and Riker has formalized the "paradox of vote-trading," demonstrating that although vote-trading is immediately advantageous to the traders, when everybody trades everybody is worse off (Riker, 1972).

The conditions under which vote-trading is Pareto-optimal constitute a marginal issue in the present discussion. In large groups (e.g., the electorate) vote-trading is difficult, if not impossible, because the participants have little information about each other's expected utilities (or intensity of preferences); in small groups, such as legislative assemblies, vote-trading is possible and actually occurs. This is also the area in which the economic theory of politics comes closest to blurring the line of distinction between exchange behavior in politics and political decision-making. Political economists are willing to concede that government also involves the legitimate use of coercion; but when coercion cannot be shown to serve economic rationality (e.g., the enforcement of contracts, the reduction of broad-incidence externalities, economies of scale), they will recommend the transfer of the activity to private bargaining and exchange. Thus, it would seem, economic rationality "legitimizes" coercion.

Political science has generally accepted Weber's definition of government and politics as involving the "legitimate monopoly of physical coercion." Under this definition, any activity, any program of action or ideology, which seeks or obtains the support of the institutions or actors possessing the legitimate authority to enforce decisions, becomes, ipso facto, political. Easton's interpretation of the political system as involving the "authoritative allocation of scarce resources" adds that the use of authority is associated with competition for, or conflict over, resources which either *are not* or *cannot* be shared by all those who seek such resources to satisfy their needs. There is broad agreement that in democratic systems the content, volume, and incidence of such allocations is generally the result of bargaining and exchange in the coalition-forming processes. This is Almond's "aggregation of interests" (Almond and Coleman, 1960) and in a logically more explicit formulation, Coleman's aggregation of power as a process oriented at maximizing control over decisions by exchanging agreements to support issues on which the partners in the exchange differ in value preference or intensity of support (Coleman, 1964, 1966). If we now combine the predecisional exchange of agreements and the postdecisional distribution of rewards, do we not arrive at a market exchange and corporation theory of government and politics? The answer depends on whether we can prove that economics and politics differ in some respect which is not a matter of degree, but of mutually exclusive properties. The remainder of this chapter is an attempt to demonstrate that a reconceptualization of "public goods" is capable of providing an unequivocal answer to this question.

There is no particular advantage to be derived from using the "language" of political science in this attempt to clarify whether or not the political system is simply a particular form of an exchange market or firm. One ought to meet the arguments of the economists on their own ground. Olson has recently stated that economic theory

> is relevant whenever actors have determinate wants or objectives but at the same time do not have so much of the means needed to achieve these ends. . . . The ends in question may be social status or political power . . . economic theory not only is, but . . . must be so general that it also applies to "goods" that are not traded in markets [and] this makes it clear that economic . . . theory is in a fundamental sense more nearly a theory of rational behavior than a theory of material goods [Olson, 1969: 141].

According to this statement, a theory of rational behavior should be able to account for both market and nonmarket "allocations of scarce resources." Thus, an attempt to point at some critical differences between economics and politics would have to take one of two possible positions: (1) political behavior is predominantly nonrational, or (2) it is necessary—and possible—to adopt the conceptual framework and reasoning of economic science to demonstrate such differences. Harsanyi has adopted a longitudinal motivational perspective to justify a position which allows for nonrational components in political behavior, but explains their presence in rational terms. Thus, individuals do not have a free, rational choice in politics, because they have undertaken personal commitments at earlier periods, and because their behavior is also guided by the desire for social acceptance. However, acquiring such commitments and conforming to specific values and behavioral patterns in order to gain social acceptance can be interpreted as an original rational choice; a purely conformist model could not explain changes in values and patterns of behavior (Harsanyi, 1969: 513-538). This position, however plausible, tends to support Olson's argument, since economic behavior is also subject to limitations imposed by earlier commitments and conformity to social values, although probably to a lesser degree than that which has been observed in political behavior. It is perhaps easier to point at a critical difference between economics and politics by applying economic reasoning in an examination of the contention that the political process is essentially an exchange phenomenon.

In economic terms, the political process can be defined as the collective supply and distribution of public goods. The concept of "public goods" requires, however, a conceptual clarification. As mentioned earlier, economists have been concerned with the economic properties of public goods. The "equal availability" of public goods was explained in terms of "jointness of supply" (or indivisibility) and the externalities attached to it, given the "impossibility of excluding" individuals from sharing the benefits arising from the production of such goods (Musgrave, 1959: 8; Head, 1962: 203; and the bibliography in Buchanan, 1968: 46-48, 74-75). Jointness of supply was associated with the physical indivisibility of the traditional public goods, although it was realized that equal availability was a matter of degree: roads and bridges have capacity limits, and a citizen's home located near the fire station is better protected than that of another citizen located some distance away. Such differences, however, merely affect the quality or the size of units of consumption, not their availability. Since most public goods exhibited both indivisibility and non-exclusiveness, it was generally assumed that the latter is necessarily a consequence of the former. Head has shown, however, that the problem of non-exclusion need not arise as a consequence of jointness of supply, and he quotes road tolls, court fees, and other admission charges. Riker and Ordeshook have developed a typology of collective (though not necessarily public) goods which explicitly distinguishes between cases in which the impossibility of excluding some persons from consumption applies and those in which it does not apply (Riker and Ordeshook, 1973: 261). It was Buchanan who made the decisive observation that technological jointness of supply is not required, as long as equal availability of the good is, or can be, provided (Buchanan, 1968: 36). Thus, the "publicness" of the good, although historically a consequence of indivisibility, is in fact *a characteristic of the distribution of the good*. Any private divisible good can become a public good if it is collectively supplied and its equal availability is provided for. This happens, in fact, when food or gasoline—which are clearly divisible goods—are rationed and made equally available by public authorities. Some public goods are not made available to the entire community, but only to specified subcategories or groups (e.g., unemployment compensation, subsidies for farmers); it is the association of "publicness" with indivisibility rather than distribution which has unnecessarily limited the denotation of the concept of "public goods."

Reconceptualizing public goods in terms of the conditions under which they are made available leads to a definition of "publicness" as the availability of *nontransferable units of consumption*. In the case of a road, bridge, or lighthouse, nontransferability is a consequence of physical or technological indivisibility. The new public goods of the welfare-state are nontransferable as a consequence of the conditions under which they are distributed. Food rations in periods of war or scarcity are an adequate example. They are physically divisible and transferable, but most governments have prohibited their transfer or sale. In other cases, there is no need for enforcement: old-age pensions or medical care cannot be transferred. We are now in a position to refute the argument that politics is essentially an exchange process. *If public goods are nontransferable, they cannot be exchanged.*

The purposes for which collective or noncollective goods are transformed into public goods vary; they can be economic (reducing externalities, natural monopolies, economies of contiguity or scale) or noneconomic (redistribution of income or wealth; welfare or social justice; integration of, or discrimination against, minorities; nationalistic or paternalistic policies). The purpose for which a public good is created determines the scope or range of its availability. However, when the good is divisible, no specific range or limit of availability can be effectively circumscribed unless the good is distributed on a nontransferable basis. In consumption terms: a unit consumed by individual A does not diminish the supply available for individuals B, C, D . . . N, because A cannot consume a unit made available for any other individual; in the case of indivisible goods, because of the properties of the goods; in the case of divisible goods, as a consequence of the conditions under which the distribution of the goods has been organized. In both cases—although for different reasons—the units of consumption are nontransferable and cannot be exchanged.

It is perhaps necessary to draw attention to the fact that from the viewpoint of public finance theory, money allocations (e.g., subsidies, pensions) are considered transfer payments, but not public goods, since they do not involve a direct use of resources by the government (Mitchell and Mitchell, 1969: 98; Wade and Curry, 1970: 7, 33). According to the preceding analysis, however, the distinction between the direct and indirect use of resources is not relevant to the criterion of transferability. A further possible source of confusion is the description of private goods as involving specific consumers who can claim exclusive possession of the goods, as opposed to public goods which are indivisible (Mitchell and Mitchell, 1969: 98; Frohlich et al., 1971: 3). This description refers obviously to the distinction between indivisible and divisible, rather than public and private goods; moreover, property rights over divisible goods are not a consequence of the characteristics of the goods. The possessor of a private good may choose to consume it or to exchange it for other private goods. A divisible public good cannot be exchanged.

Having established the distinction between economic processes involving exchangeable goods and political processes leading to the supply and distribution of nontransferable goods, we can apply economic reasoning to the analysis of political participation without the risk of a fallacious analogy between the economy and the polity. In economic terms, the various forms of political participation can be considered expressions of demands for public goods. The term "goods" applies, of course, to a variety of goods and services, money allocations, changes in allocations, regulations, rights, etc. Since public goods are not exchangeable, demands for public goods cannot be made for "retrading" purposes. This does not mean that public goods are "final" or "consummatory" values; they may very well be of only instrumental value to the beneficiary (e.g., education). Neither does it mean that in the actual political process one may not encounter demands for public goods made by individuals who are not potential beneficiaries of the demanded goods. What we have gained, however, in this formulation, is a conceptual framework which combines two levels of observation along a dimension of meanings: political participation is defined as an *individual* input into *collective* action for the supply of *public goods*. This will facilitate an application of the "logic of collective action" (Olson, 1965) to different types of distribution of public goods. It should be noted, however, that whereas Olson has been able to apply the logic of collective action to an explanation of interest group behavior and of some of the roles performed by political parties, the formulation proposed in this and in the following chapter is not intended to serve as an explanatory model. It will merely help establish criteria of functional equivalence between different types of political behavior within a conceptual framework which combines intended and observed private and public consequences.

Chapter 8

FUNCTIONAL EQUIVALENCE

Rationality, Collective Action, and Public

Goods—A Model for Assessing Functional

Equivalence in Political Participation

This chapter will introduce and discuss criteria of functional equivalence directly related to the definition of political participation as an individual input into collective action for the supply of public goods. "Function" is a generic concept which denotes the meaning an action acquires in a larger system of action and meanings, of which the actor and his framework of meanings are only a part—usually at a lower level of organization. It is in this sense that we refer, for example, to the meaning of the actions of individuals engaging in a political career in terms of a systemic recruitment function. However, the generic concept of function does not specify the "shape of the curve" of a specific functional relationship between levels of meanings, and comparisons along a functional dimension cannot be made unless the function is described at least in its most salient characteristics.

Weber's typology of meanings of actions in terms of the actor's own orientations (1947: 115-117) consisted of two variations in the application of the concept of rationality. He distinguished (1) between action that was and action that was not the result of a choice of means (habitual and emotional action being examples of the latter); and (2) between rationality in the pursuit of ultimate values *(wertrational)* and rationality in the achievement of discrete goals ordered in terms of a scale of priorities *(zwecksrational)*. By using rationality as a criterion of classification, Weber identified rationality as a dimension on which functional equivalence of individual-level meanings of action can be established. In the first part of this chapter an attempt will be made to demonstrate that rationality conceived as a means-ends relationship is an insufficient criterion for establishing equivalence of political actions —i.e., of actions with intended and observed consequences at both the individual and the collective level. Instead, a means-ends-outcomes function will be shown to be more adequate for capturing the levels of meanings involved in political participation. The second part of the chapter then applies this criterion to an assessment of functional equivalence within and across systems for different types of distribution of public goods.

Rationality and Political Participation

The literature dealing with rational behavior in economics and politics displays two somewhat different, though not unrelated, concepts of rationality. One of these concepts refers to choices, or statements of preferences, assuming a calculus of benefits, or costs (or both), depending on whether the calculus deals with a choice of goals or a choice of means (or both). Essentially, it defines rationality as *consistency* in the ranking of items on scales of expected utilities. This logical property of choices is referred to as transitivity. Preference statements of political support or indifference curves of demand in economic theory have been interpreted in terms of this assumption of consistency. Shapiro (1969) has demonstrated that voters' statements of preferences also display consistency with several mutually independent dimensions, which are applied simultaneously in the calculus of choice. Furthermore, these different dimensions (e.g., candidate's personal image, issues, party-identification) carry different weights (e.g., intensity of value-commitments, salience of issues) which are reflected in the choice. Similarly, Riker and Ordeshook (1968) have proposed a model of the rational voting decision which includes the gratification of psychological or sociopsychological needs as a component of expected utilities.

The fact that many voters do not or cannot make an issue-oriented choice, and the impact of learning processes, political socialization, and other sociopsychological factors on voting preferences, have been amply documented. A voter can be consistent with his earlier experiences, with his esteem for the opinions of some "relevant other," or with his dislike for some personality-characteristic of a candidate. Thus, consistency can be an adequate description of the relation between electoral choice and voters' value- and belief-systems. It is evident, however, that no benefit can be derived from equating consistency with rationality. The rational-choice model has been proposed as an explanation of social behavior; consistency merely indicates that when criteria for preference and preference itself can be ascertained independently of each other, the most preferred item among available alternatives is the item which ranks highest according to the individual's criteria for choice. If criteria and choice are not independently ascertained, consistency cannot be demonstrated. Equating consistency and rationality therefore reduces rationality to the choice of the most preferred item, a quasitautology of little theoretical relevance, since it hardly leaves any type of behavior that would not qualify as rational (Olson, 1965: 160, n. 91).

Riker and Ordeshook (1968) explicitly prefer the tautological interpretation of rationality, adding that "in a descriptive theory it is unwise for the theorist to impose his own interpretation of goals on the observed behavior. By doing so he falls into the trap . . . of saying that one goal is rational and another is not" and it is not possible to judge the rationality of goals. A similar argument has been put forward by Shapiro (1969: 1118-1119): "It is exceedingly problematic to choose a set of value criteria which belong to voting decisions irrespective of the nature of the voters concerned. . . . The elevation of one particular criterion above others such that choices are considered rational to the extent to which they are designed to maximize it, usually involves the pre-selection of some notion of collective rationality." Similarly, in a critical review of the major positions taken in the literature on determinants of individual choice, Riker and Zavoina (1970: 48-60) have compared the tautological ("procedural") with a narrower ("substantive") concept of rationality and claimed that the latter assumes that a particular goal (i.e., maximizing profits) is appropriate for all men in all circumstances of choice. These statements seem to imply that the refusal to accept the quasi-tautological definition of rationality is based on a "judgment of goals." There is a fairly obvious fallacy in this implication. The assumption of rationality, as an "ideal-typic" explanation of social behavior, involves *a judgment of purposiveness, not of purposes.*

The second construct of rationality incorporates a dimension which describes the relationship between choices and *outcome*. Even for Weber, rationality was more than a means-ends relationship: "The more unconditionally the actor devotes himself to [an absolute] value for its own sake . . . the less he is influenced by considerations of the *consequences* of his action. . . . From the . . . point of view [of a system of discrete individual ends] absolute values are always *irrational*" (1947: 117; italics added). In economic behavior, in a free competitive market, preferences can be translated into outcomes whenever the choices of buyers and sellers coincide; the availability of the required means is a sufficient condition for the outcome

to occur. A different situation prevails when available means are not a sufficient condition for goal-attainment, and the actor has little or no control
over the fulfillment of the remaining conditions. Even greater uncertainty
prevails when the actor has little or no information about the additional
conditions. A game of chess, or strategic decision-making, involving interaction between opponents, is an example of choice under varying degrees
of uncertainty. A further consideration is the relationship between the differential impact of different choices on the probability that the outcome will
occur. Thus, one can considerably improve the probability of winning a
fixed prize in an "honest" lottery by betting on a hundred rather than on
a single number; needless to say, the increase in the probability of winning
also decreases the utility of winning, given the cost of purchasing additional
tickets. A voter cannot improve his chances of "winning," because under
normal circumstances he cannot "purchase" additional votes. This reasoning,
however, does not usually apply to a political entrepreneur or a political
organization.

Thus, the second construct of rationality goes beyond mere consistency
and incorporates a dimension of "effectiveness"—i.e., a relation between
choice and outcome. Riker and Ordeshook (1968) have demonstrated that
the expected consequence of an act is indeed an integral part of a calculus
of voter rationality. They used the voter's perception of the closeness of an
election as an indicator of his belief about the probability that his own vote
could influence the result. Controlling for expected benefit and psychological
gratification, they showed that voting turnout was associated with belief in
the closeness of the election. This indicates that voters sometimes behave
as if their vote could influence the outcome.

In discussing the applicability of these models to political behavior it is
not necessary to assume that individuals actually calculate cardinal values
for expected utilities; the assumption of ordinal rankings will suffice, if
propositions concerning rational political behavior are to be subjected to
empirical testing (but see Stratman, 1971, for an attempt to assign cardinal
values to the components of voters' choices). Furthermore, one need not
assume that "maximizing" expected utilities implies the examination of all
theoretically possible alternatives. The actor will explore, at best, what he
considers available alternatives. Since benefit-satisficing and benefit-maximizing can be described by the same rational calculus (Riker and Ordeshook,
1973: 23), the question whether maximization is a realistic assumption need
not detain us any further.

The interpretation of the consistency model as voter rationality has perhaps been the result of borrowing the economic concept of rationality in
market exchange behavior and applying it to an act which does not share
the characteristics of economic behavior. There is only a seeming similarity

between market-decisions and decisions in political participation. First, market behavior consists of interaction; in voter behavior there is neither exchange nor interaction of any other kind. Second, the simple economic transaction occurs under conditions of certainty (at least in the short-term perspective); voting decisions involve varying degrees of uncertainty in the relationship between choice and outcome. Third, the observation that in a relatively large competitive market no single transaction will affect the price of the commodities involved and that, in the political arena, no single vote is likely to affect the outcome of an election, cannot conceal the difference between these two mechanisms of purposive behavior: the market is a series of individual transactions, whereas an election is an instance of collective action. Furthermore, the aggregative impact of individual transactions, in the competitive market model, is a continuous, flexible, and self-regulating process; the rules of aggregation of the impact of individual votes in an election are predetermined and rigid (see also Frohlich et al., 1971: 21, n. 32).

The recognition that participation in collective action involves individual and collective intended and observed consequences raises the question of the relationship between individual consistency and collective outcome. The rational voting model proposed by Riker and Ordeshook (1968, 1973) distinguishes between the private utility the political participant attaches to the choice of means (e.g., the psychological gratification obtained from the fulfillment of a civic duty) and the utility he attaches to the outcome. These utilities are additive components of an individualistic calculus and remain within the framework of the consistency-concept of rationality. Furthermore, the efficacy of a specific act of participation a_i to produce outcome O_j is defined as the difference between the probabilities the actor attaches to the occurrence of O_j should he prefer alternative a_i to alternative a_k. It is easy to demonstrate that in the case of voting, viewed as participation in collective action, this calculus remains within the consistency-concept of rationality. Since no single voter can assume that his or her choice can affect the probability of the occurrence of O_j, the estimate of the differential impact of a_i over a_k is really an estimate of the distribution of support for the competing parties or candidates in the relevant electorate. The supporter of a minority party with no serious chances of winning will not attach a high efficacy to his vote if he votes for the party he prefers, and no efficacy at all, in terms of his preferred outcome, to a vote for the majority party. Adding the psychological satisfaction derived from supporting his preferred party, as opposed to the dissatisfaction from voting for the other party, the calculus leads to a vote for the preferred party. A similar reasoning indicates that the voter who attaches a greater utility to a victory of the majority party will vote for that party. The case of a close election increases the benefit derived from participating rather than abstaining, but does not affect the choice between parties. Even if O_j is interpreted as a series of outcomes in different policy areas the calculus will remain within the consistency model, since the voter will decide according to what he considers the most salient issues or policy areas.

Had the analysis of political behavior and processes been concerned only with the logical and intrapsychic consistency of the individual actor's input, because the aggregate outcome would be some function of individual consistency, one could not reject the equation of consistency and rationality. This, however, is not the case, since collective outcomes can be completely independent of individual consistency. It is well known that the aggregate outcomes of individually consistent choices need not be consistent (Arrow, 1951; Black, 1958; Riker, 1962; Riker and Ordeshook, 1973: 78-115), and depend on the rules of summation. Furthermore, in collective action for the supply of collective goods, individual consistency and the logic of collective goal-achievement may not only be independent of each other, but may lead to contradictory cost/benefit analyses and contradictory behavior (Olson, 1965).

Riker and Ordeshook have argued that the logic of collective action is compatible with their model of rational calculus in participation. It is the private incentive to vote—supplied perhaps through political socialization—which compensates for the lack of effectiveness of the individual vote (1973: 74). There is, however, a difference between the special case of collective goods beneficial to all members of the group in Olson's analysis of collective action and the general calculus of political participation formulated by Riker and Ordeshook. In the cases to which Olson's argument applies, the selective private benefits supplied by interest groups or political parties raise the incentive to participate in action for a collective benefit and increase the probability of an optimal supply of the collective good. In the general case of a theory of voting, this positive functional relationship between private and public consequences does not necessarily prevail.

The calculus of a voting decision does not usually refer to the supply of nonexcludable public goods which are more or less equally available to all participants. If the goods are nonexcludable and beneficial to all participants, the supply of such goods will not become an issue of political conflict to be decided by the voters' choice. Neither does Hardin's interpretation of the logic of collective action as an N-person "Prisoner's Dilemma" (Hardin, 1971) reflect the calculus of the voter; first, because the cost of participation is almost zero (this does not include the cost of obtaining information, but since the impact of the individual vote is negligible, it would not be rational to incur such costs exclusively for the purpose of voting), and second, because voters do not participate in order to prevent a situation in which everybody would behave rationally—i.e., abstain—and the goods would not be supplied at all; they participate in order to support the public goods they prefer against the action, not the inaction, of others who prefer a competing set of public goods.

If there is competition between two or more groups of expected beneficiaries of alternative sets of public goods, is the voter rational if he votes for his preferred alternative, although he knows it has no chance of winning? His participation is not functional to the creation of the preferred public goods, although his calculus is consistent and he may derive some private satisfaction from making a demand for the public goods he prefers. Only under unanimous consensus are all participants consistent *and* rational, and the distinction becomes superfluous. Or, considering outcomes, one may ask to what extent the creation of some public goods is not an *unintended consequence* of the support of those participants who are motivated only by the moral or psychological incentives to participate. Under majority rule, at any given time, some participants display politically effective behavior while others can behave only consistently, but not effectively. Clearly, individual consistency and political outcomes are different criteria of evaluation; an analysis of politics as purposive behavior cannot afford to concentrate on the first criterion and disregard the second.

A means-ends-outcomes calculus by the individual voter seems possible only when the expected outcome of the behavior of other voters can be taken into consideration. The perceived closeness of an election is an example of such a situation. The expected outcome of the behavior of other participants is also a function of the distribution of the proposed public goods: hence, the possibility of a functional calculus for the individual group member with respect to his participation in the supply of collective public goods. The degree of uncertainty concerning the behavior of other participants can thus be reduced by introducing into the analysis the direction and intensity of preferences of other participants, as determined by the proposed differential distribution of public goods. It then becomes possible to identify categories of participants in terms of the range and incidence in the distribution of the benefits to be provided by the proposed public good. Within each category individuals are in the same position in terms of the required political participation (means) to achieve a given benefit (ends) with the same probability of success (results). Incentives to participate in collective action will therefore vary between categories of participants but will remain equivalent within categories. The criterion of rationality is thereby transferred from an individual consistency analysis to a functional analysis of participation in collective action. Whether or not individuals who are in the same position in terms of this means-ends-outcomes relationship actually display the same behavior is precisely the purpose of the inquiry in which this type of control for equivalence would be relevant.

Functional Equivalence in
Political Participation

The preceding discussion has suggested that political participation can be analyzed in functional terms within the framework of a cross-level conceptualization of collective action for the supply and distribution of public goods. This formulation is not a theoretical proposition; it is a statement of some of the elements of a paradigm for the study of participation. Two major elements not included in this statement are *initiative* and *organization*. Organization refers to the formally or informally institutionalized patterns of mobilization and to the rules of summation and decision-making. Initiative cannot be institutionalized, although expectations of initiative can be assigned to specific political roles and denied to others. Since initiative—i.e., leadership—is a requisite of collective action, a more complete paradigm would include three, rather than two, levels of imputation for intended and observed consequences of participation.

This does not mean, however, that the incomplete paradigm discussed in this chapter can offer no guidance whatsoever to the empirically oriented theorist. An attempt will be made to demonstrate the methodological relevance of the criterion it offers for the assessment of functional equivalence in the comparison of political behavior.

PRIVATE AND PUBLIC GOAL ATTAINMENT IN
COLLECTIVE ACTION

Participation in collective action can be analyzed in terms of the relationship between private and public goal attainment. Given the fact that the observed consequence of a vote is the registration of a demand for a public good (or for a specific cluster of public goods), one can use the meaning the voter imputes to his act as a criterion of classification. If the voter considers himself an expected beneficiary of the public goods he demands and supports, individual and collective consequences are interdependent. If the goods are provided, both collective and private goal attainment have been attained; if the goods are not provided, both collective and private goal attainment have been frustrated. If a voter lends his support to a party or candidate because he derives psychological satisfaction from participation or because he considers one candidate more "attractive" than another (but does not relate his support to a set of public goods), the resultant support for public goods is an unintended consequence of his act, private and public rewards are independent of each other, and private satisfaction can be achieved irrespective of the outcome of the collective action. These are clearly nonequivalent instances of nominally identical forms of political participation. The case of collective public goods is a special instance in which private goal achievement depends on the attainment of the collective goal but is independent of participation in collective action.

The following are some of the consequences of this distinction viewed from a collective-level perspective:

(1) If a demand for public goods has been defeated, but the number of issue-oriented opponents is smaller than the number of issue-oriented supporters (i.e., a sizable proportion of opponents did not cast issue-oriented votes), the policy has in fact been defeated by a minority, in terms of the total number of issue-oriented voters.

(2) If a demand for public goods has gained sufficient support to be translated into public policy, but less than the required number of supporters have also demanded this policy (i.e., have cast an issue-oriented vote), then the policy has been adopted by a minority, if the number of issue-oriented opponents exceeds the number of issue-oriented supporters.

(3) Among non-issue-oriented voters, psychological identifications (with party, class, ethnic group, or any combination thereof) are likely to be the most stable determinants of voting behavior. As long as issues are not sufficiently salient to bring about issue-oriented voting by a large majority of participants (as, for example, in times of social, economic, or political crisis), the supply of public goods will depend on the ability of the expected beneficiaries to enlist the support of one or another segment of non-issue-oriented voters. Whether this increases the opportunities of individual political entrepreneurs or the power of political parties depends on the resources and loyalties political parties are able to command.

The term "expected beneficiaries" would generally refer to a collection of public goods, the demand for which is supported by different groups, although not all items in this collection would necessarily be of similar salience to all groups concerned. Two groups may be mutually committed to support each other's demands, even if none of these demands is shared by members of both groups. The point to be emphasized, however, is that such exchanges of commitments can only take place between expected beneficiaries. When a group of expected beneficiaries requires the support of non-issue-oriented voters in order to win an election, it must offer these voters an opportunity to satisfy psychological and other non-issue-oriented needs which is likely to elicit their support. Thus it may be politically rational (i.e., functional), for the creation of public goods, to deliberately introduce non-issue-oriented individual-level goals and psychological needs into the political process. This is possible when the cost of participation is negligible, as in the case of voting. How the supply of public goods has been affected by non-issue-oriented support or opposition is a subject into which one may wish to inquire; it is an area in which it is possible not only to demonstrate that "politics is the art of the possible," but also to measure the extent to which this is true of any given decision. When the cost of participation is not negligible, individual-level rewards must be highly salient to elicit participation. Although a party activist or a candidate for political office has to espouse a set of public goods, he need not be, and very frequently is not, one of the expected beneficiaries. His willingness to pay the cost of participation is determined, to a great extent, by his individual-level goal orientations. If this assertion is valid, we may have to rephrase some of our questions in the study of elite recruitment and behavior in order to explore the relationship between private and public goal attainment in the behavior of political elites. Eldersveld's findings concerning the private motivations in the recruitment of party officials in Detroit (Eldersveld, 1964) clearly support this line of analysis.

RANGE OF DISTRIBUTION, UNEQUAL AVAILABILITY, AND POLITICAL PARTICIPATION

We shall now consider cases in which a public good is not made available to all members of the political system, and those in which not all units of the public good are of equal size.

When a public good is intended to be made equally available to all members of the political system, one must assume that there is a widely distributed demand for the good. This does not mean, however, that the good is equally salient to all citizens or that the cost of providing the good will be equally shared. Since taxation is only rarely submitted to the approval of the electorate, and since in the legislative process decisions on the distribution of the tax burden are usually separated from decisions on items of expenditure, individuals can only rarely use cost-benefit analysis as a guide to their participation in the demand and support for public goods. Salience, however, is not a function of cost or available resources, and it can guide the citizen's political participation.

However, when the demand is widely distributed and the good is intended to be made equally available, there will be little or no disagreement and, therefore, no need for active participation. Citizens would therefore tend to become indifferent toward voting or abstaining. Thus, when there is broad agreement and parties take similar stands on a proposed policy, one may expect a relatively low voter turnout.

The above case must be distinguished from that in which the public good, although equally available to all citizens, is not consumed in equal units at any time, but from a cumulative long-term perspective individual units of consumption will tend to cluster around the modal size. This will happen when differences in the salience and in the demand for the good, at any given time, will cancel out in the long run according to some predictable pattern. A health insurance program is a suitable example. Assuming that there is no benefit taxation—e.g., the service is supplied either free of charge or for a flat-rate fee—demand will vary according to age. In a debate whether optometric services should be included in the program and fees increased, a short-term cost-benefit analysis would lead younger people to oppose the measure and middle-aged and older people to support it. Generalizing from this example, immediate beneficiaries can be expected to actively support the supply of a public good, whereas those for whom it would represent deferred consumption would abstain from active support and might even oppose the demand. This is merely a special case of a more general phenomenon—i.e., that individuals are unlikely to reveal their real demand for equally available public goods. In the collective action leading to the supply of the good, the voter and taxpayer is concerned with minimizing the cost of providing the good since he must balance it against all other social needs, but once the good has been supplied, demand is likely to exceed the supply provided for. The practical consequences of such inconsistencies—and therefore the theoretical interest therein—are far from negligible, as demonstrated, for example, in Buchanan's study of the British National Health Service (1965). (See also Wade and Curry, 1970: 53-57.) In the present context the issue exemplifies the relevance of Olson's argument at the societal level in the special case when the equal availability of the public good is defined in terms of a cumulative long-term pattern of demand.

We may restate the case as one in which at any given time there is no demand for the good by some segment of society, but there is also a very high probability that across a calculable span of time that segment will display a demand which will fall within the modal societal range. This formulation points at another type of public goods for which the probability of a more or less equal long-term demand is very low. This refers to goods or services created for those who satisfy a set of relevant requirements, but the probability that all members of a society will at one time or another qualify for an allocation of the good is very low. Indeed, the good is created for the purpose of satisfying the demands of a specific segment of society. One may refer to these as *segmental public goods*. Unemployment benefits and subsidies for farmers are examples of segmental public goods. Applying, once more, the logic of collective action, we can distinguish between two nonequivalent cases:

(1) When the public good is intended to be equally distributed among all beneficiaries, the individual beneficiary will behave rationally if he votes and thereby registers his demand against competing claims of supporters of other segmental goods, but there is no reason why he should invest more efforts than any other expected beneficiary.

(2) When the public good is intended to be distributed according to some

discriminating criterion—i.e., when some beneficiaries expect larger and others expect smaller shares of the public good—both subsegments of beneficiaries will act rationally if they support the creation of the good; moreover, the preferred beneficiaries can be expected to actively campaign and enlist the support of others in order to protect their larger share of the good, whereas those who expect a smaller share would campaign and attempt to enlist support for an increase in their share.

POLITICAL AND NONPOLITICAL GOAL-ATTAINMENT

The theoretically most far-reaching question which arises in the comparison of political participation inquires into the reasons and purposes for which individuals and groups seek the attainment of some of their goals through collective (political) processes rather than individual action.

Individual and collective action are different ways in which individuals attempt to satisfy their needs and achieve their goals. The political system authoritatively allocates values (by creating and distributing public goods) and the need for such allocations arises when the demand greatly exceeds private supply, when there is scarcity and conflict, or when there is a widely shared demand for a redistribution of resources. In some cases, public goods reflect considerable economies of scale; in such cases, private action is not a valid alternative to collective action. No one would claim, for example, that postal services should be replaced by the personal delivery of mail. Yet, even in the case of postal services, some individuals will prefer and be able to use private channels of communication such as teleprinters or private radio stations. In this example the privately and the collectively supplied services are not really identical; the example points, however, at the importance of available means as a determinant in the choice between collective and private action, since private channels of communication are much more costly than regular postal services.

The importance of the availability of means in the choice between individual and collective action is clearly apparent in the case of public goods made available to specific subsets of society. Welfare payments to the unemployed or incapacitated are cases in which the beneficiary has no available means for individual action to satisfy his or her needs. Medical insurance is an intermediate case: the wage-earner, the salaried employee, or the aged will prefer the low-cost or free insurance supplied as a public good by public authorities, whereas people in business, the self-employed, or professionals can afford a more costly but perhaps more convenient private insurance program, even if they are eligible for a public health program (e.g., in Great Britain). There are also certain needs which can be satisfied only through political action: the prestige, power, or ability to influence political decisions which are attached to public office. In totalitarian and single-party regimes, many nonpolitical occupational careers are open only to those who engage in political activity within the ruling party.

If we conceive of collective action for the supply of public goods as an alternative to the achievement of private goals through individual action, we can evaluate political action in terms of the cost, in units of private goods, at which individual goal-achievement can be substituted for collective action. This is the most general measure of equivalence, and it can be applied both intra- and intersystemically. Intersystemically it consists in comparing "systemic rates of substitution"; within systems it consists in comparing individual availability of resources with the systemic rate of substitution.

The "systemic rate of substitution" is the *number of units of a "standard private good"* necessary to obtain, through private action in an exchange market, a good or service equivalent in size and quality to *one unit* of the corresponding public good allocated through collective action. A "standard private good" is not an empirically vacuous concept: one may choose, for example, the *modal monthly income* or the *modal level of education,* depending on the type of good under consideration. The standard private good serves the function of a numéraire. Systemic rates of substitution depend on a market situation and a political decision: the market determines the number of units of private goods necessary to obtain one unit of the desired good or service, but the size and quality of one unit of the corresponding public good are determined by a political decision. At any given time, in any given system, the systemic rate of substitution for a specific good or service is fairly stable; across systems, of course, it may vary considerably.

Although the concept of systemic rate of substitution closely resembles the concept of price—i.e., the price of a unit of public goods if supplied by the mechanism of the private market—the systemic rate of substitution is not exactly a price. A price is a measure of exchange value and assumes exchangeability, but in relating private to collective action we do not assume exchangeability as given. The rate of substitution may be infinite—i.e., no number whatsoever of standard private goods can "buy" a good or service equivalent to that supplied as a public good. Whether or not the political system has a monopoly in the supply of certain goods or services is a distinction of some relevance in cross-systemic comparisons. The monopoly of a one-party system in matters related to candidacies for political office is an obvious, almost trivial, example of the relevance of this distinction; with the increasing number and types of public goods supplied by governments on a monopolistic basis the question whether the systemic rate of substitution is infinite, a finite number, or zero in any particular area of collective action is far from trivial.

So far we have considered conditions of *supply*. Assuming that the systemic rate of substitution is neither infinite nor zero, let us examine the problem of equivalence under difference patterns of *demand*. The economic concept of "elasticity of demand" is based on the assumption that under varying prices, demand may increase or decrease. Two components are involved in this assumption: if, for example, the market price of a good will decrease, (1) more individuals may be willing to purchase the good and (2) any individual may purchase a larger number of units. For many public goods, however, the supply is limited to one unit only, and the size and quality of that unit is fixed, at least for categories of expected beneficiaries (e.g., a public housing project or social security payments). A distinction must be made, therefore, between public goods for which the demand for the first unit is elastic and those for which the demand for the first unit is inelastic. When the demand for the first unit does not vary according to price—i.e., the first unit is demanded whatever the price—the comparison between private and collective action for the attainment of the good requires the introduction of another variable: the availability of private resources.

An inelastic demand for the first (and possibly the only) unit of consumption of a good is an indicator of the high salience (or utility), of the first unit of the good. On the private action side of the comparison, we are not dealing with a willingness-to-pay curve of demand, but with a variable indicating the individual's ability to pay the market exchange price of the first unit of the good. Consequently, participation in collective action to secure the allocation of one unit of the good has to be evaluated in terms of the individual's ability to pay the market price for individual action. This criterion of evaluation is the *individual rate of substitution* between individual and collective action. Operationally, it is the ratio between the individual's score on the numéraire variable and the systemic rate—i.e., the individual monthly income and the systemic rate expressed in units of the modal monthly income, or the individual's level of education and the systemic rate expressed in terms of the modal level of education. Thus, within systems, individual participation in collective action for the allocation of goods for which the demand is inelastic can be evaluated in terms of the individual's availability of resources for private action, measured by the "rate of substitution" which defines his resources in terms of the systemic rate of substitution. Establishing equivalence for individual participation across systems involves a comparison of within-system individual rates of substitution weighted by the cross-systemic difference between systemic rates in terms of the numéraire.

When the demand for the first unit of the good is elastic, the analysis also reflects the salience or utility of the good in relation to alternative uses of the individual's resources. There will still be those who have no available resources and for whom the salience of the first unit of the good is very high. There will be others who have available resources but for whom the salience of the good is lower than that of any alternative use of their resources; they are able and willing to purchase the good on the exchange market only at a cost which is lower than the systemic rate of substitution. Faced with a choice between collective action and no supply at all, both categories will support collective action, the second category, however, only if the cost of collective supply does not exceed the price this category is able and willing to pay on the exchange market. Common to both categories is the fact that their real demand for the good cannot be assessed on the exchange market. Only a third category—i.e., those who are able and willing to pay the systemic rate (or even more) for the supply of the good through private action—can express its real demand for the good on the exchange market. Members of this category will support collective action if the salience of the good is higher than that of an alternative investment of the resources needed to cover their share of the cost of collective supply.

Since two out of these three categories of expected beneficiaries cannot express their demand for the good on the exchange market, the assumption of elasticity of demand does not provide any additional criterion of differentiation between participants in collective action. Some public goods are actually supplied only to those whose demand for the first unit of the good is assumed to be inelastic (segmental public goods) and the size of the only unit of general public goods (i.e., goods made available to all members of the community) often tends to be below the level at which elasticity of demand would justify differential availability.

Chapter 9

CRITERIA OF SUBSTANTIVE EQUIVALENCE

In the preceding chapters a distinction was made between political and economic behavior in terms of procedures of goal attainment (collective action as opposed to exchange transaction) and the nontransferability of public goods. This distinction is congruent with the mainstream of empirical and normative political theory because it is predicated on both forms of behavior and the normative validity attached to the outcomes of action channeled through procedures of collective decision-making. It is also congruent with the observation that any area of life, any subject matter in which there is conflict over scarce resources, can become the object of political action. One rather obvious concomitant of this observation is the view that neither behavioral nor institutional political science can address itself to the substantive issues of politics or suggest a systematic interpretation of the history of political events.

This chapter will explore whether it is possible to go beyond the formal, procedural and normativist interpretation of politics in order to develop substantive criteria of equivalence for comparative political analysis. Undertaking this exploration does not imply agreement with the contention that empirical political science is inquiring into problems which are socially and politically marginal, if not irrelevant, and that the behavioral approach is essentially conservative. One must recognize that the substance of politics does not easily lend itself to empirical generalizations and theory-building;

even conscious attempts to address the question of "what" in the mapping sentence "who gets what, when and how" have resulted, so far, only in performance models in terms of functions conceptualized at high levels of abstraction. Furthermore, although system-theoretic approaches are primarily goal-attainment rather than goal-setting models, political behavior, conceptualized as collective behavior, does indeed occur only in systems.

One of the most persistently—and yet unsuccessfully—pursued attempts to analyze politics in substantive terms has consisted in considering politics as involving the use of *power*. Political philosophers, sociologists, and quantitatively oriented political scientists alike have hoped to construct a theory of politics based on what has been intuitively perceived as the major resource in politics: the ability to exercise influence and obtain compliance. Yet, as increasing attention was devoted to this search, the operational concept of power became increasingly elusive. No attempt will be made here to review this literature; it will suffice to indicate what seem to be sufficient reasons for abandoning the pursuit of a substantive theory of politics based on the concept of power.

"Power," like "energy" in physics (and "life" in biology), is an analytical construct. One can observe what is imputed to power, a manifestation of power, but not power per se. Furthermore, power is generally defined as a relation between power holders and those upon whom it is exercised. These two statements already indicate some of the fundamental difficulties encountered in attempts to operationalize and measure power.

(1) If power is revealed only in some behavioral manifestation, can we identify it only *after* it has been exercised and perhaps expended? Yet, the problems that one would wish to study are those in which power is considered a potentiality—i.e., before it has been exercised.

(2) Many authors, including Dahl (1957), have suggested that power could be measured as the difference between two conditional probabilities: the difference between the probability that B does x if A does w and the probability that B does x if A does not do w. The operationalization of this formulation raises some difficulties to which we shall return shortly; here one may wish to ask a more general question: what does the use of a power concept add to the stated conditional probability of the occurrence of two events? Following March (1955) and Simon (1957), Riker (1964) has argued—I believe conclusively—that power and *cause* are closely related concepts: "Power is potential cause," or "power is the ability to exercise influence while cause is the actual exercise of it." Given the multivariate structure of determination in the social universe and the difficulties encountered in making causal inferences, there can be little reason to

expect a substantive theory of politics based on the even more slippery concept of *potential cause*—i.e., power.

(3) Those who apparently are unconvinced by this reasoning have focused on a number of aspects of power relationships, which reflect the complexity of social interaction but have contributed little to an agreement on an operational definition of power. Considering the power relationship from the viewpoint of A and from the viewpoint of B leads to contrasting conceptualizations; combining the viewpoints of both A and B transforms the impositional aspect of power into an exchange transaction. A may have to overcome the resistance of B (i.e., some interests of B would have to be sacrificed) but A will not be able to do so unless he has something B wants even more and cannot get elsewhere. Even physical coercion has been construed as an exchange relationship: in exchange for the wallet, the gunman offers his victim physical safety. Admittedly, this is an asymmetrical exchange transaction (Blau, 1964; Litt, 1973) because the victim attaches "greater utility" to survival or safety than does the gunman to any single wallet; however, with perhaps the exception of the limiting case of survival or physical safety, how can we draw the line between symmetry and asymmetry, between exchange and coercion, if there is no interpersonally valid unit of measurement for the comparison of utilities? Even the utilities any single individual attaches to alternative outcomes cannot be easily measured and thus one of the major dimensions of power in unilateral power situations—the opportunity cost of refusing compliance (which Harsanyi, 1962, considers the "strength" dimension of power)—does not lend itself to operational measurement.

Reciprocal power situations can be conceptualized as bargaining situations and have been analyzed in terms of strategies of rational behavior in two- and n-person bargaining game theories. Yet, irrespective of whether game-theoretic models do or do not approximate political behavior, or at least behavior in committees or legislative assemblies, the major potential contribution of these approaches would be in the areas of the "who" and the "how," rather than the "what" of politics.

(4) A further difficulty is revealed by the operationalization of power formulations based on the concept of probability. A probability measurement is construed as the proportion p of all cases n in which compliance (or noncompliance) has been observed. Probabilities are thus calculated in terms of observed empirical frequencies; "potential power" is inferred from previously exercised actual power. However, if power presupposes the ability to withhold rewards in case of noncompliance—i.e., if it presupposes resources controlled by A and needed by B, the probability formulation of power based on past performance necessarily implies that the exercise of power by A does not diminish his supply of, and control over, the relevant resources.

If, on the other hand, the resources on which A's power is based are divisible and expendable and the exercise of power involves the distribution of such resources as rewards, then the higher the frequency of observed cases in which power has been exercised by A, the lower the supply of such resources available to A and the smaller the "amount" of his power.

Since this reasoning seems to run counter to most definitions of power, are we to conclude that a power relationship exists only when the resources available to A consist of nondivisible goods? It is possible to argue that the very act of compliance by B enables A to replenish his supply of the relevant resources or even to increase it; this would imply, however, that the act of compliance constitutes a source of power for B: (a) if the act of compliance generates a supply of the relevant goods, B can choose to generate this supply for the benefit of anyone who offers him a greater reward (and A would have no power over him); and (b) if only A can benefit from the resources generated by the compliance of B, B actually exercises power over A.

(5) The preceding observation also suggests that the analogy between the role of power in society and in politics and the role of money in the economy is somewhat misleading. Unlike money, power has only very limited liquidity (i.e., generalizability or transferability), since power depends on specific relations (Martin, 1971). One may argue, however, that power shares some of the characteristics of monetary *credit:* both power and credit can be increased through reputation. An individual or a corporation known to be considered trustworthy by one bank is likely to receive similar recognition—and credit—from another bank without any actual change in his or its financial holdings. Similarly, the very exercise of power by A over B may create or enhance A's reputation for obtaining compliance, thus making it unnecessary for A to display the resources on which his power rests in order to obtain compliance from C, D, or E. Stated in Dahl's terms, A can broaden the extension of his power without a change in the base of his power. In Harsanyi's model this would denote decreasing values on the opportunity-cost curve.

Thus a power base can consist of (a) divisible and expendable resources; (b) indivisible nonexpendable resources (e.g., expertise, authority) and (c) reputation (the measurement of which may reveal that it is both divisible and expendable). Needless to say, each of these types of resources affects the power-holder's ability to increase the amount, strength, and extension of power in a different manner. It follows that evaluating probabilities of the future use of power from frequencies of the past exercise of power requires information on the type of power base, on the interchangeability of power resources, and on the shape of the opportunity-cost curve. Furthermore, as

Simon has pointed out, the expectations—concerning the power base of A—of those to be subjected to his power, as well as A's evaluation of their "zone of acceptance" of his power, also contribute to the probability of A's future use of power.

It is probably safe to assume that "power" is a generic term applicable to a number of different multidimensional social relationships. The common denominator of these relationships is the commonplace observation that among individuals, groups, and organizations there is inequality in the ability to "cause" social action and to determine its outcomes. However, what is the reason to believe that all such inequalities will result in political action? Are there no power relationships in the private lives of men and women? If a power is a relationship between resources, goals, actions, and outcomes, the study of *political power* should perhaps proceed in the direction of examining specific types of resources, their exchangeability, and their relevance to collective action for the supply of specific types of public goods.

The preceding discussion should not be interpreted as a rejection of the conflictual model of politics, which is predicated on the assumption of unequal distribution of resources, including the resources which constitute the bases of power. Indeed, it is possible to argue that the procedural-normativist definition of politics assumes that collective action is required when the expected beneficiaries of public goods do not possess the necessary power to seek and obtain the expected benefits through individual action or exchange transactions, and that collective action generates, combines, and organizes the power necessary for the supply and administration of public goods.

However, this is not the only possible interpretation of the function of power in a collective-action-for-public-goods model of politics. For Parsons (1967), power is a generalized circulating medium, within the political system but also over its boundaries, which secures the performance of binding obligations in a system of collective organization when the obligations are legitimized with reference to their bearing on collective goals. This conceptualization—as most of its critics have pointed out—is based on an assumption of consensus of some kind between power-holders and those subordinate to them.

Conflictual and consensual models of the political system are not the only available alternatives. They do refer, however, to different levels of analysis: the consensual model implies a system-level, the conflict model a subsystem- or possibly even an individual-level perspective. A third alternative is suggested by a psychological model of political man. Which of the available models of politics is more likely to lead to a substantive interpretation of political behavior? This discussion can be usefully conducted in terms of the different *models of man* associated with the major positions advanced in recent attempts to examine the differences between political and other types of social behavior and the relationship between politics and the social sciences.

There are essentially only three criteria for a classification of the major models for the study of politics: (1) the choice of the unit of analysis—i.e., actors or groups of actors as opposed to systems or communities; (2) assumptions about the integrative as opposed to the conflictual characteristics of politics; and (3) the motivations of political man—i.e., the predominance of psychological, sociopsychological, or rational determinants of political behavior. One should hasten to add that these are complementary rather than mutually exclusive approaches. Men act as individuals or as members of groups, but politics is predicated on a decision-making system. Systems tend to be integrative and stabilizing, but the need for integration and stability arises from the presence of differences and conflict. Finally, men often proceed rationally in their participation in collective processes, but they will also tend to be consistent with sociopsychologically learned value systems and personality-determined propensities. For purposes of an economical manipulation of variables, empirical theories have emphasized one or another of these aspects. We can retrace in these theories the images of *homo sociologicus, homo economicus,* and *homo psychologicus.* If it is true, however, that we are too frequently "specialists by default" (Greer, 1969a: 53)—i.e., it is not that we know much about our subject, we are just ignorant of everything outside it—why have we been unable to propose a model of *homo politicus* without borrowing from the metatheoretical assumptions of the disciplines studying man's nonpolitical behavior?

Greer believes that it is, indeed, neither possible nor desirable for political science to be delimited by some analytical model or theory. He subscribes to the view that there are really only two basic analytical schemes in the study of human behavior—the psychological and the sociological. Olson (1969: 147), on the other hand, believes that the major distinction, in the social sciences, is to be made between sociology and economics. "Sociology [is] the discipline that studies the formation and transmission of wants or beliefs of all kinds, and economics [is] the discipline that studies the ways in which people strive to obtain whatever it is they want." The two disciplines also differ in terms of method, of preconceptions concerning the role of rationality and, needless to say, in the substantive conclusions they draw about the same problems.

What role do these different approaches assign to politics? Although couched in somewhat different terms, their conceptualizations of politics (and political science) are strikingly similar. For Greer, "Political science focuses primarily upon the formal organizations of the *public control system* and their interaction with the relevant environment. As such, it provides a needed *corrective to economic determinism* on one hand, and an apolitical study of organizational evolution and *societal trends* on the other" (1969a: 56; italics added). For Olson, the "economic ideal" is one of conditions for an efficient and optimal allocation of resources; the "sociological ideal," one of maximizing integration and minimizing alienation. "If either of these ideals were attained, the society would be a nightmare in terms of the other. *The choice of a position along the continuum between the economic and the sociological ideals must, of course, be made by the political sytem*" (1969: 159, italics added). Thus both positions ascribe the role of politics to system-level "needs" for control or choices of equilibria and, consequently, have no use for a motivational syndrome that could be ascribed to *homo politicus*.

Let us now take a closer look at the motivational assumptions underlying the models of sociological and economic man. Systemic sociological theory treats man as a "role-taker," as conforming to a prevailing value system and socioculturally determined expectations about behavior. In this image, man is a "thoroughly oversocialized, conformist creature." In an attempt to translate this image into a motivational syndrome, Dallmayr (1970), following Zetterberg (1957) and Wrong (1961), suggests that the *quest for social approval* comes close to qualifying as the major motivational theorem in sociology. "The maximization of approval . . . could be viewed as the counterpart in sociological theory to the maximization of profit in economic theory."

Economic man has been described as the gain seeker and maximizer (or satisficer) of utilities. This model has been extended to behavior going beyond that of "traditional economic man," who was assumed to be interested only in material gain. The new economic man "may have any values whatever, from altruism to hedonism, but so long as he does not utterly squander his resources in achieving these values his behavior is still economic" (Homans, 1961: 79). There are two components in this model: (1) an assumption of consistency-rationality in the selection of ends—i.e., a transitive set of preferences, and (2) a cost-minimizing or benefit-maximizing strategy in the selection of means.

In contradistinction to sociological man, who adapts to his social environment or seeks its approval, economic man employs the "best" available strategy for obtaining what he wants. Stated more appropriately: the model postulates man's *ability* to pursue his goals in a consistent, benefit-maximizing manner. In very crude terms, this is the psychology of the pain and pleasure principle. It describes a self-serving strategy of behavior, even when it refers to nonmaterial values; as a behavioral model it indicates individualistic criteria for individual behavior. Exchange theories postulate that exchanges will continue so long as the actors involved find it profitable. Social exchange is therefore often interpreted as a socially integrative mechanism, a position which does not take into account those situations in which exchange ceases to be profitable for some of the actors involved and a different mechanism of allocation is resorted to.

A comparison of the two models indicates that they are based not only on different human characteristics, but on different types of human characteristics. "Sociological man" represents a ubiquitous aspect of man's life in groups and societies. Its counterpart in psychology is the universal need for belonging and acceptance. "Economic man" reflects the ability to engage in a specific type of strategies. Its counterpart in psychology—and this involves some stretching of the analogy—is the reward/punishment principle in learning—i.e., a behavioral pattern displayed by animals with various degrees of learning ability. For man, the ability to learn and the potentiality of rational behavior seem to be neurobiological givens. They are instrumental in need satisfaction, but do not constitute substantive needs which human beings seek to satisfy. Since sociological and economic man reflect different types of human characteristics, would a model of political man draw upon yet another type of characteristics?

There have been numerous attempts to interpret political man in sociological and economic terms. The ethnic voter, the party identifier, and the alienated protester are examples of sociological man in politics. The vote-trading members of a legislature, or the party leaders trading programs for votes in Downs' economic model of democracy are examples of economic man in politics. Several quite explicit formulations of a different model of political man have been proposed by those who subscribe to a conflict theory of politics. Dahrendorf (1959) has consistently argued that every political organization exhibits a dichotomous distribution of power and authority, that there is a zero-sum element implicit in the power relationships of the political arena and that interest groups engage in conflict over the preservation or change of the status quo. Although couched in macrosociological terms, Dahrendorf's theory of conflict and constraints assumes an image of man engaged in maintaining or improving his position in society, of man the power wielder or power seeker. Commenting on this image, Dallmayr (1970) has added the epithet of "man the maximizer of self-determination," a concept further developed by Renshon (1974) as denoting a basic need to gain control over one's physical and psychological life space. There is a scarcity of positions in which individuals enjoy the advantage of being able to shape their own lives and the direction of society. "From this scarcity arises a struggle of wills . . . which is primarily a contest over the extent and direction of self-determination and self-realization" (Dallmayr, 1970: 472). Riker's politically rational man, who would rather win than lose, is consistent with the image of the power seeker, since "the man who wants to win also wants to make other people do things they would not otherwise do" (Riker, 1962: 22).

The power motivation model of political man, which has a long tradition in political philosophy, refers primarily to elites and aspiring elites. In a contemporary version, Lasswell (1960) has formulated the model in psycho-analytic terms. Yet, consistent with Lasswell's observation about the functional diversity of power-relevant roles, recent research has shown that there is little evidence to substantiate the assertion that a power motivation—i.e., a political motivation according to this model—is characteristic of political elites only (Czudnowski, 1975). At this point, however, the argument loses its force and the reasoning becomes ambiguous, because in the above statement "political elites" are identified according to institutional criteria and the fact that nonpolitical elites may also be power-motivated does not prove that the model of power-oriented *homo politicus* is not useful. Have we not encountered sociological and economic man in the arena institutionally defined as politics without denying the usefulness of these models in sociologically and economically defined areas of social behavior?

The real difficulty with a psychological, motivational model of political man derives from the need to relate personal, private meanings of action to the collectivity-oriented frame of reference of politics. Lasswell was fully cognizant of this difficulty when he posited a displacement of private motivations onto public objects; his formulation remains, however, within the scope of individual psychology. Different psychological theories have injected their perspectives into the study of social behavior, and the political scientist is now able to draw different psychological and ideological profiles of his version of *homo politicus,* depending on the psychological theory he subscribes to (Anderson, 1973). Although the field known as political psychology is a "pluralist universe" (Greenstein, 1973), it can be described as inquiring into the functions that political beliefs, attitudes, and behavioral involvement serve in the "psychic economy" of the individual (Smith, 1973). It therefore necessarily accepts definitions of politics drawn from outside the field of psychology.

It will be argued, in the remainder of this chapter, that psychological theory can contribute a useful perspective in the search for substantive criteria of equivalence in the comparison of political behavior. However, no psychologically defined motivational syndrome can serve as a model of political man and, therefore, as a criterion defining political behavior, unless one chooses to restrict the denotation of "political man" to the power seeker. The political system, however, is not merely an arena in which individuals seek to satisfy their need for power or deference. Although his personal motivations may vary considerably (e.g., a sense of citizen-duty, the benefit expected from a demanded public good, a quest for status, influence, or power), political man is the participant, at different levels of involvement, in collective action for the ultimate purpose of supplying and administering public goods. Since groups compete in their collective actions for the use of limited resources to be applied to alternative (or mutually exclusive) public goods, this definition posits a conflict model of politics. Thus the substance of politics remains undetermined by this definition of political man; let us attempt therefore to approach the problem from a different angle.

The empirical political scientist is necessarily Janus-faced; he must observe both the individual and the system and account for the interaction between individual and systemic variables. One of the constraints of this research posture is the inability to allow both individual and systemic variables to vary along a dimension of time, because the units of time relevant for individual change and for systemic change may differ considerably. For the individual, relevant units of time for the study of uniformity or change can be determined by applying "historical time" (i.e., the occurrence and sequence of political events) to "relative time" (i.e., stages in the individual's life cycle). Political systems, on the other hand, have sometimes changed very slowly across a number of generations, whereas at other times they have been subjected to successive changes of considerable extent during the lifetime of a single generation (e.g., the Weimar Republic, post-World War II France). For theoretical purposes, however, the analyst is free to allow for variation along the time dimension using the units of time relevant at each level of observation. Stated otherwise, he may conduct a comparative study of change by observing the variation in psychological, attitudinal, and behavioral variables across the stages in the life cycle of individuals, and the political history of groups, strata, classes, and systems across extended periods of time. What insights can the psychological perspective offer to the social and political historian, and what evidence of interest can the political psychologist find in cross-generational units of analysis? Political scientists should be in a position to capitalize on this set of potential intellectual transactions, provided they can avoid reductionism and cross-level fallacies. In recent years, one particular theory of human motivation has stirred the curiosity of political scientists who have been tempted to explore the possible theoretical linkage among human motivation, a historical perspective on behavior, and a science of politics. The motivational theory is Maslow's hierarchy of human needs.

In *Human Nature in Politics,* Davies (1963) has interpreted political beliefs, attitudes, and behavior in terms of a hierarchy of needs, with examples drawn from fields as widely separated as experimental psychology, psychobiography, and political history. Davies' interpretations alternate between individual- and aggregate-level analyses, between single events and periods of history, but the primary unit of analysis is, explicitly or implicitly, the individual and his political behavior. Arguing from a normative position, Bay (1968) has shown the relevance of Maslow's theory in an evaluation of contemporary political issues. Knutson's *Human Basis of the Polity* (1972), the first American empirical study inspired by Maslowian theory, inquires into the association between need-satisfaction and politically relevant beliefs and attitudes. Inglehart's study of "The Silent Revolution in Europe" (1971) relates economic development, through Maslowian theory, to changes in political values and attitudes. Davies, Bay, and Inglehart clearly suggest that political issues, and the underlying value systems, can be interpreted as reflections of basic human needs and that these needs constitute a sequential hierarchy. "A consideration of the basic needs and of their priority may help explain many phenomena that hitherto have not made much sense in relation to each other . . . the hierarchization of needs may help explain different stages of political development and help determine approximately the order in which different kinds of politics are likely to emerge" (Davies, 1963: 63).

Earlier attempts to relate systemic variables to psychological characteristics of individuals have been made by psychologists, sociologists, and cultural anthropologists and are reflected in studies of "national character," "culture and personality," and "modal personality" (for an assessment of this literature, see Inkeles and Levinson, 1969). The relevance of these studies for the present discussion derives from the personality theories from which they proceed. Freudian psychoanalytic approaches, positing that man is driven by instincts while society and civilization are possible only at the price of instinctual frustration, were ill-fitted to provide a link between psychological and systemic variables. The neo-Freudians added concepts such as "individual security system" (Kardiner, 1939, 1945) and self-realization (Fromm, 1941, 1947) and Erikson (1950) introduced the psychoanalysis of ego identity and development. It was the transition from a psychology of *traits* to personality theories of *needs* which facilitated a developmental interpretation of psychological determinants of behavior. Some studies, however, focused on the predominance of a particular need; of these, the best known is probably McClelland's (1961) analysis of the relationship between the achievement need and economic development. Other studies have combined a number of needs considered as characteristic of the modal personality type of a people: Inkeles et al. (1958), for example, described the central needs and modes of need satisfaction of the Russian personality and found considerable incongruence between this personality syndrome and the Soviet sociopolitical regime. Different need inventories have been proposed by psychologists, but it is Maslow's parsimonious and hierarchical list of needs which lends itself best to a substantive interpretation of politics.

Exploring whether a developmental motivational theory is likely to facilitate a more systematic interpretation of certain trends or sequences of events and, conversely, whether sequences of events at the aggregate or systemic level are congruent with Maslow's theory of needs, does not imply that anthropomorphic characteristics are being imputed to aggregates or systems. The polity will be considered to consist of individuals and groups, and a set of authoritative rules for authoritative collective decision-making. This does not preclude recognition of the fact that groups and aggregates, unlike individuals, display a (social) structure in terms of the distribution, among members, of certain relevant characteristics. Furthermore, the polity will be considered as an organization—i.e., a structure of political roles. Thus it becomes necessary to make a distinction between the politics of rules and organization, the politics of substance, and the politics of individual role-seekers and role-holders in the decision-making structure.

Let us now turn to Maslow's theory of motivation. It represents a "growth-oriented" or dynamic "humanistic" psychology. In contradistinction to what Maslow considers atomistic and theoretically unsound lists of human needs or drives, it focuses on five "basic need areas": (1) physiological needs (survival); (2) safety needs (security, stability, protection, freedom from anxiety and fear, need for structure, order, law); (3) belongingness and love needs (affection, a place in one's family, group, neighborhood, clan, gang, work-team, class, territory); (4) esteem needs—from others and self-esteem (status, recognition, attention, appreciation, dominance, need for adequacy, achievement, competence, confidence); (5) self-actualization (self-fulfillment, to become actualized in what one is potentially, to become more and more of what one is capable of becoming).

This, however, is not just another list of needs. The developmental aspect of the theory is based on Maslow's observation "that the human being is never satisfied except in a relative or one-step-along-the-path fashion, and . . . that wants seem to arrange themselves in some sort of hierarchy of prepotency" (Maslow, 1970: 25). This hierarchy of prepotency follows the order in which the needs have been listed above. It means that *only after a more basic need has been satisfied does the next need become a motivating force*. The following are some examples of the application of this hierarchy of prepotency to situations in contemporary society. The unemployed worker who is concerned about the supply of shelter and food for his family will accept any sufficiently rewarding and immediately available job, without making demands for job security. The employed but "migrant" worker will seek stability and security before he becomes concerned with social belongingness. The immigrant who has found stable employment will seek social acceptance by his new environment before he becomes motivated by a need for appreciation or deference. Fulfillment of the four basic needs represents incipient self-actualization. "Growth in self-actualization leads to increased creativity, increased awareness of self and others, increased universality in thought and values, and increased curiosity." The self-actualizer is "growth-motivated" rather than "deficiency-motivated." He is more tolerant, assesses the world more realistically, and is concerned with his environment and with his relation to it (Knutson, 1972: 87). Early gratification of the four basic needs also makes the self-actualizer more capable of tolerating subsequent threats to, or thwarting of, these needs.

Maslow also discusses cognitive needs—the need to know, to understand, analyze, relate, systematize—which also form a small hierarchy of their own, but are not part of the hierarchy of basic needs. Davies groups the need for knowledge with a need for power into a category of instrumental needs (1973: 7), in which he also includes the need for security, thus disputing its status of basic need in Maslow's hierarchy.

These are the central features of a motivation theory developed by Maslow from clinical and experimental observations in psychology. Its relevance to the major concepts and findings in the sociopsychological literature on politically salient beliefs and attitudes has been discussed by Knutson (1972). Here we shall be concerned with the usefulness of the theory of a hierarchy of needs in the quest for substantive criteria of equivalence in the comparison of political behavior. We shall examine, in empirical studies and historical data, some of the differences in substantive political concerns between different types of political actors and attempt to relate such differences to need-levels in Maslow's hierarchy. To begin with, we shall briefly review an area of inquiry which has received considerable attention from American political scientists in the 1960s: the contrasting profiles of "professional" and "amateur" politicians.

The "amateur" profile was first developed in Wilson's (1962) study of the political clubs in Chicago, New York, and Los Angeles. The "amateur" finds intrinsic rewards in politics: the determination of public policy on the basis of principles. He conceives politics in terms of issues: substantive (e.g., liberalism) or procedural (e.g., reformism). The "professional" expects extrinsic rewards of power, income, or status, and views politics in terms of "winning an election" or in terms of party interests which usually involve appeals to, and compromises with, specific interest groups. This description of the two contrasting profiles of politicians has been confirmed in a number of subsequent studies ranging from party committeemen in New York (Hirschfield et al., 1962) and ward leaders in Columbus, Ohio (Hofstetter, 1971), to National Convention delegates of the Republican Party in 1964 and the Democratic Party in 1968 (Soule and Clarke, 1970; Polsby and Wildavsky, 1971). The amateurs are the idealistic campaign workers for Barry Goldwater or Eugene McCarthy. Polsby and Wildavsky describe them as "purists," whose attitudes toward politics have strongly moralistic overtones, whereas the professionals believe in incremental policy changes through bargaining. It has also been shown, however, that the "new style" of politics represented by the amateurs was associated with a change in the sociodemographic profile of urban politicians: they were young, well educated, and "recruited" from middle- and upper-middle-class occupations.

Thus the politics of reform, of support for principles of party organization associated with uncompromising stands on issues, the politics of "purposive incentives" as opposed to "solidary" or "material" incentives of the professionals (Clark and Wilson, 1961; Conway and Feigert, 1968), reflect to a large extent the political involvement of members of the middle class who are relatively prosperous—i.e., economically secure and socially established. The incentives of the professionals reflect the politics of welfare, of demands for economic security, and of ethnic solidarity, which often overlap in the demographic context of large urban centers in the United States; they also reflect the pragmatic politics of patronage necessary for the maintenance of the organization and the winning of elections. For the idealistic reformer, as well as for the "game politician," politics is a "mode of self-expression and self-realization" (Rogow and Lasswell, 1963).

These differences have often been referred to as differences in political style. Although "political style" has never been clearly defined, the term seems to refer to a personal input into role performance in areas not structured by the set of expectations defining a role. Amateurs and professionals, however, appear to have different expectations about the role itself. This is possible because there can be no generally accepted set of specific expectations attached to roles in the subsytem of society which deals precisely with those issues on which there is conflict of interests, goals, and values. In comparing amateur and professional styles, we are in fact examining different values and goals, not differences in the manner in which a role with generally accepted expectations is being performed by different actors. We are examining different views of what politics is or should be, in terms of substance, rules, organization, and office-holding alike, and these views correspond very closely to different motivational levels in Maslow's hierarchy of basic needs.

The politics of material and solidary incentives tend to benefit those who seek to satisfy their needs for economic and social security, as well as their needs for social acceptance. The reform politics of the amateurs, opposing the morally if not otherwise "corrupt" establishment, reflect a melioristic concern for principles characteristic of self-actualizers. The active spokesmen of reform politics, and apparently also the strata whose support they seek and obtain, have satisfied their lower-level needs and are politically motivated by a need for self-actualization. In terms of individual participants, there can be some overlap or combination of characteristics drawn from both sides of this ideal-typic dichotomy: the long-established leader of a "professional" political organization may have become a self-actualizer. At the public-policy level, however, the distinction remains valid.

This interpretation suggests that the hierarchy of needs is reflected not only along the growth-continuum of individual motivational development, but also in terms of the contrasting characteristics of the political action engaged in by different groups or strata of society. Of equal interest are the consequences of psychic deprivation, interpreted in terms of Maslow's need theory. If an individual experiences a deprivation of a lower-level need, especially in the period of personality formation, this need will motivate his behavior long after the need has eventually been satisfied. Thus "it may come about that the insecure adult remains insecure even when offered safety, belongingness and love, though the already secure person can retain his security in the midst of a threatening, isolating and rejecting environment" (Maslow, 1952). Independent of Maslowian theory, the concept of psychic deprivation has guided social and political psychologists in their studies of dogmatic, authoritarian, esteem- or power-seeking political actors. An unsatisfied need is assumed to "color" or "flavor" the individual's behavior in all relevant situations or areas of life. Combined with socialization theory, the psychic deprivation theory has enabled Inglehart to demonstrate the relevance of the need hierarchy to the study of intergenerational changes in political value systems.

Recent studies of the political implications of lower-level need satisfaction have been prompted by the observation that radical protest movements among college students recruited their membership (and not just their leaders) from highly educated upper-status families. Flacks (1967) notes, among other factors,

> a particular trend in the development of the family: namely the emergence of a pattern of familial relations, located most typically in upper middle class, professional homes, having the following elements: (a) a strong emphasis on democratic, egalitarian interpersonal relations; (b) a high degree of permissiveness with respect to self-regulation; and (c) an emphasis on values other than achievement; in particular on the intrinsic worth of living up to intellectual, aesthetic, political, or religious ideals.

Following Parsons and Eisenstadt, Flacks emphasizes the sharp disjunction between the values and expectations embodied in the family and those prevailing in the occupational sphere. And he adds: "This is the first generation in which a substantial number of youth have both the impulse to free themselves from conventional status concerns and can afford to do so . . . they are a 'liberated' generation; affluence has freed them, at least for a period of time, from some of the anxieties and preoccupations which have been the defining features of American middle class social characteristics"

(1967: 61). We easily identify the Maslowian argument that after security, belongingness, and esteem needs have been satisfied, behavior is motivated by self-actualization needs.

While Flacks' observations are derived from two studies of relatively small samples of students, Inglehart's (1971) cross-national study conducted in 1970 reports findings based on six Western European cross-sectional samples ranging from 1,230 cases from the Netherlands to 2,046 cases from France. The data are responses given in opinion polls and do not reflect issues which have motivated active political participation. For this analysis, respondents were classified according to the priority they assigned to two issues reflecting material security ("acquisitive values") as opposed to political participation and freedom of speech, which Inglehart interpreted as "postbourgeois" values (there were four mixed-response categories expressing preference for one acquisitive and one postbourgeois value). Although the pair of acquisitive values predominated across the six nations by a ratio of 3 : 1, the most recently formed age-cohorts, socialized entirely under conditions of rising affluence without major economic dislocations, displayed the highest proportions of pure postbourgeois and the lowest proportions of acquisitive preferences in all six nations. The oldest age-cohorts displayed the reverse pattern. Furthermore, the distribution of value preferences varied across nations in a fashion reflecting the economic history of the given nation. High absolute levels of wealth in a given nation at a given time were associated with high proportions of postbourgeois respondents among age-cohorts socialized under those conditions, and higher rates of economic growth were associated with large increases in the proportion of postbourgeois respondents across that nation's age groups. Lower socioeconomic groups selected acquisitive values more frequently than upper socioeconomic groups, and, conversely, the latter chose postbourgeois values more frequently than the former. On the whole, the relationship between age-cohorts and value priorities persisted after socioeconomic status was controlled for.

Commenting on the long-term political consequences of these intergenerational changes, Inglehart believes that they might (a) "encourage the development of new parties responsive to emerging value cleavages"; and (b) "lead to a realignment of the social bases of existing parties ... eventually ... tending to reverse the traditional alignment of the working class with the Left and the middle class with the Right [since] upper status respondents are far likelier than lower status respondents to support a set of post-bourgeois principles which seem more compatible with parties of movement than with parties of order" (1971: 1009). The data on current party support provide tentative evidence for these hypotheses, moderately in the cases of Britain and Belgium, sizably for the Dutch, German, and Italian samples, and most impressively in the case of France. Moreover, even when parental party preference is controlled for, a postbourgeois value preference often leads to a defection from religious or conservative parties to parties of the Left (Italy: 33%; Netherlands: 44%; Germany: 54%; and France: 70%).

Of similar interest is the fact that the separatist movements in Belgium—both Flemish and Walloon—draw their strength disproportionately from the postbourgeois type. "The Flemish separatists clearly are not seeking economic gains. Indeed, they seem prepared to sacrifice them for what they regard as cultural and humanitarian gains." What these movements share with the New Left is their basis of recruitment and the function—suggested in Inglehart's interpretation—of satisfying needs for belongingness, self-esteem, and self-actualization, thus "shifting the emphasis from economic issues to life-style issues." Political participation thus becomes motivated by successively higher levels of needs in Maslow's hierarchy.

Another study of European age cohorts using the more traditional concept of class-based partisan preferences (Abramson, 1971) showed a decrease in class-based partisanship (and in the case of Germany, a far less sharp increase) between 1955 and 1965 among members of the age group born between 1926 and 1934, in comparison with the increasing (or relatively stable, in the case of Britain) class-base of partisanship among members of the older age cohorts.

Partisan preference and (objective) class-status are indirect and somewhat ambiguous "measurements" of value preferences. Even Inglehart's direct measure is not devoid of ambiguities, although it has been validated by a high association of postbourgeois values with support for student demonstrations. The data also tend to support Inglehart's intergenerational—rather than life cycle—explanation of changes in value preferences, and of the "advance" from lower- to higher-level needs as determinants of political attitudes.

At the elite level, a study of Israeli legislators' orientations toward political careers at their initial recruitment into political office (Czudnowski, 1972) revealed a polarization of motivations between legislators of higher and those of lower social status at initial recruitment. One-half the legislators in the high-status category had sought a political career in order to exert influence and gain a position associated with power, and another thirty-six percent in this category had approached a political career with expressive, ideological orientations. Among the lower-status group, fifty-four percent had been motivated by needs for material security (especially among new immigrants), and another twenty-three percent had sought upward mobility in terms of social status. Thus high-status candidates in initial recruitment had been motivated by self-actualization needs, whereas those of lower status had sought the satisfaction of lower-level needs. This study also revealed that higher-level basic needs were associated with initial entry into politics at higher levels of office in the structure of political offices, whereas lower-level basic needs motivated those who entered politics at lower levels of office. This more than suggestive parallelism between the hierarchy of levels of entry into the structure of political offices, the social stratification system, and the distribution of dominant motivations in recruitment reflects perhaps the characteristics of a system adjusting to large-scale immigration. Under more stable conditions, a more complex stratification system and a differently structured party system, this parallelism may be less apparent or not prevail at all. Yet, this study provides empirical support for the theory of a stratification of basic needs and its relevance in the realm of politics. The proposition that individuals with different motivations will seek different types of political positions is not new (Lasswell, 1954; Browning and Jacob, 1964; Browning, 1968). However, the finding that, after these positions had been assigned to their location in the hierarchy of offices, the motivations of their incumbents (in initial recruitment) displayed the order posited in Maslow's theory, seems to provide an outside criterion of validation for one of Maslow's basic propositions.

The studies discussed so far suggest that the hierarchy of basic human needs is reflected not only in the sequential stages of individual psychological development, but also (a) in intergenerational changes of predominant values associated with systemic (economic) conditions facilitating the satisfaction of lower-level needs; and (b) in a vertical dimension of social stratification. It is hardly surprising that needs motivating political involvement should be associated with social position; however, if the prepotency of a particular need usually denotes the prior satisfaction of lower-level needs, the members of a society also constitute a stratification system in terms of those of their basic needs which (might) motivate them to participate in the political process. Furthermore, if the prepotency of a need is associated with social position, stratification in terms of prepotency of needs should correspond to the social stratification system.

In modern societies, social stratification systems are complex; different criteria serve as guidelines for both subjective and objective assessments of social position and the degree of experienced, observed, or expected mobility adds further complexity to the general pattern and to the determination of any individual position therein. Criteria of stratification and the specific indicators of such criteria vary across nations and cultures, and have varied considerably across different periods of economic, social, and political development. So have the substantive issues of politics. However, if this diversity could be interpreted in terms of the basic needs which motivated the substantive demands, social movements, political struggles, institutional arrangements, and political careers across nations and stages of development, one would gain a criterion for comparing the substantive issues of politics in terms of equivalence on a fairly stable ordinal and sequential scale of basic human needs. What this type of analysis is capable of contributing to systematic comparative research and empirical theorizing is a subject worth exploring. The present discussion will have served its purpose if it can marshal additional evidence to support the plausibility of this thesis and point out some of the difficulties resulting from the need for both contextual and longitudinal interpretations of the motivational determinants of political behavior.

Additional evidence for a hierarchical and sequential ordering of motivating needs in political behavior can be found in the politics of ethnic and immigrant groups. Considerable attention has been devoted to the political behavior of such groups in polyethnic and immigrant societies. Thus it has been possible to document some of the critical stages in the processes of their integration into the sociopolitical networks of the absorbing societies at least as far as the United States, and more recently Israel, are concerned. In a very real sense, however, these processes epitomize a recurrent pattern in modern Western political history: the successive ascension to full citizenship and political participation of social strata which had previously been unable to participate in the processes leading to the authoritative distribution of scarce resources. The successive demands made by new groups entering the political arena could be indicative of a sequence of needs motivating political action.

Ethnicity has been interpreted to include a number of ascriptive characteristics such as race, religion, tribal, national, or cultural ancestry. For the present purpose it is not necessary to distinguish among these categories; let us consider ethnic politics as the politics of minority groups seeking integration and participation in the political system of a nation-state without abandoning their specific identity.

In his recent attempt to reinterpret American ethnic politics by comparing the earlier experience of the European immigrants with the "new ethnic politics" involving radicalism and separatism, Litt (1970) summarizes the prevailing theories and available findings by pointing at the association of ethnic political behavior with two major types of goals: (1) economic sustenance and advancement, and (2) psychic rewards of status and esteem. The first stage in the political involvement of ethnic groups is motivated by economic deprivation. Urban political machines and, more recently, governmental agencies have provided employment and channels for economic and social advancement to members of immigrational groups and racial minorities deprived of alternative opportunities. In this process immigrants from different countries have often competed with each other for the control of local party and patronage positions, the groups motivated by the more basic needs of survival and security (i.e., the more recent waves of immigrants) eventually replacing those who had become more economically self-sufficient and therefore less dependent on public employment.

However, the political pull of ethnicity did not recede after the initial satisfaction of economic needs. Litt offers several explanations for the persistence of ethnic politics; they all seem to reflect situations in which the lower-level needs of some members of a group gradually combine with the higher-level needs of other members of the same group. (1) Relative differences in the economic position of groups, and of members within groups, persist for long periods of time. Immigrational generations within a specific ethnic group also differ in their levels of socioeconomic advancement. Thus lower-level needs will continue to motivate some members of the group. (2) However, the dominant social and economic characteristics of a group produce policies that are displayed even by group members of different social and economic accomplishment. Litt cites the example of the lower-middle-class orientation of Catholics and professional class orientation of Jews in the United States, to which one may add the lower-class-oriented platforms of black leaders who have personally achieved a comfortable middle-class status. Among immigrants, after survival and security needs have been satisfied to an acceptable degree, political behavior is motivated by ethnic group solidarity, which reflects the need for belongingness.

This interpretation does not imply that ethnic consciousness and group solidarity appear only after the gratification of material needs; only at the latter stage, however, do they motivate political behavior. The tendency for an ethnic group to display shared political orientations overriding many individual differences in socioeconomic status has also been furthered, at least in the United States, by attachments to the political party which provided the initial material benefits and opportunities for advancement. The persistence of such loyalties beyond the "political memory" of a generation and their transmission to the immediately following generation can probably be explained only by introducing additional variables, including a traditional culture, the persistence of ethnic antagonism, or a rigid stratification system.

The next stage in ethnic politics is the emergence of ethnically identified leaders seeking and achieving political office. These are group leaders with sufficient skills, education, organization or financial support to translate ethnicity into political power. They are supported by those who are motivated by group solidarity, as well as by others who seek status recognition for their group by the larger society through the public acceptance of some of their co-ethnics. The length of time required to reach this stage has varied considerably, but ethnic politics becomes more prevalent as more members of the group attain a socioeconomic status that qualifies them for political positions according to the criteria of eligibility in the larger community, which are also the criteria bestowing recognition on the ethnic group.

The dominant groups in the community, the ruling majorities or coalitions, have often tried to retain their power by offering political status recognition to individual members of ethnic or immigrant groups without the group's participation in the choice of these individuals. These were token recognitions of status through the selection of "pseudo-representatives." They were capable of drawing the support of group members motivated by the need to seek and express group solidarity, but did not satisfy those who sought recognition of group status and positions of influence independent of the patronage of the majority. When ethnic groups are denied recognition and esteem through integration and representational politics, they will (1) either withdraw into apathy, or (2) establish nonpolitical organizations to enhance their self-esteem, or (3) more or less overtly reject the system which institutionalizes or tolerates discrimination by the larger society.

In terms of motivations, ethnic politics qua group politics, cannot transcend the level of status and esteem needs (which include influence and power). The next level of motivations in the hierarchy of needs—self-actualization—cannot be easily conceptualized in a meaningful manner for social groups and other types of aggregates. Such group-related political attitudes as nationalistic chauvinism, racism, or expansionism would not qualify as reflecting "group-level" self-actualization under Maslow's humanistic and universalistic, and growth- rather than deficiency-motivated definition of self-actualization. Neither are these common attitudes among ethnic minorities.

Ethnic leaders who have received status recognition for themselves and for their group may wish to pursue even higher levels of need satisfaction. They may be able to achieve such gratifications even in politics, but as individuals and not as representatives of their groups. Group members will continue to consider such activities of their leaders as rewards of esteem for the group. This is even more obvious when established leaders seek—or are compelled to seek—an alternative career, albeit prestigious, outside the political arena. A different pattern obtains when ethnic leaders in political positions seek to entrench themselves in these positions in the face of mounting pressure from other groups, because (1) they may not have opportunities or resources for an alternative career, or (2) their group still lags behind other groups in terms of economic advancement, and the pressure from new groups may pose a threat to the ability to bridge the existing gap.

It is in this last pattern that we encounter a need motivation not easily categorized in terms of Maslow's hierarchy. Is the demand for better education, for more efficient social services, etc., motivated primarily by status and esteem needs—i.e., the desire to catch up with higher strata on the social ladder—or by safety needs, in order to protect a relative position on the ladder in the face of economic or technological changes which benefit the upper strata or damage them less severely? All deprivations are relative, but is the behavior aimed at improving one's position motivated primarily by the deprivation or by its relativity? Perhaps these are inseparable motivational components constituting a very frequently encountered determinant of political behavior in modern societies, a need activated only after esteem and status needs have initially been satisfied (e.g., subjective competence, political efficacy). Perhaps the theory of successive need prepotencies ought to include socioculturally and technologically determined "levels of satisfaction," as well as a dimension of time—i.e., a dimension of social change.

The need to add a time dimension to the motivational analysis of politics has already become apparent in Inglehart's study of value changes in post-World War II Europe. Litt's interpretation of ethnic politics in America offers another opportunity for a word of caution against too simplistic an application of motivational theory to complex and overlapping stages of development. The phases of ethnic acculturation and integration referred to in the preceding pages correspond to what Litt has called "the politics of accommodation." He distinguishes among three methods of accommodation: (1) divisible political rewards to the few combined with recognition of the ethnic group; (2) collective welfare benefits in which public resources are used to satisfy broad-scale group needs, and (3) the inclusion of ethnic group criteria in "enduring social, economic and political patterns of distributing benefits." Litt points at the fact that divisible benefits and recognition politics were the dominant strategy before World War II, to which collective welfare programs for mass aid (through federal subsidies) were added in more recent years. This should not be interpreted, however, as a reversal of the sequence of need prepotency—i.e., recognition taking precedence over material needs, since these different "strategies of accommodation" were applied to different groups at different times. Before the New Deal, massive welfare programs were neither salient nor acceptable government policies in the United States, a fact which did not prevent urban party organizations from performing such welfare functions on a smaller scale, especially with regard to immigrational ethnic groups. Furthermore, although recognition politics is probably the most inexpensive strategy for the absorbing society and its organizations, the success of this strategy depends—as Litt himself points out—"on the ability of the political economy to provide long-term material benefits. . . . When the means of social and economic advancement are not available on a mass scale to ethnic group members . . . psychic recognition does not suffice" (1970: 63, 65).

Mass immigration in Israel has followed a similar pattern. In the pre-independence period political parties, the unions and agricultural settlements provided most immigrants with the basic resources required for their survival and trained them for appropriate occupational roles. After 1948, most of these services were provided by the government, after welfare-state policies had been generally accepted and institutionalized. Within the absorption agencies—the unions, parties, and local government—the politics of "ethnic recognition" developed at a somewhat later stage, but once established, ethnic politics intensified as a consequence of the cultural diversity of the mass of immigrants and the political culture of proportional representation. At the local government level, and within the party organizations, the politics of recognition were soon superseded by the politics of distribution in which ethnic representation gained effective *influence;* at the national level, however, recognition politics persisted because the real power remained in the hands of party organizations, and conflicts over power and policy influence were contained within these organizations.

Black nationalism represents a deviation from the pattern of accommodation politics. As Litt points out, the Black Muslim movement has been striving primarily to create a new identity for a people who have been deprived of any worthwhile self-identity. In this respect black separatism also differs from the nationalism of historical communities not only in Europe, but also in Asia and Africa. The politics of nationalism emerges only after a population has achieved a sense of historical *and* cultural identity. Black "nationalism" is therefore a potential rather than an actual national movement. What matters here is the fact that a search for identity needs to be interpreted in terms of basic human needs.

Identity, and identity crises, are concepts borrowed from psychology. Their application to politics indicates, according to Pye (1969: 110), "the need to expand our study of nationalism to include quite specifically the psychological dimensions of the individual's feeling toward membership in the polity." Pye describes four types of identity crises experienced by developing nations. The first relates national identity to territorial boundaries, the second to social stratification, the third refers to a possible conflict between ethnic identity and commitments to a "common national identity" (which could mean either a shared past or a shared polity), and the fourth refers to the contradictions arising from the sudden encounter between traditionalist societies and modern ways of life. However, these sets of incompatibilities reflect the identity crises of members of groups rather than of individuals.

An identity crisis can perhaps be defined operationally as an incongruence between shared central existential beliefs and perceptions of social and political conditions undermining these beliefs. Ethnic or national identity refers to beliefs about one's membership in a group defined by shared historical experiences, values, customs, etc. The perceived conditions underlying such incongruences are the result of specific patterns in the distribution of values: material goods, services, security, social acceptance, status, esteem, or opportunities for social and economic advancement. More specifically, such patterns of distribution are perceived as denying a group (defined by racial, ethnic, or cultural characteristics) full membership in the social and political community. In the case of "black nationalism," some members of the group sought to dissociate themselves from the larger society and its political system by redefining their identity in terms of new or previously nonarticulated *allegiances.* The politics of identity crises are the politics of frustrated belongingness at the group level, caused by insufficient satisfaction of certain basic *individual needs,* as a consequence of group-discriminating distributions of values. Thus group-level "needs" can arise in response to *group-specific deprivations of individual need-satisfaction.*

It was pointed out earlier that from the viewpoint of a hierarchy and sequence of needs, the sociopolitical integration of ethnic minorities and immigrant waves epitomizes the successive accession to citizenship and political participation of the lower social strata in modern Western history. Let us recall some of the stages, trends, and episodes of this process in Western Europe in order to examine the usefulness and the limitations of this analogy.

In the feudal systems which preceded absolutist rule and the rise of modern nations, politics consisted of jurisdictional disputes and their settlement by compromise or the force of arms. The actors in these disputes were the rulers and the landed nobility, the source of authority was a grant of "immunity" and the authority included judicial and administrative powers over the territory held in "fief" and all its inhabitants. Under these conditions, there was no distinction—in the modern sense—between government and politics. Social protest took the form of demanding recognition for new autonomous jurisdictions by direct action, but success depended on the wealth and high rank of the families leading these urban revolts. When such favorable conditions did not obtain, social protest took place outside the "political system"—i.e., outside the framework of jurisdictional demands, in the form of social banditry, millenarian movements, populist legitimism, or combinations thereof (Bendix, 1969: 39-65).

Evidently, seeking the satisfaction of basic needs through political action is predicated on the existence of a political system in which such action is both feasible and legitimate. The democratic revolution therefore began with a struggle for citizens' rights. This was preceded and facilitated by the rise of absolutist rule, which destroyed the feudal jurisdictional structure and brought all people under a supreme central authority. These developments set the stage for the struggle to transform the "subjects of one king" into the "citizens of one nation." Thus, historically, the demand for political rights, for a dissociation of political participation and influence from social rank, preceded the politics of economic needs. Yet, it is also true that the legal equality in national citizenship was first demanded and achieved by the bourgeois leaders of the French Revolution. This was an enlightened and wealthy bourgeoisie, whose major grievance was its exclusion from political influence. For the leaders of this class, the struggle against the ancien régime was a demand for status, influence, and power, not for economic advancement or security. The achievement of a constitutional monarchy offered them precisely these rewards. Although it temporarily lost these advantages to a more radical faction, the upper bourgeoisie regained its position in the Napoleonic regimes, which were ushered in by the very ideologue of protest in 1789, the Abbé Sieyès. In England, the commercial and industrial middle classes gained access to political influence through the Reform Act of 1832, but not until the second Reform Act, of 1867, did the urban electorate increase considerably.

During the first half of the nineteenth century, the condition of the industrial working class became a subject of increasing social agitation, both in England and on the continent. Although it expressed itself in different philosophies and strategies, and although most of the leadership was provided by middle-class intellectuals, this movement derived its strength from the ability to mobilize a significant section of the working class in its earliest political attempts to satisfy basic needs for economic survival and security under the developing industrial revolution. This period witnessed, especially on the continent, some temporary alliances between the "forces" of nationalism, republicanism, liberalism, democratization, and socialism, but the economic goals which working-class leaders attempted to achieve through political action were almost invariably defeated. These attempts ranged from Babeuf's insurrection in 1796 and Blanqui's revolutionary involvements between 1832 and 1848, through Louis Blanc's "national workshops" intended to provide employment (rather than relief payments, which they actually did) to all unemployed workers in Paris under the provisional Republican government of 1848, to the demand for universal manhood suffrage promoted by the Chartist movement in England. The proponents of "industrial action" denounced the "hollowness" of "merely" political reform demanded by the Chartists. Represented in England by Owenism, Trade Unionism, the cooperative movement, and the Christian Socialists, industrial action progressed slowly but proved to be successful and lasting, and it was the Trades Union Congress which, half a century later, took the steps toward the organization of a national Labor Party.

On the continent, the revolutions of 1848 were halted and beaten back everywhere. In Central and Eastern Europe, 1848 accomplished what 1789 had done for France: the abolition of the feudal system. Peasants and workers were free to move, and emigration was soon to become a substitute for seeking economic and social relief in their own countries. In France, the

Constitution of 1848 established universal suffrage and the King of Prussia, followed by other German monarchs, temporarily granted similar rights. The results of the only presidential election held in the Second Republic are indicative of the reluctance of the lower classes to follow the lead of radical reformers: the socialist candidate received 40,000 votes, the middle-class democrat, 400,000; General Cavaignac, who had crushed the Paris uprising, received about one and a half-million votes, but five and a half-million peasants, workers, and bourgeois elected Louis Napoleon. It was not for political representation, but for the right to work, for an organization of labor capable of providing employment, that the Parisian workers had entrenched themselves behind their barricades.

The delay in the development of working-class political parties during the second half of the nineteenth century has been explained by improved standards of living, economic expansion, an increasing wage-differentiation between skilled and unskilled workers, and direct governmental action to ameliorate the conditions of the working classes. It was in the last third of the nineteenth century that governments first undertook a comprehensive regulation of society. This was generally a period in which the drift from laissez faire toward increased organization of interests and government regulation was greatly accelerated in response to industrial growth and technological advance. Government intervention to improve the conditions of the workers proceeded from different political motivations. First introduced in England, Factory Acts regulating working hours and safety conditions were adopted throughout Western Europe as part of a *liberal* approach to social policies. When Bismarck embarked in the 1880s on a policy of supplying social insurance through legislation and government regulation, covering sickness, accidents, old age, and disability (thus establishing the first welfare state in history), his motivations were associated with a "preventive war" against the Social Democratic Party (SPD). In 1878 a repressive law had been adopted which considerably curbed the activities of the SPD, and the state insurance program was intended not only to alleviate the condition of the workers, but also to demonstrate that this could be done by the state without the participation of the workers' party which refused to accept the social and economic foundations of this state. This caused the SPD to adopt an even more strongly Marxist program. However, as it gained in membership and support (it obtained 29% of all votes in 1912), the SPD in fact adopted a strategy of "peaceful class warfare." It was the strong and centralized party organization which enabled it to take advantage of universal suffrage in order to build a new power base.

Political organizations, and especially mass parties, are a modern phenomenon, but so are mass societies and mass participation. No collective action is possible without a modicum of organization, or at least leadership.

Let us note, however, that "organization" and "leadership" are group phenomena and do not correspond to any basic individual need. The purposes for which groups organize and select leaders will generally reflect unsatisfied basic needs, but organization and leadership are "group needs"—i.e., types of action each group member feels or agrees are necessary if group members are to pool some resources and coordinate their actions. The political salience of organization per se has, of course, not escaped the attention of popes and emperors alike, not to mention military commanders of all times. It was not until the nineteenth century, however, that the right to associate and organize for political purposes became a salient and explicit demand of the working classes. After the right to organize was achieved, it served purposes as different as the economic action of Trade Unions, the parliamentary action of Labor Parties, the Second International, and the "general strike" as an economic or political weapon. Thus, the satisfaction of certain instrumental "group needs" has been a prerequisite for the ability to seek individual substantive need satisfaction through politics.

The preceding glimpses into nineteenth-century working-class history in Western Europe seem to suggest that the appearance, acceptance, and development of Socialist and Labor Parties occurred only after the most pressing problems of economic survival and welfare encountered by the emerging working class had been acknowledged and given minimally acceptable solutions by either the cooperative movement, the Trade Unions, or state action taken by upper- and middle-class governments. Was this due (1) only to the opposition and the delaying tactics of the upper and middle classes while the ideological leaders of the working classes offered utopian or anarchistic solutions, or (2) was it also a consequence of the psychological difficulty, postulated by Maslow, of seeking long-term and higher-level goals of social justice at the societal level as long as immediate and personal economic survival and welfare remained the most pressing problems? These are hypotheses which need not be mutually exclusive; at this level of longitudinal and cross-national generalization, and with the type of data available, they will probably remain within the realm of speculations about one segment of nineteenth-century history. The theory of a hierarchy of needs emerges, however, as a plausible interpretation.

One may, of course, consider trade unionism and cooperativism to be political phenomena, since they involve collective action. The results of such action may be collective or divisible goods; however, they will always be private, not public, goods. This line of distinction can be drawn from a different perspective: political participation is directed at the decision-making process of a political system, and not merely at contractual agreements between interested parties. Political participation involves the need to take stands and act on issues reflecting not only the interests of one's own group, but also those of any other group, as well as problems faced by the entire community.

Thus the ability of a social group or organization to get its representatives appointed or elected to political office denotes not only the recognition or acceptance of the legitimacy of its interests, it also confers upon that group an increment of *status:* the status of participant in decisions affecting all other groups and the entire community, and the *influence* associated with it. Maslow's need hierarchy indeed postulates a progression from needs which are primarily self-oriented to needs reflecting first the individual's integration in society and then his concern for that society.

If ideologies are at all reflective of the perspective of specific social groups in given historical situations, in terms of their relevant needs or interests, is the transformation of utilitarian philosophical radicalism into the humanitarian or idealist liberalism of J. S. Mill and T. H. Green not indicative of a similar shift from self-oriented to other-oriented motivations of the politically enfranchised bourgeoisie? Needless to say, attempts to interpret historical development or change in terms of a simple "model of human nature" (in the present case, Maslow's hierarchy of needs) would be as oblivious of the contextual determinants of behavior as utilitarianism itself. What is discussed here, however, is neither a philosophy of history nor a psychological theory of politics; it is merely an exploration into the issue of providing substantive criteria for classifying and comparing political behavior. Indeed, it should be emphasized that the above-mentioned "modernization of liberalism" occurred only after the enfranchisement, by a Conservative government, of a sizable segment of the English working class (in 1867) which felt safer with Disraeli's party controlled by landlords than with a party led by the spokesman for industrial employers. Thus a situation developed in which either liberalism, as a party and as a doctrine, adjusted to the needs of the working class, or the working class would not be liberal (Sabine, 1951: 590).

When such specific historical situations are integrated into a developmental perspective on the relationship between social stratification and politics, it is possible to interpret not only the political attitudes of upwardly mobile invididuals, but also the "political memories" of generations and social classes in terms of the prepotency of unsatisfied lower-level needs in later stages of motivational development—i.e., long after such needs have eventually been satisfied. The previously mentioned electoral victory of Louis Napoleon illustrates this statement. The peasants, by far the most numerous social group, "still feared the reestablishment of an aristocratic and clerical régime that would reimpose feudal dues ... conversely, they had acquired a very acute sense of their property rights and, particularly since 1848, it had become easy to rouse in them an irrational fear of 'the Reds' " (Néré, 1962: 300). The same "memories" account for their increasing support of republican candidates after the 1871 election which had created a Chamber with a heavy (though divided) royalist majority. What motivational theory, or even socialization theory, cannot explain are the reasons for which "political memories" persist across a number of generations in some cases but do not persist in others. Only in the context of social stratification and political configurations, viewed along a dimension of development and change—or absence of change—can one find hypotheses for the explanation of such differences.

The period between the establishment and the collapse of the Second International in 1914 is likely to be a fertile ground for the study of the psychological concomitants of the sociology of leadership in the political movements of the working class: support for doctrinaire Marxism as opposed to "possibilism" (Brousse) and Revisionism (Bernstein), the debate between the French and the German socialist leadership, the Millerand "affair," the Fabian Socialism of the Webbs, the predominance of national over working-class solidarity, especially in the German SPD. The period following World War II offers additional examples of a "progression" from politics reflecting lower-level needs to higher-level need satisfaction among the Labor Parties in Western Europe. Attlee's government in Britain accomplished the institutionalization of the welfare state, reflecting the social and economic security needs of an enlarged working class and a new lower-middle class. Only thereafter could the party leadership, under Gaitskell and Wilson, proceed to elicit the support of broader strata by substituting the image of a national, pragmatic party for that of a class-oriented and union-related political organization. General acceptance, social influence, and political power replaced the earlier welfare-economics motivations of political action. The French Socialist Party, a substantial faction of the Italian Socialist Party, and, somewhat later, the German SPD adopted a similar profile.

The changes in political values and programs which have been attributed here to the sequential order of the hierarchy of needs, have been interpreted by Duverger (1954) as reflecting a continuous tendency of political parties to move from the Left to the Right, from reformist to conservative positions, while new parties appear on the left wing of the ideological spectrum.

It is a fairly common occurrence that reformist or revolutionary parties become conservative once the reforms or revolutions they have fought for are accomplished: they move from the Left to the Right, leaving a gap which is filled by the appearance of a new left-wing party that in its turn evolves in the same way. Thus after an interval of twenty or thirty years the Left of one period becomes the Right of the next [1954: 235].

Duverger's observation seems to identify the evidence for Maslow's proposition that lower-level needs which were not satisfied at the time of their earliest prepotency in motivational development will continue to determine value preferences and to motivate behavior after they have eventually been satisfied. However, this tendency toward conservatism is incapable of accounting for the "development" from security- to acceptance-needs satisfaction, and from self-oriented to society-oriented value preferences.

There is one easily apparent criticism of Maslowian interpretations of the substance of politics. The hierarchy and sequence of needs represent stages of motivational development in the life cycle of the individual; the level at which needs are considered satisfied is therefore contingent upon the prevailing state of technology and of socially or culturally acceptable expectations and solutions. When one applies the hierarchy and sequence of need satisfaction across generations, especially in periods of relatively rapid economic and technological change, one inevitably encounters situations in which previously attained levels of need satisfaction are no longer considered sufficient. This occurs especially when the benefits or the costs associated with such changes are unequally distributed between different segments of society or sectors of the economy. Development and modernization are misleading concepts if they are interpreted as involving a terminal state of affairs in which a society would be "developed" or "modern." Both concepts denote relative distances from a *moving target*. It is also obvious, at least to some social groups or generations, that economic development and rising standards of living are not irreversible processes, and that individual or collective action may become necessary to restore previously attained levels of economic welfare. Stated otherwise, survival and security needs may regain prepotency long after higher-level needs have been satisfied. Does this observation undermine the rationale for an attempt to consider need levels as criteria of substantive equivalence of political action?

As far as political participation is concerned, in both the demand and the support categories, the rationale for this attempt seems to be independent of the fact that "development" occurs in stages and that the need hierarchy and sequence can be reactivated at lower need levels. A basic need is considered a psychological "universal." A need for security, for example, was once satisfied through the protection a feudal lord was bound to grant to his tenants; today we seek physical security through law enforcement agencies and economic and social protection through social security programs, health insurance, and unemployment compensation. If the determinants of behavior follow the pattern of the need-hierarchy model, the need for security, if reactivated, will always have prepotency over needs for belongingness, status, or influence, regardless of the state of technology or of the social structure. If the stability of this hierarchy can be demonstrated, need levels would provide substantive criteria of equivalence in comparing political participation and specific political decisions.

In examining system performance—i.e., decision-making across a period of time rather than individual decisions, the motivational hierarchy model ceases to be a reliable predictor of sequences of substantive political concerns. At the system level, the configuration and sequence of substantive political decisions is determined by structural characteristics of the social and political systems, rather than by the need levels of their component groups, strata, or sectors. Different groups can be motivated in their political demands by needs at different levels in the need hierarchy. Which of these types of demands will be responded to during any particular period depends on the resources the governing elites can command, on their ideological commitments, as well as on their strategies for the enhancement—or at least the protection—of their positions in the political structure.

Encouraged by theories of economic development, students of "political development" in the new states in Asia and Africa believed they could discern a pattern of stages, or at least a sequence of crises, in the politics of the developing areas. The crises associated with political development have been identified as pertaining to *identity, legitimacy, penetration, participation,* and *distribution* (Verba, 1971b: 299). Commenting on the "crises and sequences" approach to the study of political development, Verba indicates that he "can find no clear logical structure among" the five problem areas, and that "they do not easily or naturally form a sequential pattern." The absence of a logical structure among the five problem areas can perhaps be explained, in part, by the fact that these areas have been defined in terms of different levels of imputation. Whereas identity and participation are individual- or group-level concepts, legitimacy and penetration are system-level concepts. Only distribution can have both system-level and individual-level referents. Students of development have also drawn attention to the consequences of the accumulation, or overlap, of unsolved crises; but while it is true that from the viewpoint of the ruling elites such crises are indeed cumulative, they may involve different subsets of society.

One way of overcoming the problem of different levels of imputation is to consider all five areas of crises problems of *distribution*. The advantage of this conceptualization would derive from the fact that "distribution" is an empirically empty concept unless one specifies *what* it is that is expected to be distributed in a different manner: incomes, social benefits, opportunities for social advancement, the power positions of elites, affective support for the regime, citizen influence on decisions concerning distribution, the implementation of authoritative decisions, or feelings of social acceptance and political recognition despite racial, tribal, ethnic, or religious differences. Only conflicts between nation-states cannot be easily conceptualized in terms of domestic patterns of distribution. After distributional problems have been described in substantive terms, they can be interpreted as reflecting levels of basic needs. This, in turn, will facilitate the testing of Maslow's model of a hierarchical sequence of need prepotency, as far as citizen demands and supports are concerned, in transitional, developing societies and nations.

Following Almond's functional approach to political analysis and his conceptualizations of systemic capabilities, the works sponsored by the Committee on Comparative Politics of the Social Science Research Council have attempted to adapt a function-performance model to a developmental perspective. In doing so, they have de-emphasized structural characteristics of social and political systems. This departure from predominantly structural models—of which the Lipset-Rokkan historical typology of social cleavages and political parties is still the most comprehensive and elaborate example— has necessarily led to a focus on system-level dimensions of performance. The major exception in this area is the addition of an operationalized and researchable construct of political culture. System-level dimensions of performance are theoretically useful if they can be operationalized in measurable terms and imputed to specific substantive areas of social and political life (Groth, 1971). They do not reflect, however, the manner in which the consequences of performance have been distributed between the affected groups. Since political decisions are at least temporary settlements of conflicting claims over scarce resources, collective actions and their outcomes cannot be meaningfully compared unless the substance of such outcomes can be assigned or otherwise imputed to the affected segments of society. Socio-structural concomitants of political conflict, and measurements of substantive system performance are necessary elements of any set of statements intended for cross-systemic comparison. What this chapter has attempted to explore is the possibility of using levels in the need hierarchy as criteria for establishing substantive equivalence between the performance statements in such comparisons.

CONCLUSION

Comparing political behavior is the method of empirical political science; comparing behavior across systems is the method for developing and testing general theoretical statements about political behavior. This book has been concerned with an examination of several elements of a general paradigm for political science. The examination has been conducted in terms of methodological issues: units of analysis, the relationship between actor and environment, the meanings of intended and observed consequences of behavior, individual and collective levels of interpretation, and problems of functional and substantive equivalence in cross-systemic comparisons.

This methodological posture has been helpful in directing attention toward the dependence of both theorizing and data interpretation on the characteristics of political behavior included in the paradigmatic assumptions of the discipline. The paradigm examined in this book identifies multilevel structures of social and political organizations, levels of meaning, and patterns of interaction in collective behavior as empirically given "settings" within which political behavior has to be interpreted. The single most important function of a paradigm is to provide a general definition of the subject matter to which the discipline addresses itself. Thus, the science of economics studies the benefit-maximizing behavior of producers and consumers in market exchange. The paradigmatic definition of politics adopted in this book is "collective action for the supply and distribution of public goods." The term "public goods" stands in contradistinction to market exchange, since it implies the non-transferability of goods and services and assumes the mechanisms of authoritative allocation and enforcement.

It is suggested that the acceptance of this paradigmatic definition will facilitate the integration of existing theoretical approaches. In addition to the study of the organization of collective action—which has been the province of institutionalist political science and of coalition theory—political science is concerned with the "how" and the "what" of politics. This study has explored two major explanations of the "how": sociopsychological and rational-behavior theories. In cross-systemic comparisons, such explanatory analyses are subject to the requirement of functional equivalence. Concerning the "what"—i.e., the substance of politics—the most frequently held position states that since any subject matter can become the object of authoritative decision-making, there can be no general, substantive theory of politics. In this book an attempt has been made to integrate the goals of collective action (as an alternative to individual action) into the hierarchical sequence of Maslow's theory of basic human needs, thus providing the empirical theorist engaged in cross-systemic and longitudinal comparisons with a modicum of substantive criteria of equivalence.

One important component of the patterns of interaction in political behavior has not been discussed in this book: the role of political elites in initiating and organizing collective action. This writer will not be suspected of ignoring the role of elites and elite recruitment in the political process. The presently available knowledge on elites justifies the inclusion of elites and elite roles in the paradigm of political science. It seems, however, that this would not require any modification of the paradigmatic elements discussed in this book, since the "who" in politics is always implicitly included in the questions of "how," "what," and "what for."

Unchallenged high-level theories are characteristic of well-developed fields of scientific inquiry. Such formal theories are either derived from, or validated by, substantive and testable theorizing at lower- and middle-range levels of generalization. Political science has not sufficiently advanced in substantive theorizing at these levels. For such further efforts to yield cumulative knowledge, one must seek comparability across systems and theoretical linkages among different forms, aspects, and areas of political behavior. The first requirement—comparability—is itself predicated on a postulated or hypothesized framework which would provide such linkages. Empirical research is necessarily conducted primarily for purposes of lower- and middle-range theorizing; only if it is comparatively oriented can it be forced into conceptual moulds which seek anchorage in a common general paradigm.

BIBLIOGRAPHY

ABRAMSON, P. R. (1971) "Social class and political change in Western Europe." Comparative Political Studies 4: 561-587.

ADELMAN, I. and C. T. MORRIS (1965) "A factor analysis of the interrelationship between social and political variables and per capita gross national product." Quarterly Journal of Economics 79: 555-578.

——— (1967) *Society, Politics and Economic Development: A Quantitative Approach.* Baltimore: Johns Hopkins.

ALFORD, R. (1963) *Party and Society: The Anglo-American Democracies.* Chicago: Rand McNally.

ALKER, H. R., Jr. (1964) "Regionalism Versus Universalism in Comparing Nations." In B. Russett et al., *World Handbook of Political and Social Indicators.* New Haven: Yale University Press.

——— (1965) *Mathematics and Politics.* New York: Macmillan.

——— (1966) "Causal Inference and Political Analysis." In J. Bernd (ed.) *Mathematical Applications in Political Science,* II. Dallas: Southern Methodist University Press.

——— (1969) "A Typology of Ecological Fallacies." In M. Dogan and S. Rokkan (eds.) *Quantitative Ecological Analysis in the Social Sciences.* Cambridge, Mass.: MIT Press.

ALLARDT, E. (1964) "Social sources of Finnish Communism." International Journal of Comparative Sociology 5: 49-72.

——— (1966) "Implications of Within-Nation Variations and Regional Imbalances for Cross-National Research." In R. Merritt and S. Rokkan (eds.) *Comparing Nations: The Use of Quantitative Data in Cross-National Research.* New Haven: Yale University Press.

——— and P. PESONEN (1967) "Cleavages in Finnish Politics." In S. M. Lipset and S. Rokkan (eds.) *Party Systems and Voter Alignments.* New York: Free Press.

ALMOND, G. A. and J. S. COLEMAN (1960) *The Politics of Developing Areas.* Princeton: Princeton University Press.

ANDERSON, W. (1973) *Politics and the New Humanism.* Pacific Palisades, Calif.: Goodyear.

ARIAN, A. (1973) *The Choosing People: Voting Behavior in Israel.* Cleveland: Case Western Reserve University Press.

ARROW, K. J. (1951) *Social Choice and Individual Values.* New York: John Wiley.

BANKS, A. S. and P. M. GREGG (1965) "Dimensions of political systems: factor analysis of *A Cross-Polity Survey.*" American Political Science Review 59: 602-614.

BARBER, J. A., Jr. (1970) *Social Mobility and Voting Behavior.* Chicago: Rand McNally.

BARNES, S. H. (1966) "Ideology and the organization of conflict: on the relationship between political thought and behavior." Journal of Politics 28: 513-530.

BAUMOL, W. J. (1967) Welfare Economics and the Theory of the State. Cambridge, Mass.: Harvard University Press.

BAY, C. (1968) "Needs, wants and political legitimacy." Canadian Journal of Political Science 1: 241-260.

BENDIX, R. (1969) Nation-Building and Citizenship. Garden City, N.Y.: Doubleday.

——— and S. M. LIPSET (1957) "Political sociology." Current Sociology 6: 79-99.

BERELSON, B. and G. A. STEINER (1964) Human Behavior. New York: Harcourt, Brace & World.

BERELSON, B., P. LAZARSFELD, and W. McPHEE (1954) Voting: A Study of Opinion Formation in a Presidential Campaign. Chicago: University of Chicago Press.

BERRY, B.J.L. (1960) "An Inductive Approach to the Regionalization of Economic Development." In N. Ginsburg (ed.) Essays on Geography and Economic Development. Chicago: University of Chicago Press.

BILL, J. A. and R. L. HARDGRAVE, Jr. (1973) Comparative Politics: The Quest for Theory. Columbus, Ohio: Charles E. Merrill.

BLACK, D. (1958) The Theory of Committees and Elections. Cambridge: Cambridge University Press.

BLALOCK, H. M. (1964) Causal Inferences in Non-Experimental Research. Chapel Hill: University of North Carolina Press.

——— (1966) "The identification problem and theory building: the case of status inconsistency." American Sociological Review 31: 52-61.

——— (1967a) "Status integration and structural effects." American Sociological Review 32: 790-801.

——— (1967b) "Status inconsistency and interaction: some alternative models." American Journal of Sociology 73: 305-315.

BLAU, P. M. (1960) "Structural effects." American Sociological Review 25: 178-193.

——— (1964) Exchange and Power in Social Life. New York: John Wiley.

BOYD, R. W. (1969) "Presidential elections: an explanation of voting defection." American Political Science Review 63: 498-514.

——— (1972) "Popular control of public policy: a normal vote analysis of the 1968 election." American Political Science Review 66: 429-449.

BOYNTON, G. R., S. C. PATTERSON, and R. HEDLUND (1969) "The missing link in legislative politics: attentive constituents." Journal of Politics 31: 700-721.

BRETON, A. (1966) "A theory of the demand for public goods." Canadian Journal of Economics and Political Science 32: 455-467.

BRODBECK, M. (1963) "Meaning and action." Philosophy of Science 30: 309-324.

BRODY, R. A. and B. I. PAGE (1972) "Comment: the assessment of policy voting." American Political Science Review 66: 429-449.

BROWNING, R. P. (1968) "The interaction of personality and political system in decisions to run for office: some data and a simulation technique." Journal of Social Issues 24: 93-109.

——— and H. JACOB (1964) "Power motivation and the political personality." Public Opinion Quarterly 28: 75-90.

BUCHANAN, J. M. (1965) The Inconsistencies of the National Health Service. London: Institute of Economic Affairs, Occasional Paper 7.

——— (1968) The Demand and Supply of Public Goods. Chicago: Rand McNally.

——— and G. TULLOCK (1962) The Calculus of Consent. Ann Arbor: University of Michigan Press.

BURNHAM, W. D. (1965) "The changing shape of the American political universe." American Political Science Review 54: 7-28.
——— (1968) "American voting behavior and the 1964 election." Midwest Journal of Political Science 12: 1-40.
——— (1974a) "Theory and voting research: some reflections on Converse's 'Change in the American Electorate'." American Political Science Review 68: 1002-1023.
——— (1974b) "Rejoinder to 'Comments' by Philip Converse and Jerrold Rusk." American Political Science Review 68: 1050-1057.
——— and J. SPRAGUE (1970) "Additive and multiplicative models of the voting universe: the case of Pennsylvania: 1960-1968." American Political Science Review 64: 471-490.
BUTLER, D. E. and D. E. STOKES (1969) Political Change in Britain: Forces Shaping Electoral Choice. New York: St. Martin's Press.
BWY, D. P. (1968) "Political instability in Latin America: a cross-cultural test of a causal model." Latin American Research Review 3: 17-66.

CAMPBELL, A. and D. E. STOKES (1959) "Partisan Attitudes and the Presidential Vote." In E. Burdick and A. J. Brodbeck (eds.) American Voting Behavior. New York: Free Press.
CAMPBELL, A. and H. VALEN (1966) "Party Identification in Norway and the United States." In A. Campbell et al., Elections and the Political Order. New York: John Wiley.
CAMPBELL, A., G. GURIN, and W. MILLER (1954) The Voter Decides. Evanston: Row, Peterson.
CAMPBELL, A., P. CONVERSE, W. MILLER, and D. E. STOKES (1960) The American Voter. New York: John Wiley.
CAPECCHI, V. and G. GIORGIO (1969) "Determinants of Voting Behavior in Italy: A Linear Causal Model of Analysis." In M. Dogan and S. Rokkan (eds.) Quantitative Ecological Analysis in the Social Sciences. Cambridge, Mass.: MIT Press.
CATTELL, R. B. (1949) "The dimensions of culture patterns by factorization of national characters." Journal of Abnormal and Social Psychology 44: 443-469.
CLARK, P. B. and J. Q. WILSON (1961) "Incentive systems: a theory of organizations." Administrative Science Quarterly 6: 134-137.
COLEMAN, J. S. (1964) "Collective decisions." Sociological Inquiry 34: 166-181.
——— (1966) "Foundations for a theory of collective decisions." American Journal of Sociology 71: 615-627.
CONVERSE, P. (1958) "The Shifting Role of Class in Political Attitudes and Behavior." In E. Maccoby et al. (eds.) Readings in Social Psychology. New York: Holt.
——— (1966) "The Concept of a Normal Vote." In A. Campbell et al., Elections and the Political Order. New York: John Wiley.
——— (1972) "Change in the American Electorate." Pp. 263-337 in A. Campbell and P. E. Converse (eds.) The Human Meaning of Social Change. New York: Russell Sage.
——— (1974) "Comment on Burnham's 'Theory and Voting Research'." American Political Science Review 68: 1024-1027.
——— W. MILLER, J. RUSK, and A. WOLFE (1969) "Continuity and change in American politics: parties and issues in the 1968 election." American Political Science Review 63: 1083-1105.
CONWAY, M. M. and F. B. FEIGERT (1968) "Motivation, incentive systems and the political party organization." Journal of Politics 31: 1035-1062.

COOMBS, C. H. (1953) "Theory and Method of Social Measurement." In L. Festinger and D. Katz (eds.) *Research Methods in the Behavioral Sciences*. New York: Dryden.

CURRY, R. L., Jr. and L. L. WADE (1968) *A Theory of Political Exchange*. Englewood Cliffs, N.J.: Prentice-Hall.

CZUDNOWSKI, M. M. (1968) "A salience dimension of politics for the study of political culture." American Political Science Review 62: 878-888.

——— (1972) "Sociocultural variables and legislative recruitment." Comparative Politics 4: 561-587.

——— (1975) "Political Recruitment." in F. Greenstein and N. Polsby (eds.) *Handbook of Political Science*, 2. Reading, Mass.: Addison-Wesley.

DAHL, R. A. (1957) "The concept of power." Behavioral Science 2: 201-215.

DAHRENDORF, R. (1959) *Class and Conflict in Traditional Society*. Stanford: Stanford University Press.

DALLMAYR, F. R. (1970) "Empirical political theory and the image of man." Polity 2: 443-478.

DAVIES, J. C. (1963) *Human Nature in Politics*. New York: John Wiley.

DEUTSCH, K. W. (1960) "Toward an inventory of basic tools and patterns in comparative and international politics." American Political Science Review 54: 34-57.

DOGAN, M. (1967) "Political cleavage and social stratification in France and Italy." In S. M. Lipset and S. Rokkan (eds.) *Party Systems and Voter Alignments*. New York: Free Press.

——— (1969) "A covariance analysis of French electoral data." In M. Dogan and S. Rokkan (eds.) *Quantitative Ecological Analysis in the Social Sciences*. Cambridge: Cambridge University Press.

DOWNS, A. (1957) *An Economic Theory of Democracy*. New York: Harper.

DREYER, E. C. (1971-1972) "Media use and electoral choices: some political consequences of information exposure." Public Opinion Quarterly 35: 544-553.

DUNCAN, O. D., R. P. CUZZORT, and B. DUNCAN (1961) *Statistical Geography: Problems in Analyzing Areal Data*. New York: Free Press.

DUVERGER, M. (1954) *Political Parties, Their Organization and Activity in the Modern State*. New York: John Wiley.

DYE, T. (1966) *Politics, Economics and the Public: Policy Outcomes in the American States*. Chicago: Rand McNally.

ECKSTEIN, H. (1963) "A Perspective on Comparative Politics, Past and Present." In H. Eckstein and D. E. Apter (eds.) *Comparative Politics*. New York: Free Press.

ELDERSVELD, S. I. (1964) *Political Parties: A Behavioral Analysis*. Chicago: Rand McNally.

ERIKSON, E. H. (1950) *Childhood and Society*. New York: W. W. Norton.

EULAU, H. (1962) *Class and Party in the Eisenhower Years: Class Roles and Perspectives in the 1952 and 1956 Elections*. New York: Free Press.

——— (1963) *The Behavioral Persuasion in Politics*. New York: Random House.

——— (1969) *Micro-Macro Political Analysis: Accents of Inquiry*. Chicago: Aldine.

FIELD, J. O. and R. E. ANDERSON (1969) "Ideology in the public's conceptualization of the 1964 election." Public Opinion Quarterly 33: 380-398.

FLACKS, R. (1967) "The liberated generation: an exploration of the roots of student protest." Journal of Social Issues 23: 52-75.

FLANIGAN, W. and E. FOGELMAN (1967) "Patterns of political development and democratization: a quantitative analysis." Presented at the 1967 Annual Meeting of the American Political Science Association, Chicago, September.

FROHLICH, N., J. A. OPPENHEIMER, and O. R. YOUNG (1971) *Political Leadership and Collective Goods.* Princeton, N.J.: Princeton University Press.

FROMM, E. (1941) *Escape from Freedom.* New York: Farrar & Rinehart.

——— (1947) *Man for Himself.* New York: Farrar & Rinehart.

GALTUNG, J. (1967) *Theory and Methods of Social Research.* New York: Columbia University Press.

GIBSON, Q. (1960) *The Logic of Social Inquiry.* London: Routledge & Kegan Paul.

GILLESPIE, J. V. and B. NESVOLD, eds. (1971) *Macro-Quantitative Analysis: Conflict, Development and Democratization.* Beverly Hills: Sage Publications.

GLASER, B. G. and A. L. STRAUSS (1967) *The Discovery of Grounded Theory.* Chicago: Aldine.

GOLDBERG, A. S. (1966) "Discerning a causal pattern among data on voting behavior." American Political Science Review 60: 913-922.

GOLEMBIEWSKI, R. T., W. A. WELSH, and W. J. CROTTY (1969) *A Methodological Primer for Political Scientists.* Chicago: Rand McNally.

GOODMAN, L. A. (1953) "Ecological regressions and behavior of individuals." American Sociological Review 18: 663-664.

GREENSTEIN, F. I. (1973) "Political Psychology: A Pluralistic Universe." In J. N. Knutson (ed.) *Handbook of Political Psychology.* San Francisco: Jossey-Bass.

GREER, S. (1969a) "Sociology and Political Science." In S. M. Lipset (ed.) *Politics and the Social Sciences.* New York: Oxford University Press.

——— (1969b) *The Logic of Social Inquiry.* Chicago: Aldine.

GRIMSHAW, A. D. (1973) "Comparative Sociology: In What Ways Different from Other Sociologies?" In M. Armer and A. D. Grimshaw (eds.) *Comparative Social Research: Methodological Problems and Strategies.* New York: John Wiley.

GROTH, A. J. (1971) *Comparative Politics: A Distributive Approach.* New York: Macmillan.

GURR, T. R. (1972) *Polimetrics: An Introduction to Macro-politics.* Englewood Cliffs, N.J.: Prentice-Hall.

——— and C. RUTTENBURG (1971) "The Conditions of Civil Violence: First Tests of a Causal Model." In J. V. Gillespie and B. Nesvold (eds.) *Macro-Quantitative Analysis: Conflict, Development and Democratization.* Beverly Hills: Sage Publications.

HABERMAS, J. et al. (1961) *Student und Politik.* Frankfurt: Neuwied.

HARDIN, R. (1971) "Collective action as an agreeable n-Prisoner's Dilemma." Behavioral Science 16: 472-481.

HARMAN, H. H. (1967) *Modern Factor Analysis.* Chicago: University of Chicago Press.

HARSANYI, J. C. (1962) "Measurement of social power, opportunity costs, and the theory of two-person bargaining games." Behavioral Science 7: 67-80.

——— (1969) "Rational choice models of political behavior vs. functionalist and conformist theories." World Politics 21: 513-538.

HEAD, J. G. (1962) "Public goods and public policy." Public Finance 17: 203-205.

HEMPEL, C. (1965) *Aspects of Scientific Explanation.* New York: Free Press.

HIRSCHFIELD, R. S., B. E. SWANSON, and B. D. BLANK (1962) "A profile of political activists in Manhattan." Western Political Quarterly 15: 489-506.

HOFSTETTER, R. C. (1971) "The amateur politician: a problem in construct valida-
tion." Midwest Journal of Political Science 15: 31-56.
HOLT, R. T. and J. M. RICHARDSON (1970) "Competing Paradigms in Comparative
Politics." In R. T. Holt and J. E. Turner, The Methodology of Comparative Research.
New York: Free Press.
HOLT, R. T. and J. E. TURNER (1970) The Methodology of Comparative Research.
New York: Free Press.
HOMANS, G. C. (1961) Social Behavior: Its Elementary Forms. New York: Harcourt,
Brace & World.
HOPKINS, T. K. and I. WALLERSTEIN (1967) "The comparative study of national
societies." Social Science Information 6: 25-58.
HUME, D. (1952) A Treatise of Human Nature. LaSalle: Open Court Publishing House.
(Originally published in 1739).
HYMAN, H. H. (1959) Political Socialization: A Study in the Psychology of Political
Behavior. New York: Free Press.

INGLEHART, R. (1971) "The silent revolution in Europe: intergenerational change in
post-industrial societies." American Political Science Review 65: 991-1017.
INKELES, A. and D. J. LEVINSON (1969) "National Character: The Study of Modal
Personality and Sociocultural Systems." In G. Lindzey and E. Aronson (eds.) The
Handbook of Social Psychology, 4. Reading, Mass.: Addison-Wesley.
INKELES, A., E. HANFMANN, and H. BEIER (1958) "Modal personality and adjust-
ment to the Soviet socio-political system." Human Relations 11: 3-22.

JANDA, K. (1971) "A technique for assessing the conceptual equivalence of institutional variables across and within culture areas." Presented to the 1971 Annual Meeting of the American Political Science Association, Chicago, September.

KAPLAN, A. (1964) The Conduct of Inquiry. San Francisco: Chandler.
KARDINER, A. (1939) The Individual and His Society. New York: Columbia University
Press.
––– (1945) The Psychological Frontiers of Society. New York: Columbia University
Press.
KATZ, D. and R. L. KAHN (1966) The Social Psychology of Organizations. New York:
John Wiley.
KESSEL, J. H. (1968) The Goldwater Coalition. Indianapolis: Bobbs-Merrill.
––– (1972) "The issues in issue voting." American Political Science Review 66: 459-
465.
KIRKPATRICK, S. A. and M. JONES (1970) "Vote direction and issue cleavage in
1968." Social Science Quarterly 51: 689-705.
KNUTSON, J. N. (1972) The Human Basis of the Polity. Chicago: Aldine-Atherton.
KROEBER, A. L. (1948) Anthropology. New York: Harcourt, Brace & World.

LaPIERE, R. T. (1934) "Attitudes vs. action." Social Forces 13: 230-237.
LASSWELL, H. D. (1960) Psychopathology and Politics. New York: Viking Press.
––– (1948) Power and Personality. New York: Viking Press.
––– (1954) "The Selective Effect of Personality on Political Participation." In R.
Christie and M. Jahoda (eds.) Studies in the Scope and Method of the Authoritarian
Personality. New York: Free Press.
––– (1968) "The future of the comparative method." Comparative Politics 1: 3-18.

LAZARSFELD, P. F. (1958) "Evidence and Inference in Social Research." In D. Lerner (ed.) *Evidence and Inference.* Boston: American Academy of Arts and Sciences.

——— (1959) "Problems in Methodology." In R. Merton et al. (eds.) *Sociology Today: Problems and Prospects.* New York: Basic Books.

——— and A. H. BARTON (1951) "Quantitative Measurement in the Social Sciences." In D. Lerner and H. D. Lasswell (eds.) *The Policy Sciences.* Stanford: Stanford University Press.

LAZARSFELD, P. F. and A. MENZEL (1961) "On the Relation Between Individuals and Collective Properties." In A. Etzioni (ed.) *Complex Organizations: A Sociological Reader.* New York: Holt, Rinehart & Winston.

LENSKI, G. (1967) "Status inconsistency and the vote: a four-nation test." American Sociological Review 32: 298-301.

LIEPELT, K. (1971) "The Infra-structure of Party Support in Austria and West Germany." In M. Dogan and R. Rose (eds.) *European Politics.* Boston: Little, Brown.

LINZ, J. (1969) "Ecological Analysis and Survey Research." In M. Dogan and S. Rokkan (eds.) *Quantitative Ecological Analysis in the Social Sciences.* Cambridge, Mass.: MIT Press.

——— and A. DE MIGUEL (1966) "Within-Nation Differences and Comparisons: The Eight Spains." In R. Merritt and S. Rokkan (eds.) *Comparing Nations: The Use of Quantitative Data in Cross-National Research.* New Haven: Yale University Press.

LIPSET, S. M. and S. ROKKAN (1967) *Party Systems and Voter Alignments: Cross-National Perspectives.* New York: Free Press.

LIPSET, S. M., P. F. LAZARSFELD, A. H. BARTON, and J. LINZ (1954) "The Psychology of Voting: An Analysis of Political Behavior." In G. Lindzey and E. Aronson (eds.) *The Handbook of Social Psychology.* Reading, Mass.: Addison-Wesley.

LITT, E. (1970) *Ethnic Politics in America.* Glenview, Ill.: Scott, Foresman.

——— (1973) *Democracy's Ordeal in America.* Hinsdale, Ill.: Dryden.

LOPREATO, J. (1967) "Social mobility and political outlooks in Italy." American Sociological Review 32: 586-592.

McCLELLAND, D. C. (1961) *The Achieving Society.* Princeton, N.J.: D. Van Nostrand.

McCLOSKY, H., P. J. HOFFMAN, and R. O'HARA (1960) "Issue conflict and consensus among party leaders and followers." American Political Science Review 54: 406-427.

MARCH, J. G. (1955) "An introduction to the theory and measurement of influence." American Political Science Review 49: 431-451.

MARGOLIS, J. (1955) "A comment on the pure theory of public expenditure." Review of Economics and Statistics 37: 347-350.

MARTIN, R. (1971) "The concept of power: a critical defense." British Journal of Sociology 22: 240-256.

MASLOW, A. A. (1952) *The Security-Insecurity Inventory.* Stanford: Stanford University Press.

——— (1970) *Motivation and Personality.* New York: Harper & Row.

MAYER, L. C. (1972) *Comparative Political Inquiry.* Homewood, Ill.: Dorsey.

MERKL, P. H. (1970) *Modern Comparative Politics.* New York: Holt, Rinehart & Winston.

MERRITT, R. (1970) *Systematic Approaches to Comparative Politics.* Chicago: Rand McNally.

——— and S. ROKKAN, eds. (1966) *Comparing Nations: The Use of Quantitative Data in Cross-National Research.* New Haven: Yale University Press.

MILBRATH, L. W. (1965) *Political Participation: How and Why Do People Get Involved in Politics?* Chicago: Rand McNally.

MILLER, W. E. and D. E. STOKES (1963) "Constituency influence in Congress." American Political Science Review 57: 45-56.

MITCHELL, W. C. (1969) "The Shape of Political Theory To Come." In S. M. Lipset (ed.) *Politics and the Social Sciences.* New York: Oxford University Press.

——— and J. M. MITCHELL (1969) *Political Analysis and Public Policy.* Chicago: Rand McNally.

MULLER, E. N. (1970) "Cross-national dimensions of political competence." American Political Science Review 64: 792-809.

MUSGRAVE, R. (1959) *The Theory of Public Finance.* New York: McGraw-Hill.

NAGEL, E. (1961) *The Structure of Science.* New York: Harcourt, Brace & World.

NAROLL, R. (1970) "Galton's Problem." In R. Naroll and R. Cohen (eds.) *A Handbook of Method in Cultural Anthropology.* Garden City, N.Y.: Natural History Press.

NERE, J. (1962) "The French Republic." In F. H. Hinsley (ed.) *The New Cambridge Modern History,* 11. Cambridge: Cambridge University Press.

NIE, N. H., G. B. POWELL, and K. PREWITT (1969) "Social structure and political participation." American Political Science Review 63: 361-378, 808-832.

OHLIN, G. (1968) "Aggregate Comparisons: Problems and Prospects of Quantitative Analysis Based on National Accounts." In S. Rokkan (ed.) *Comparative Research Across Culture and Nations.* The Hague: Mouton.

OLSON, M., Jr. (1965) *The Logic of Collective Action.* Cambridge, Mass.: Harvard University Press.

——— (1969) "The Relationship Between Economics and Other Social Sciences." In S. M. Lipset (ed.) *Politics and the Social Sciences.* New York: Oxford University Press.

OSGOOD, C. E., G. J. SUCHI, and P. H. TANNENBAUM (1957) *The Measurement of Meaning.* Urbana: University of Illinois Press.

PAPPI, F. U. (1970) "Wahlverhalten und Politische Kultur." In F. Hermens et al. (eds.) *Politik und Wähler,* 1. Meisenheim am Glan: Anton Hain.

PARSONS, T. (1967) "On the Concept of Political Power." In *Sociological Theory and Modern Society.* New York: Free Press.

PHILLIPS, D. L. (1971) *Knowledge from What?* Chicago: Rand McNally.

PIERCE, J. G. (1970) "Party identification and the changing role of ideology in American politics." Midwest Journal of Political Science 14: 25-42.

POLSBY, N. W. and A. B. WILDAVSKY (1971) *Presidential Elections.* New York: Scribner's.

POMPER, G. M. (1969) "Controls and influence in American elections (even 1968)." American Behavioral Scientist 13: 215-230.

——— (1972) "From confusion to clarity: issues and American voters, 1956-1968." American Political Science Review 66: 415-428.

POPPER, K. (1957) *The Poverty of Historicism.* Boston: Beacon Press.

——— (1959) *The Logic of Scientific Discovery.* London: Hutchinson.

PRICE, D. (1968) "Micro and Macro Politics." In O. Garceau (ed.) *Political Research and Political Theory.* Cambridge, Mass.: Harvard University Press.

PRZEWORSKI, A. and G. SOARES (1971) "Theories in search of a curve: a contextual interpretation of left vote." American Political Science Review 65: 51-68.

PRZEWORSKI, A. and H. TEUNE (1966) "Equivalence in cross-national research." Public Opinion Quarterly 30: 551-568.
——— (1970) *The Logic of Comparative Social Inquiry.* New York: Wiley-Interscience.
PYE, L. W. (1969) "Identity and the Political Culture." In L. Binder et al., *Crisis and Sequences in Political Development.* Princeton, N.J.: Princeton University Press.

RENSHON, S. A. (1974) *Psychological Needs and Political Behavior.* New York: Freedom.
RePASS, D. E. (1971) "Issue salience and party choice." American Political Science Review 65: 389-400.
RIKER, W. H. (1962) *The Theory of Political Coalitions.* New Haven: Yale University Press.
——— (1964) "Some ambiguities in the notion of power." American Political Science Review 58: 341-349.
——— (1972) "The Paradox of Vote Trading." Presented at the 1972 Annual Meeting of the American Political Science Association, Washington, D.C.
——— and P. C. ORDESHOOK (1968) "A theory of the calculus of voting." American Political Science Review 62: 25-42.
——— (1973) *An Introduction to Positive Political Theory.* Englewood Cliffs, N.J.: Prentice-Hall.
RIKER, W. H. and W. J. ZAVOINA (1970) "Rational behavior in politics: evidence from a three-person game." American Political Science Review 64: 48-60.
ROBINSON, W. S. (1950) "Ecological correlations and the behavior of individuals." American Sociological Review 15: 351-357.
ROGOW, A. A. and H. D. LASSWELL (1963) *Power, Corruption and Rectitude.* Englewood Cliffs, N.J.: Prentice-Hall.
ROKKAN, S. (1962) "The Comparative Study of Political Participation." In A. Ranney (ed.) *Essays on the Behavioral Study of Politics.* Urbana: University of Illinois Press.
——— ed. (1968) *Comparative Research Across Cultures and Nations.* The Hague: Mouton.
——— (1970) *Citizens, Elections, Parties: Approaches to the Comparative Study of the Processes of Development.* New York: David McKay.
——— and H. VALEN (1960) "Parties, elections and political behavior in the Northern countries." In O. Stammer (ed.) *Politische Forschung.* Cologne: Westdeutscher Verlag.
——— (1970) "The mobilization of the periphery." Chapter 6 of S. Rokkan, *Citizens, Elections, Parties.* New York: David McKay. (Originally published in 1962.)
ROSENTHAL, H. (1969a) "The electoral politics of Gaullists in the Fourth French Republic: ideology or constituency interest?" American Political Science Review 63: 476-487.
——— (1969b) "Size of Coalition and Electoral Outcomes in the Fourth French Republic." In S. Groennings et al. (eds.) *The Study of Coalition Behavior.* New York: Holt, Rinehart & Winston.
——— and S. SEN (1969) "Candidate selection and voting behavior in France." Public Choice 6: 71-92.
ROTHENBERG, J. (1969) "The Process of Group Choice in a Legislative Context." In G. T. Guilbaud (ed.) *La Decision: Aggregation et Dynamique des Ordres de Preference.* Paris: Centre National de la Recherche Scientifique.
RUMMEL, R. J. (1963) "Dimensions of Conflict Behavior Within and Between Nations." In L. von Bertalanffy and A. Rapoport (eds.) *General Systems Yearbook,* 8. Ann Arbor, Mich.: Society for General Systems Research.

RUMMEL, R. J. (1966) "The Dimensionality of Nations Project." In R. Merritt and S. Rokkan (eds.) *Comparing Nations: The Use of Quantitative Data in Cross-National Research*. New Haven: Yale University Press.

RUNCIMAN, W. G. (1969) *Social Science and Political Theory*. Cambridge: Cambridge University Press.

RUSSETT, B. M. (1967) *International Regions and the International System: A Study in Political Ecology*. Chicago: Rand McNally.

——— et al. (1964) *World Handbook of Political and Social Indicators*. New Haven: Yale University Press.

SABINE, G. H. (1951) *A History of Political Theory*. London: George Harrap. (Originally published in 1937.)

SAMUELSON, P. A. (1955) "Diagrammatic exposition of a theory of public expenditure." Review of Economics and Statistics 37: 350-356.

——— (1958) "Aspects of public expenditure theories." Review of Economics and Statistics 60: 332-338.

SARTORI, G. (1969) "From the Sociology of Politics to Political Sociology." In S. M. Lipset (ed.) *Politics and the Social Sciences*. New York: Oxford University Press.

SCARROW, H. A. (1969) *Comparative Political Analysis: An Introduction*. New York: Harper & Row.

SCHEUCH, E. K. (1966) "Cross-National Comparisons Using Aggregate Data: Some Substantive and Methodological Problems." In R. Merritt and S. Rokkan (eds.) *Comparing Nations: The Use of Quantitative Data in Cross-National Research*. New Haven: Yale University Press.

——— (1969) "Social Context and Individual Behavior." In M. Dogan and S. Rokkan (eds.) *Quantitative Ecological Analysis in the Social Sciences*. Cambridge, Mass.: MIT Press.

SCOTT, W. A. (1969) "Attitude Measurement." In G. Lindzey and E. Aronson (eds.) *The Handbook of Social Psychology*, 2. Reading, Mass.: Addison-Wesley.

SEARS, D. O. (1969) "Political Behavior." In G. Lindzey and E. Aronson (eds.) *The Handbook of Social Psychology*, 1. Reading, Mass.: Addison-Wesley.

SHAPIRO, M. J. (1969) "Rational political man: a synthesis of economic and social-psychological perspectives." American Political Science Review 63: 1106-1119.

SHARKANSKY, I. (1967) "Government expenditures and public services in the American states." American Political Science Review 61: 1066-1077.

SHEVSKY, E. and W. BELL (1955) *Social Area Analysis: Theory, Illustrative Application and Computational Procedures*. Stanford: Stanford University Press.

SIMON, H. A. (1957) *Models of Man*. New York: John Wiley.

SMITH M. B. (1973) "Political attitudes." In J. N. Knutson (ed.) *Handbook of Political Psychology*. San Francisco: Jossey-Bass.

SOARES, G. and R. HAMBLIN (1967) "Socio-economic variables and voting for the radical Left: Chile, 1952." American Political Science Review 61: 1053-1065.

SONQUIST, J. A. and J. N. MORGAN (1964) "The detection of interaction effects." Survey Research Center Monograph 35, University of Michigan Institute for Social Research.

SOULE, J. W. and J. W. CLARKE (1970) "Amateurs and professionals: a study of delegates to the 1968 Democratic National Convention." American Political Science Review 64: 888-898.

SPIRO, M. E. (1961) "Social Systems, Personality and Functional Analysis." In B. Kaplan (ed.) *Studying Personality Cross-Culturally*. New York: Harper & Row.

SPROUT, H. and M. SPROUT (1965) *The Ecological Perspective.* Princeton, N.J.: Princeton University Press.

STRATMAN, W. C. (1971) "A Concept of Voter Rationality." Presented at the 1971 Annual Meeting of the American Political Science Association, Chicago.

STOKES, D. E. (1965) "A Variance Components Model of Political Effects." In J. M. Claunch (ed.) *Mathematical Applications in Political Science,* 1. Dallas: Arnold Foundation.

——— (1966) "Some dynamic elements of contests for the presidency." American Political Science Review 60: 19-28.

——— (1969) "Cross-Level Inference as a Game Against Nature." In J. Bernd (ed.) *Mathematical Applications in Political Science,* 4. Charlottesville: University of Virginia Press.

TANTER, R. (1965) "Dimensions of conflict behavior within and between nations, 1955-60." Peace Research Society Papers 3.

——— (1966) "Dimensions of conflict behavior within and between nations, 1958-60." Journal of Conflict Resolution 10: 41-64.

THOMPSON, K. (1970) "Cross-National Voting Behavior Research: An Example of Computer-Assisted Multivariate Analysis of Attribute Data." Sage Professional Papers in Comparative Politics 01-003.

THORSON, T. L. (1970) *Biopolitics.* New York: Holt, Rinehart & Winston.

TOULMIN, S. E. (1961) *Foresight and Understanding: An Enquiry into the Aims of Science.* Bloomington: University of Indiana Press.

TULLOCK, G. (1970) *Private Wants and Public Means.* New York: Basic Books.

VERBA, S. (1969) "The Use of Survey Research in the Study of Comparative Politics: Issues and Strategies." In S. Rokkan et al., *Comparative Survey Analysis.* The Hague: Mouton.

——— (1971a) "Cross-National Survey Research: The Problem of Credibility." In I. Vallier (ed.) *Comparative Methods in Sociology.* Berkeley: University of California Press.

——— (1971b) "Sequences and Development." In L. Binder et al., *Crisis and Sequences in Political Development.* Princeton, N.J.: Princeton University Press.

——— and N. H. NIE (1972) *Participation in America: Political Democracy and Social Equality.* New York: Harper & Row.

——— and J-O. KIM (1971) "The Modes of Democratic Participation: A Cross-National Comparison." Sage Professional Papers in Comparative Politics 01-013.

WADE, L. L. and R. L. CURRY (1970) *A Logic of Public Policy.* Belmont, Calif.: Wadsworth.

WAHLKE, J. C., H. EULAU et at. (1962) *The Legislative System: Explorations in Legislative Behavior.* New York: John Wiley.

WALDMAN, S. R. (1972) *Foundations of Political Action.* Boston: Little, Brown.

WEBER, M. (1947) *The Theory of Social and Economic Organization.* New York: Oxford University Press.

WILSON, J. Q. (1962) *The Amateur Democrat.* Chicago: University of Chicago Press.

WRONG, D. H. (1961) "The oversocialized concept of man in modern sociology." American Sociological Review 26: 183-193.

ZELDITCH, M., Jr. (1971) "Intelligible Comparisons." In Vallier (ed.) *Comparative Methods in Sociology.* Berkeley: University of California Press.

ZETTERBERG, H. L. (1957) "Compliant actions." Acta Sociologica 2: 179-201.

ZOHLNHOFER, W. (1965) "Parteiidentifizierung in der Bundesrepublik und den USA." In E. K. Scheuch and R. Wildenmann (eds.) *Zur Soziologie der Wahl.* Koln: Westdeutscher Verlag.